FORGOTTEN PEOPLE

THE STORY OF CAREBY, HOLYWELL & AUNBY

THREE LINCOLNSHIRE VILLAGES BOUND TOGETHER IN HISTORY

Barbara Cooper

HARESLEAP BOOKS

PUBLISHED BY:

PACIFIC STUDIO

Designed and published in the UK in 2011 by
Pacific Studio, Mallard's Peak, Careby, Lincolnshire PE9 4EB

ISBN 978-0-9568754-0-2

Front cover painting of Careby School by Geoff Forman
Reproduced with kind permission of Jonathan and Mrs Forman

CONTENTS

Contents

FOREWORD

Grateful thanks are offered to the people in and around Careby, Holywell and Aunby who supplied many of the photographs and tolerated my prying and questioning. I thank them most sincerely. I am indebted to my husband Dave for his endless encouragement and hours of painstaking research. Thanks must also go to Marie and Richard Turpin and Stuart Rowley for their assistance and input. Particular thanks to Ian Wilson of Pacific Studio – based in Careby – who has scanned and edited many of the photographs, diagrams and maps, and laid out the text ready for printing.

Forgotten People is intended as an enjoyable read with the dramatisation of real events in history. Where possible I've used the names of those involved.

Without the foresight of Mrs Agatha Fane and her husband, the Hon. Mountjoy John Charles Wedderburn-Fane, this book could not have been written. Before leaving Holywell Hall they deposited the Holywell Records with Lindsey County Council in 1934. The records were listed and arranged principally by Mr B. C. Duddles before the outbreak of WWII. At a later date the records were transferred to Lincolnshire Archives and thanks are given to the staff at Lincoln for their help, advice and permissions.

It is inevitable that a book like this that has involved so much translation, deciphering, memories and interpretation may contain errors. If there are any I accept sole responsibility for them.

Barbara Cooper
Careby, July 2011

Careby, 1980

INTRODUCTION

FASCINATING FAMILY TIES – the Hatchers, the Reynardsons and the Fanes connect Careby, Holywell and Aunby. A tyrant of a king, a Russian Prince and a Member of Parliament have strong links here. On the northern boundary is the scene of a glorious industrial revolution.

Ask anyone who regularly travels along the B1176 between Stamford and Grantham and they will tell you that Careby, if they remember it at all, is two sharp bends and a railway bridge. If you can find one of the residents they will tell you that Careby is a quiet, rural village of less than eighty people, with a pretty church tucked away and supporting a community that until the last few years has had strong links to dairy, arable and sheep farming.

Take a walk past the old school with its elegant chimney pots; glance opposite at Corner Cottage with its picturesque garden then over the railway bridge into the village street. You'll see the village hall, closed since the fifties and sometimes known as the 'tin hut', standing in the field opposite where the village pub, The Reynardsons Arms once stood. A few cottages farther on, curving privet hedges hide an ancient farm, The Elms.

Next door you'll see that Careby Manor overlooks a street that no longer exists. Beyond is almost concealed Gardener's Cottage, then the Rectory, hidden in a garden lovingly created by Victorian Rector and benefactor, John Birch-Reynardson. The Millennium lych gate leads to St Stephen's, secluded from the lane and close to the river. The south-facing porch of this Norman Church is another reminder the village once faced into the sun.

Linger on the bridge. Behind a high stone wall is a fine house now bearing little resemblance to village children's much loved Little Paddocks where donkeys and foals lived with Daphne Fane. The lane ends here but not so long ago it meandered steeply upwards to the long dismantled windmill and on to

Witham-on-the Hill. Now the track is overgrown and impassable, overlooked by Park Farm, the new house on the side of the hill.

If you return to the main Stamford Road, four stone cottages built for paupers stand on waste ground after the building of the railway. A mile further on you will see a ford and the pretty stone Spurr Bridge. Walk along the narrow lane and past a scattering of houses to Aunby Manor; this hamlet has a history few suspect. Then continue along the byway to Holywell, a jewel of a place hidden with lakes and wooded valleys, bursting with wild life and bound with ancient rites, castles and Roman connections.

Stamford Road Careby

CAREBY… THE ELMS

Careby used to be a village where land mattered a great deal. In the Middle Ages only nobles, lords, knights and churchmen are listed as dealing with land, transferring land, the conditions land was held and the right to hunt on it. Villagers did not matter. The Lord of the Manor controlled the people and all the lands. They built farmhouses for their tenants.

In Careby The Elms is the oldest farmhouse in the village. Much later, Ancaster Estate built or rebuilt both Warren and Marshall's Farms.

The Elms, Careby

Bob Creasey is not one of the parish's 'Forgotten People'. Born in 1926 he lives at The Elms with Margaret whom he married in 1954. Bob inherited the farm from his father Charles who came to Careby in 1914.

Before that time the farm was home to John Goodwin Grummitt and his wife Helen.

Bob and Margaret have spent much of their lives caring for Careby and Careby Church, Bob being Churchwarden at times between 1952 and 2009 with a total of thirty-nine years of faithful service. Margaret was Treasurer of the Parochial Church Council from 1955 to 2010. Both have been actively involved with long-term money raising events for the fabric of the church.

The beautiful gardens of The Elms are the venue for the Long Lazy Lunch held every summer in a giant marquee.

It is likely that The Elms was Colton's Farm, as detailed in the 'Survey of Careby Manor'[1] in 1735. The farmhouse is Grade II listed; the style indicating it was built between 1633 and 1666, perhaps originally as two cottages. Alterations have been carried out during the mid 1800s and again in the 20th century.

Built of colour-washed, coursed limestone rubble, the two-storeyed house has a five-bay front and timber lintels. Both the house and garden face south.

The upper flooring is constructed of lime-ash. From as early as the 15th century to reduce the danger of fire, lime-ash floors were laid because the commonest cause of fire in houses without thatched roofs was a spark falling between floorboards.

The lime-ash flooring was made from the limekiln's residue after burning. (The nearest limekiln was at Pickworth). Mixed with gypsum plaster until moist, the lime-ash was rammed down on a bed of straw or reeds and wetted laths. Sometimes a mixture of one-third lime, one-third well-sifted coal ash and one-third loamy clay and horse dung was used instead.

Bob grew up with seven brothers and sisters. With his sister Betty they have many memories of the village. As children, friends with Tony Sharpe, Tom and Nancy Watts, the Birch and the Buxton children they gravitated towards the churchyard, the river and the hillside to play in Careby Wood.

Careby Folly

At the top of the hill stood a well-loved landmark – an old stone folly. Children believed a secret tunnel led to the church and then on to Holywell. Betty

Bob Creasey on his tractor

1...   *Survey of Careby Manor, page 137*

Memories of the Village

The Folly on the hillside overlooking Careby village, and Joanne Fenn standing in one of the doorways

remembers the building as square with the roof like a pyramid and surrounded by hawthorn trees.

In reality, the Earl of Ancaster commissioned the folly. Serving as a summerhouse for the inhabitants of Grimsthorpe Castle, in fine weather residents and visitors would ride or drive along the old coach road, cross the Witham road and on to the folly for picnics.

The folly gradually fell into decline. Sadly, quite recently it was dismantled and removed by the present landowner.

In summer, Bob and his friends swam in the river, racing in the horse pond and sheepwash created by wooden boards. They'd catch fish, particularly bullheads and grandfathers. Sometimes sticklebacks would float into jam jars.

The girls made daisy chains in the churchyard, picked primroses and buttercups that carpeted the Church paddock or hunted for pretty stone flowers that had fallen off the gravestones into long grass.

The boys played hockey, rounders and cricket in the village field and sometimes the older members of the community, particularly the Barneys, would join in. Bob can remember his father gathering sticks from hedges and fashioning hockey sticks for them to use.

In winter the boys harpooned fish through holes in the ice. Skating on the Rectory Lake or on low-lying land near the river was an opportunity for some to wear their new ice skates.

Careby children became arch enemies with children from Little Bytham and Castle Bytham.

'We wouldn't go to either village on our own because we'd be chased out. Oh no, we daren't go down there alone.'

A gang of Little Bytham boys often gathered on the railway bridge.

'We girls were too scared to try and cross the bridge on our own and even in twos or threes they'd tease us.'

Flitting was a favourite memory. 'When news of a family moving out circulated round the school, we'd be very excited. If someone were flitting, then after school we would all race down to see if the house was empty. If it was…'

Lodge Farm

One murky August evening five boys jogged along the Holywell Road. When they came to the clump of pine trees on the left, the eldest glanced behind. 'All clear,' he said. 'No-one's about. Come on. Let's do it.'

All of them dodged down the track towards Lodge Farm. Grass fields away to their left, corn too wet to cut to their right. They slowed down for the youngest, five-year-old Harry lagging behind.

'Come on 'arry, catch up. Watch out for some nice big stones. The Beasleys have flitted. Now's our chance.'

'Wait for me! I can't go no faster. What's flittin'?'

'Don't you know? They've gone, silly. Flitted. Gone.'

The other boys ran ahead. Lodge Farmhouse stood square, grey and squat. Invitingly empty. The windows stared blackly in the evening dusk as if waiting.

Eddie threw the first stone. There was a satisfying clatter as the glass shattered and fell.

'Go on. You next Davy; you're a good shot. Aim for that window up there.'

Another crash. Then another. And another.

There were so many panes to shatter that the boys began to run out of stones.

'Harry. Go and collect some more. You're useless at this. So far you've not hit anything.'

'I can do it. Give me another chance. I want another go. Please.'

Arthur led him right up to the window close to the front door. 'Go on then. Chuck that stone with all yer strength.'

Ah. What a wonderful tinkle of breaking glass.

Harry jumped up and down. 'See. I can do it. I did it. I did it!'

With only a post office near the bridge and a butcher's shop within the Willoughby Arms, villagers learnt to be self-sufficient. A gentleman from the International Stores in Stamford walked from village to village, taking orders for groceries to be delivered weekly. Some villagers paid a weekly visit to Stamford by bus but the main form of transport in and out of the village was by train. With no road haulage, the railway yard was an extremely busy place with grain, sugar beet, vegetables and animals produced in Careby moved to Peterborough to be sold on.

Tramps sometimes lived in the spinney at the bottom of the hill on the Stamford Road. No child would venture there. Instead they bought sweets from the Post Office run by the Parker sisters. Standing in the front garden near to the road junction was the telephone box with the adjacent post box a target for fireworks on Bonfire Night.

The Post Office was formerly The Reynardsons' Arms with William Pope first mentioned as landlord in the census of 1841.

Painting of The Reynardsons Arms by Geoff Forman
With the permission of Jonathan and Mrs Forman

By 1851 there is no mention of him. His forty-five year old wife Elizabeth had taken over as landlady. Like many other families in the village she provided lodgings for several railway workers as well as accommodation for her nephew and a servant.

When she died in 1881 the inn was closed.

The old inn and the adjoining cottage were finally sold and pulled down in the sixties and Dick Wood built The Chestnuts above the old cellar of the inn. A haulage business was run from the premises with three lorries parked next door on waste ground attached to the blacksmith's shop. In autumn villagers continued to gather nuts from the almond tree that stood on the site.

Blacksmith Joe Buxton lived with his wife and six children at 66 Stamford Road. He shod horses and mended machinery in the smithy beside the railway. Much respected as a blacksmith at Holywell Hall, his funeral was held in Holywell Church.

Tom Pick who lived in Linnet Cottage with his wife Bella kept pigs in the range of buildings next to the blacksmith's shop. He worked in the butcher's shop run by Medwells at the Willoughby Arms. Then in the years up to his retirement Tom became a driver for a railway supervisor.

Tom and Bella started married life in one of the two Dog Kennel Cottages, since converted to Walnut Cottage next to Marshall's Farm. Bella took over the Post Office and ran it from their new home on Church Road when their friends Mr and Mrs Thornhill left the village.

Bob Creasey recalls his father walking down to the Willoughby Arms. Outbuildings there later accommodated prisoners of war.

'It was a rough pub in those days where they used to play dominoes. In the winter it was always cold. I remember my father used to take one or two logs with him to put on the fire. The beer was kept in the cellar and Mrs Medwell would bring it up in a jug. She had to pour it from a great height to get any sort of head on it. Major Hoare's gamekeeper George Sutton who lived at Keeper's Cottage at Holywell during the war; he used to ram the poker into the fire. When it was red-hot he put it into his beer to warm it.'

Pete Woodcock with his motorbike

Major Hoare, tenant of Holywell Hall, ran the Home Guard. Charles Creasey was a staunch member. One night whilst the Major was driving home in dense fog with only a glimmer of light from the war's compulsory shielded headlights, George was summoned to get out of the car.

'George, I want you to walk ahead and guide us,' commanded the Major.

George did so, groping his way with the car creeping along behind him.

Cars were a rare sight: motorbikes more common, particularly amongst young men.

15

Little Bytham station in the 1950s, looking south towards Essendine.

The platforms were reached directly out of the booking hall over a footbridge.

'If we wanted to go to Bourne we'd hitch up the pony and trap then drive down the street to cross the river and up the hillside to Witham. Journeys to Stamford and further away were by train from Little Bytham Station, changing at Essendine for Stamford. For holiday treats we would go on trips to Skegness and Wicksteed Park. Our mother would organise two buses for both parents and children.

'Electricity was slow to come to Careby, introduced in the fifties. Before that we had Calor gas. Before then, oil lamps. Except for the Rectory. That had its own generator installed by the new owners, the Fanes.'

MARSHALL'S FARM

The farmhouse is now home to Mr and Mrs Fuller.

Marshall's Farm and two sets of farm buildings were erected by the Earl of Ancaster who acquired some Careby Manor lands after they were sold in 1754.

When the farm was sold during WWII it was bought by Tommy Atkinson of Greatford Manor. The sale included land up to Careby Wood and Dog Kennel Cottages. Mr Atkinson also bought the sole cottage to survive a 1920s' fire in the terrace of four stone cottages to the west of The Elms. The surviving cottage was tenanted by Peter Woodcock's father who worked for Tommy Atkinson.

Along with his parents, brothers and sisters, Peter grew up at 59 Careby, later renamed Thistlecroft.

Peter's grandfather, with the help of ponies, sometimes carted stone down the track from the quarry in The Warren.

Pete Woodcock on the left
with Pete Jones in 1956

Haymaking in the 1920s
With permission of Karen Cunningham

The hillside rang with shouts of children playing. In snowy weather they tobogganed down steep Careby lane. If a visit to Bourne was desired the track that led through The Warren saved villagers cycling all the way round to Little Bytham to join the Witham road. Old maps show the well-used track running from Marshall's Farm where Ancaster Estate's carthorses were stabled following their wash down in the horse wash, through The Warren and past Warren Farm.

Several farms in Careby Parish were named after the tenants who lived there and Marshall's Farm was no exception. In 1898 it became the home of Ancaster's tenant farmers William and Clara Marshall. They had six children between the ages of thirteen and one year and a granddaughter of four months.

In May 1899, Lord Willoughby employed new gamekeeper Henry Plum. One of Plum's first tasks was to implement the Ground Game Act of 1880 and set rabbit traps easily identifiable by the Ancaster blacksmith's mark.

Shortly afterwards a trap went missing from a gateway close to Marshall's Farm.

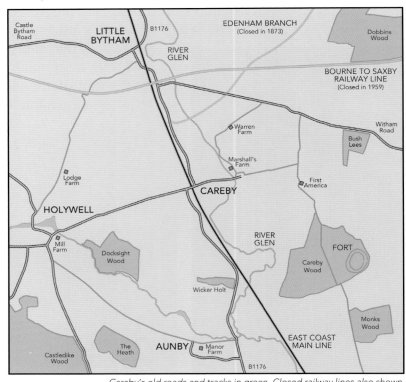

Careby's old roads and tracks in green. Closed railway lines also shown.

'William Sneath?'

The farm stockman lifted his head and leaned on his pitchfork. Having turned most of the newly cut hay he could do with a rest. 'That's me sir. What can I do for you?'

'You work for William Marshall. Is that correct?'

'Aye.' He removed his cap and wiped sweat from his brow.

'You live at Dog Kennel Cottages. Right?'

'Aye.' He looked inquiringly at the man before him. He'd never seen him before but had his suspicions. He concentrated on his boots.

'I expect you know who I am. Henry Plum. Gamekeeper on the Ancaster Estate. Have you seen any of the rabbit traps I've set?'

'No sir.'

'Are you sure? I left one over there.' Frowning, he nodded towards the farm gateway. 'It's gone missing.'

'Well I haven't seen it. Nothing to do with me.'

Henry Plum wasn't convinced and kept regular watch on Sneath for the next few months, even resorting to hiding behind trees on the hillside. One foggy January morning he begged Police Constable Carter to accompany him. With a bit of luck Sneath would be caught in the act.

'Look! There's Sneath. What did I tell you? I knew it was 'im. What are you going to do about it?'

The policeman laid a hand on Plum's arm, restraining him from erupting out of the ditch. 'Nothing yet. Hold on. Let's see what he's up to.'

'You can see what he's up to. Anyone creeping in and out of the hedges near Careby Wood is up to no good.' Plum stood up. 'Look! He's carrying a rabbit. If that isn't enough evidence…'

Plum and Carter rose in the fog to confront Sneath as he approached the red brick buildings close to First America field.

'Leave this to me.' Police Constable Carter stepped forward. 'Now Sneath. Explain yourself.'

Sneath shrugged.

'Open your coat.'

Reluctantly Sneath unbuttoned his coat. Bulging from two large pockets sewn into the lining were two freshly killed rabbits. The man averted his eyes. 'I ain't done nothing wrong. They're Mr Marshall's traps.'

'We'll see about that. Let's go and ask him.'

'Have a heart. I've got a wife and two young 'uns to feed.'

The Ground Game Act, September 7th 1880, was an Act for the better protection of occupiers of land against injury to their crops from Ground Game…

Every occupier of land shall have, as incident to and inseparable from his occupation of the land, the right to kill and take ground game, concurrently with any other person who may be entitled to kill and take ground game on the same land.

There were several provisions.

The occupier himself shall kill and take ground game only by himself or by persons duly authorised in writing…

William Marshall denied any knowledge of Sneath's actions and the matter went to court in January 1900.

WARREN FARM

The Earl of Ancaster also built WARREN FARM, the home of Carol and David Yiend. Visiting Europe in the 1840s, Lord Ancaster liked the towers on the schlosses so much that he reproduced them above the roofs of Warren Farm. The adjacent stone barn may have been used as a slaughterhouse and is estimated to be of the much earlier Queen Anne period.

Warren Farm
With permission of David Yiend

In the 1920s, James Kerfoot tenanted both Warren Farm and Marshall's Farm.

Haymaking at Warren Farm –
James Kerfoot holding the horse, with brother John.
With permission of Karen Cunningham

CAREBY... CORNER COTTAGE

Aubrey Fenn
and the newly
completed
Corner Cottage

Newly married Aubrey Fenn purchased one of a pair of toll cottages in 1970. With the help of friends, he spent every evening and weekend converting the property opposite the schoolhouse for his wife Celia and baby Joanne. He extended the two-bedroomed cottage into a four-bedroomed home with stone bought from a man who'd pulled down a house in Witham.

To finish off the front garden of their newly named Corner Cottage, Aubrey bought some of the coping stones from the platform edge of the recently closed Little Bytham Station and laid a path to their front door.

Little Bytham Station – 60013 Dominion of New Zealand on the London bound Elizabethan express

The Rectory

Chris Isaac with his children

The Rectory is a Grade II listed building rebuilt by Thomas Boyfield in 1827 at a cost of £400. It became the home of village parson Reverend Deverell.

In 1952 the Church Diocese sold the Rectory to Mrs Agatha Fane and her husband Anthony Mountjoy-Fane. They had lived at Aunby after leaving their long-standing family home at Holywell Hall.

Mrs Fane eventually sold the rectory in 1977 to Mr and Mrs Forrow. Four years later Adrian and Christine Darby and their children became the new occupants. In 2007 Chris and Emma Isaac bought the property and moved in with their children Isabella, Anastasia and Reuben.

In 1844 at the age of twenty-eight, John Birch-Reynardson, who'd studied at Corpus Christi College, Cambridge became rector and benefactor of Careby and Holywell. Holywell Church together with one hundred and seventy-seven acres of Glebe land separated from Castle Bytham came under his auspices too.

As a young man while living at Holywell Hall John Birch-Reynardson discovered and catalogued thousands of documents relating to Careby Parish. His interest in history became well known and in 1855 he became involved in the excavation of a deserted medieval village at Aunby.

Charles Chambers strode into the kitchen at Aunby House. A lad of twelve years old hovered in the doorway. Mary, a servant girl little more than a child was clearing plates away from the table.

A tall upright man approaching fifty, Chambers surveyed his men, their elbows propped on the scrubbed pine. 'Come on now. No time to waste. Let's get to work lads.'

Four farm labourers scraped back stools and stood up.

'They've not finished their breakfasts yet.' Maria frowned and shushed two children playing and giggling on the floor.

The farmer shrugged then folded his arms. Muscles rippled beneath his shirt. 'They've been in here too long already.' He surveyed them with eyes like currants.

Robert Littledyke the eldest at twenty-four, young'uns George and Mowbray and Charlie Miller who acted younger but wasn't.

'Right lads,' Chambers said mildly, his face suddenly relaxing into a smile. 'There's a good harvest coming this year. We need to extend the stackyard. Start levelling the ground today.'

In single file everyone trooped outside, pulling on caps and shrugging into waistcoats.

The farmer turned to the lad still hovering as if he didn't know what was expected. 'And you, John Cotton, if you're here to learn, you can clean out the stables. Then fetch a shovel and join 'em. There'll be no better way to start than by getting a few blisters.

Robert and Charlie took turns to loosen the surface for the other two to scrape off and load into the cart. Soon, young John's hands were too sore to hold a shovel.

Robert shook his head. 'Yer soft, you are. And that's a fact. You'd better be in charge of leading the horse then. You can empty the cart.'

The men bent over their shovels again, ignoring the heat.

'Watch out chaps.' Mowbray wiped sweat from his brow just as Charles Chambers rode into the stackyard.

Nostrils flaring, his horse breathed hard under the noonday sun.

Robert got on well with Mr Chambers. He suspected he'd just returned from Stamford. Leaning on his shovel, he pushed his cap to the back of his head then nodded towards the dry loamy ground ahead of him.

'We've come across too big a stone to move, sir. Almost broke my spade.'

'I can see it.' The farmer slid down from his horse, handing the reins to Mowbray. A large stone slab jutted a couple of inches above the surface of the earth.

Robert squatted down and brushed his hand across it. 'Look here sir. There's some sort of carving…'

'Let me see.' Charles Chambers tugged up the knees of his trousers then knelt down, smoothing his hand where Robert indicated. He sighed and looked up. The labourers watched him carefully.

'Stop work for now lads. This will need investigating.' He paused as if thinking then straightened up. 'I know just the person to deal with this. Mowbray, hop up on that horse and ride as fast as you can to the Rectory. The Reverend should be involved. Ask him if he'll come.'

John Birch-Reynardson arrived in his carriage. Francis Eborn his coachman wheeled the horse to a halt by the front door and the Rector stepped down, black robes rippling in the welcome breeze, his face eager for news. He turned back. 'Thank you Francis. I won't be long.' He smiled down at the farmer. 'Now, Mr Chambers, young Mowbray Cox tells me you have something interesting to show me.'

'That I have. If you'd like to follow me Reverend.' The farmer led the way across the road to the stackyard. His men were still scraping and clearing the ground. They stretched and stepped back, glad of the opportunity to rest.

The Rector stared down, nodding his head slightly. 'That is a coffin lid if I'm not mistaken.' He glanced at the farmer. 'Sorry. You'd better call a halt to the work. I will need to obtain permission to move this.'

Mr Chambers gnawed at his bottom lip. 'We need this space for harvest, Reverend. Is there any way of speeding things up?'

The Rector nodded. 'I'll see what I can do.' He looked round. 'Have you found any more?'

Young John piped up. 'We found three more over here, your Reverend.'

The Rector went to the Hundred Rolls, manuscripts in the possession of the Hatcher family at Careby a century before and kept in the muniment room at Holywell.

Charles Chambers' face was expectant. 'Did you discover anything Reverend?'

John Birch-Reynardson steepled his fingers and beamed. 'Indeed I did. I found an agreement between Holywell and Aunby made in 1626 when sheepwalks were broken up for corn. But no mention of any building.'

'So...?' Chambers could tell by the Rector's face that he had found something else.

'I discovered a document - it was in Latin of course. It tells us that in 1274 Adam de Saint Laudo was in possession of Aunby as subinfeudatory of Lord Walter de Colville.'

'Subinfeu… As long ago as that?'
'St Laudo came here under circumstances strongly suggestive of there being a residence upon the manor.'
'What? Here, you mean?'
'Certainly a dwelling of considerable importance that warranted a chapel and burial place.'

With permission obtained, John Birch-Reynardson and Charles Chambers' workforce excavated four stone coffins.[2]

Thirty-three skeletons, a coat of arms,[3] and some fragments of mullions and tracery of windows were discovered.

In *'Holywell and the Birch-Reynardsons'*, Mildred Phillipson of Castle Bytham wrote…

'According to the census of 1851 Careby Rectory did not appear to be occupied but in 1861 John Birch-Reynardson was in residence with his sister Emma Lucy and a staff of five - lady's maid, cook, housemaid, footman and groom. By 1871 John had married Sophie, sister Emma had departed, the servants remained much as before.

'A personal account book covering the years 1854 to 1863 has survived. It is most meticulously kept, even the smallest items of expenditure are listed separately…

'The account book begins in 1854 and large (for those days) sums of money were spent on household equipment, pointing to the possibility that John Birch-Reynardson set up house on his own for the first time in that year. Sums were expended on carpets (£95 in this one year), housepainting, (£47), glass, china, plated goods, cutlery, cocoa mats, a lamp, a barometer, greenhouse piping (£37 5s. 8d.) Portland cement, a knife board, linen (£52 9s. 0d), Carter's seeds and manure.

2… Kettles the builders incorporated the four stone coffin lids into the river bridge at Careby sometime in the 1920s. Discovered by Reverend Stanley Hoar during rebuilding of the present bridge in the eighties, they are now stored by the east wall of the church.

3… The Coat of Arms has been erected on the wall of Careby Church.

'In addition sums were paid to tradesmen - a cabinet maker, (£60), silversmith and upholsterer. Odd items of interest were £5 19s. 6d. for Moselle wine, £6 for three dozen sherry, £1 for fireworks and 2s. 6d. each for Christmas boxes to the postman and Thomas Wilford…

'During that one year 1854, John Birch-Reynardson made donations or subscriptions to the following charities or societies:

'Archaeological Institute £1, Church Missionary Society 10s. 6d. Fieldsaw Ragged School £1, Royal Free Hospital £1, Additional Curates Society £1, Widows of Clergy £1 1s., Ireland £5, Asylum for Idiots 10s. 6d. Society for the Propagation of the Gospel £1 10s, Patriotic Fund £5, Castle Bytham School Feast 5s. 0d. and Careby Poor Rate £2 15s. 4d.

'According to White's Lincolnshire 1856, Careby Rectory was worth £400; with a tithe rent of £368 and eighty acres of glebe land. During the ten years covered by the account book the lowest annual expenditure was £1,035, the highest £1,805.

'When John Birch-Reynardson died on 25 May 1914, Stamford Mercury for that week published the following obituary notice.

"There passed away on Monday night one of the most venerable personalities in the county – the Rev. John Birch Reynardson…

"His care for his parishioners was truly fatherly, but apart from this he had been a public-spirited benefactor in a variety of ways. By his death the Stamford Infirmary and other charitable institutions have lost a munificent and warm-hearted supporter, for his life seemed largely devoted to alleviating the lot of the unfortunate, both inside and outside the parochial circle. He carried out at his own expense many schemes for the benefit of the inhabitants of the locality in which he lived, and prior to the inauguration of the Board Schools he bore the expense of the education of the majority of the children in a 'Dame School'. He personally assumed the responsibility of the construction of the present road from Careby to Holywell.

"A Churchman of the old school, his sympathies with his neighbours were real and *broad and his loss to Careby and the locality generally may well be said to be irreparable...*

"Probably few Rectory houses in the country can lay claim to such delightful attractions as those at Careby Rectory, and the deceased gentleman's extreme pride in his home was quite natural. As an amateur gardener he formerly excelled, and his grounds contain many specimens of rare plants; the effect is perfectly charming. It has been said he planted every tree in the garden. He took exceptional pleasure in his beautiful lake, and displayed keen interest in any scheme for the adornment of the Rectory and its environs. He boasted a splendid aviary, in which there are foreign specimens and in one large apartment in the house was a collection of trophies[4], weird, beautiful or grotesque, quite sufficiently large to warrant the description of an elaborate private museum".'

John Birch-Reynardson, being a scholar, was fascinated by history and on discovering the Hatcher documents instated a Muniment Room at his family home, Holywell Hall. No doubt this was where he first kept the collection of weapons before he set up Careby Museum and where in the 1830s he drew up the elaborate catalogue.

In 1855/6 John Birch-Reynardson oversaw the renovation of Careby Church. He managed without an architect and the north aisle was rebuilt. By 1861 the church had been re-pewed and restored for one hundred and fifty sittings. At that time Careby was populated by one hundred and eight souls.

Anticipating the arrival of the railway the Rector also organised the selling of Glebe land near Little Bytham Station.

In 1862 he married Sophie Wynyard then set about extending his garden. Coming to an arrangement with his mother at Holywell, they exchanged lands and buildings in Careby and Aunby. The Rector was given land surrounding the

4... *Careby Rectory Museum. In 1936 nephew William Birch-Reynardson donated JBR's collection of flintlock pistols, tinderboxes and local finds to Pitt Rivers Museum in Oxford.*

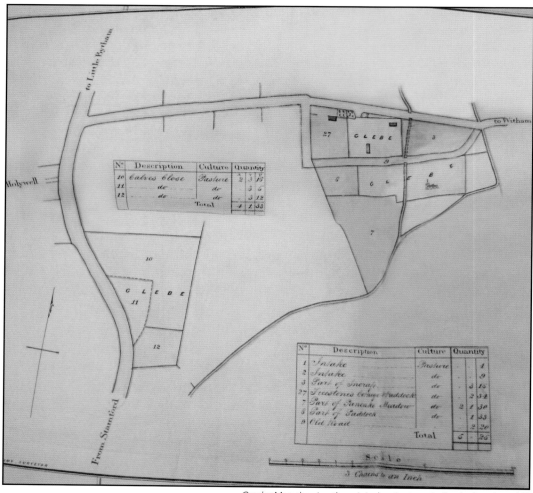

Nº	Description	Culture	Quantity		
			A	R	P
10	Calves Close	Pasture	2	3	15
11	do	do		3	5
12	do	do		3	12
		Total	4	1	33

Nº	Description	Culture	Quantity		
1	Intake	Pasture			1
2	Intake	do			9
3	Part of Snerap	do		3	15
27	Treestenes Cottage Paddock	do		2	34
7	Part of Rerrett's Meadow	do	2	1	30
8	Part of Paddock	do		1	33
9	Old Road			2	20
		Total	5		25

Scale

3 Chains to an Inch

Careby Map showing the original main street in Careby (numbered 9).
This was re-routed to accommodate John Birch-Reynardson's rectory garden,
and the route can be seen in the photograph on the right leading to the bridge.

Church. It included Freestone's Cottage where agricultural worker William Freestone lived with his wife Sarah and young daughter Mary during the 1840s, together with a paddock to the rear of Gardener's Cottage, increasing the size of the rectory garden. In return he gave his mother three Calves' Closes (behind The Elms) and land at Aunby.

Ancient Careby village had faced Aunby. Paddock Old Road ran across the front of east-facing Careby Manor before winding behind the rectory then across two branches of the River Glen before proceeding up the hill to Witham.

JBR's view of Careby Church from his beloved garden, 1914
with permission of Alan and Clare Price

The Rector provided the present road leading to the river bridge. The old road bridge to the east of the rectory garden became his private footbridge to the church.

With two rounded arches, triangular cutwaters and low sidewalls this bridge has large square piers. Set at an angle, the walls support collared ball finials.

Developing the rectory garden became one of the Rector's greatest joys.

In turn, head gardeners Alexander Reed, William Laskey and Frederick James Cannell tended the garden, orchard, greenhouse and water fountain. Laskey and Cannell, also Careby's Parish Clerks lived in Gardener's Cottage.

In 1890 when his wife Sophie died, the Rector unusually positioned her grave to face west and overlooking their beloved garden. To the rear of the marble headstone he planted an ornamental holly tree.

When John Birch-Reynardson died in 1914 at the age of ninety-eight his nephew the Reverend Edwin Thomas Birch-Reynardson conducted the funeral. Eight neighbouring clergymen attended the service and Careby School children sent a wreath in the form of a harp with a broken string.

The Rectory, Careby, 1915

John Birch-Reynardson

Between 1900 and 1911 Welsh curate Reginald Pearce shouldered most of John Birch-Reynardson's duties. He lived at the east end of four terraced cottages now known as Thistlecroft.

The 1901 Census records the Rectory household. Butler Henry Horne and housekeeper Elvira Riggs – formerly Sophie's lady's maid tended the Rector, a visiting policeman and his wife from Cape Town. Susan Aster was the cook, Martha Baxter the housemaid, Ellen Marshall the kitchen maid and there was a boy aged sixteen called Bruce Baldwin. Night nurse was Martha Garner.

John Birch-Reynardson is remembered with a wall tablet in the church he so faithfully served for seventy years. In 1918 a new heating system was installed in the church as a memorial to him.

Formerly a footman for a magistrate in Hampshire, the Rector's butler Henry Horne lived at the rectory for at least three decades. He was registered as Henry Horn Huckins in 1843.

Described as a complex character he was, in the words of his grandson, 'a right rogue. Overtly respectable, he sang in the choir but had a jacket with special pockets for hares.'

Henry returned to Hampshire in 1875 to marry Elizabeth Walter. After their wedding Elizabeth came to live at 16 Church Road, Careby and next door to curate Reginald Pearce. They had three children, Elizabeth (Bessie), Henry Frank and Ellen. In 1914 Ellen married Reginald Pearce; by then he was residing at the Rectory.

Henry Horne
With permission of
Alan and Clare Price

33

John Birch-Reynardson's strong signature is recorded on their marriage certificate.

When Henry Horne retired he rejoined his wife and they lived in the curate's former cottage because the remainder of the terrace had burned down.

Henry Horne died in 1927. His wife died in 1933 at the age of ninety-one. They'd lived in Careby for over fifty years.

The wedding day of Henry Horne's eldest daughter Elizabeth (Bessie). Elizabeth his wife is seated
With permission of Alan and Clare Price.

CAREBY...   OLD GLEN COTTAGE

Rectory Buildings, built for the previous rectory about two hundred years earlier are constructed from local limestone and brick. With stabling and four stalls for horses and a coach house for two small carriages, the outbuildings were built around the stable yard.

The groom's cottage had been home to John Birch-Reynardson's coachman, Francis Eborn.

More recently, during and after the war, Arthur Ellerby who was gamekeeper to Anthony Mountjoy Fane lived there. His wife Granny Ellerby, a member of Careby Mother's Union looked after the bread and wine for church communion. When Arthur died she stayed on in the cottage. Grandchildren stayed with her and slept through the noise of a bomb landing near Lodge Farm, the aftershock blowing tiles from the roof.

In the 1980s Jeff and Judy Midwood converted the by then, derelict property and renamed it Old Glen Cottage. It is now the home of Richard and Marie Turpin.

Granny Ellerby
With permission of Richard Clarke

Reverend Charles W. E. Cleaver   1923-35

With robes flowing, Reverend Cleaver left the Rectory and walked over the ornamental bridge through the churchyard and into the church.

Clutching a halfpenny for the collection, Betty Creasey sat with her brothers and sisters in the front two pews, intently staring up as he delivered his sermon. Reverend Cleaver always delivered this from the second pulpit. Sunday Service was attended by almost thirty worshippers. Teachers at Careby School Mrs Bewley and Mrs Capper took turns as organists. If not enough air was pumped into the bellows the only sound was the keys being pressed.

The Reverend Cleaver's car outside the Rectory in 1925

Reverend Cleaver's parishioners were dismayed when he retired. In 1935, obviously affected, he preached his farewell sermons at both Holywell and Careby Churches, making a special effort to say goodbye to every individual.

The Hall staff decorated Holywell's pretty church and Mr and Mrs C. Hoare of Holywell Hall were present. At Careby, ex-Servicemen and the Cricket Club were well represented. Mr Thornhill and Mr Carter read the lessons.

Reverend Cleaver died in 1936.

Reverend Smith became Careby's next rector. Owner of two cars, an Austin Ruby for parish visits and a prized red Alvis, he became involved with Careby's Farm Camp during the war.

Careby Farm Camp

As a result of negotiations between Sheffield's Firth Park Grammar School and Kesteven War Agricultural Committee, Brian Hall, now residing in Northborough, came to Careby Farm Camp with other thirteen to sixteen year old boys. They were based at the Village Hall.

Brian says that Firth Park School was located north of Sheffield in the catchment area for boys living on council estates so both the opportunity to go to the Grammar School and to come to Careby were opportunities not to be missed. Visiting Careby in September 1944, he was lucky to come. A boy in Form 3A had an infectious disease so his Form 3B were summoned to go to Careby instead.

With only a few hours notice the boys gained their parents' permission and packed their bags ready for the journey by train that evening. Careby was a welcome change from the damage inflicted on Sheffield by the Luftwaffe.

Next morning the boys woke to the sound of heavy bombers flying over the village hall. The sorties were a precursor to operation Market Garden. [5]

Work started on Monday. Brian opted to join onion pickers at Thurlby, leaving his friends to pick spuds or pull flax for the duration of their stay. All the time he was conscious of a continual stream of Dakota transport aircraft, (DC3's) towing gliders full of airborne troops or ferrying much needed supplies to the beleaguered division in Arnhem. When damaged aircraft returned to local airfields the boys could hear supply parachute cables swishing through the air beneath the planes.

Brian collected engine numbers from trains running on the East Coast Main Line, including grey painted steam engines (war utility), streamlined 10000 and Eighth Army. The hot evenings and weekends were spent at Holywell Lake, either in the punt found on the bank or swimming in deep water near the

5... *Operation Market Garden - an exercise carried out in an effort to bring the war to a close, fought in the German occupied Netherlands (Arnhem) to secure a series of bridges. The British met with early success but the operation ultimately failed.*

sluice gate opposite Mill Farm. Boys billeted at the Hall shared the huge stone bath. The less fortunate took their soap to the lake.

Listening to the radio, Brian heard about Dim Out, signifying, he thought, an end to Black Out. But after dark he spotted a lone aircraft flying up the railway line with all its interior lights blazing.

Brian has kindly supplied the following evocative articles written by boys who attended the Camp.

The Farm Camp at Careby 1942 *by I.R.W. Lower 6th Arts*

An advance party, consisting of six boys in charge of Messrs Tomlinson and Pascoe, went to Careby by road on Friday, August 14th to make preparations for the main body travelling the following day. From the station we had a walk of half a mile to Careby Village Hall, which was to be our home for the next month. As our bags and cases were fully packed with various goods and chattels we were very pleased indeed to see the place. A few boys were there to greet us and soon everyone had commandeered a bunk for himself. The afternoon was occupied with filling of palliasses with straw from a nearby farmyard, the securing of blankets and the making up of beds in general. Fountain pens and pencils were busily engaged in writing letters home to announce safe arrival.

Next came our first "Farm Camp" meal which, judging by the remains was heartily enjoyed by all. Various odd tasks and games filled in the evening until, to the accompaniment of many 'planes constantly roaring over and the regular thundering of expresses on the London Main Line only thirty yards away, we settled down finally to a rather restless slumber.

Next day, volunteers worked on camp sanitation; some enjoyed minor bicycle excursions into the surrounding district; others chatted of farmers and the farms. In the evening a good number attended Careby Church whilst a few others went to the

Wesleyan Chapel in Little Bytham. From the former it was reported that the singing was greatly enhanced and at the latter the morning Sunday School was increased by nearly 100%!

On Monday morning many convoys of bicycles set off in good time for their respective farms to arrive for 8a.m. They returned home (perhaps not so fast) shortly after 5p.m. and many were the stories told that evening. How I'd been driving a tractor; how I'd worked a binder; how I'd been 'turning' peas (it was a noted district for the growing of peas), how I'd been 'stooking' sheaves of corn; and generally how all thought their particular farm must be the best in the neighbourhood.

On the whole the week passed slowly and by the end of it we had lost one or two boys who did not take to the new life and returned home. Most of us were ready for Saturday afternoon, several taking the opportunity of visiting Stamford, mostly by cycle but some by bus. The entrance to the town was through a quaint narrow street that eventually broadened out to become the main shopping thoroughfare, the modern effect being produced by a Woolworth's (which was of course, patronised.)

At the beginning of the second week harvesting in the district was in full swing and it was necessary for us to put in some hard work but however tired we might have been, one could always see, of an evening, a number of boys playing with a football in the field adjoining the Hall, darkness alone stopping play. One continual source of interest was the trains

The Elms
With the permission of Nino and Penny D'Anna

on the London Scotland line just over the road from the camp, on which numerous 'stream-lines' went up and down each day. Many famous trains and engines were seen, including "The Flying Scotsman" and the record breaker, "Mallard".

An A4 streamlined locomotive at Careby on a London bound express

In the month we were there it only once really rained. The farmers were very satisfied and grateful for our work and showed it in many acts of kindness in addition to our "pay envelopes!" The Stamford newspaper printed a short appreciation of our work and indeed the only grumble was that we were not allowed to stay another week to complete our task. This could not be, despite the strenuous efforts of the Rector of Careby to lengthen our stay.

We "struck camp" on September 12th. The bunks had been in tiers of three and those who had occupied the lowest looked on in horror at the ease with which they were dismantled, though this was well known to those who had erected them after much struggling. A Main Line train was specially stopped for us by the kindly effort of a Careby inhabitant and we arrived back in Sheffield bronzed and fit, having accomplished three main objects - helped the Nation's War Effort, benefited in body and mind by the change and earned for the School the respect of many new friends.

The Reverend Smith, Rector in 1944

For Farm Campers Only – 1943 *by Deric King*
(A pupil who attended Camp the previous year.)

FIRST, MORE OF A WARNING THAN A HINT.

    1. A farm camp is not a holiday camp.

    2. Farming is sheer unadulterated HARD WORK. As the school is only able to run one camp this year, it is imperative that everybody stays the full time. We cannot afford to have anybody going home after a few days, because they "don't like it."

SO:

    3. If you MUST go to the cinema twice a week DON'T go to Careby.

    4. If you MUST have fish and chips for supper every night – DON'T go to Careby and above all

    5. If you can't stand up to eight hours solid work a day, then for your own sake, have your holiday at HOME.

BUT:

If you do want to do one of the most important jobs of the war, if you want a complete change of life for a month in the heart of the country, THEN, if you are allowed, GO, by all means.

NOW HERE ARE SOME PRACTICAL SUGGESTIONS AND ADVICE FOR THIS YEAR'S NEW RECRUITS.

Sort your luggage carefully and cut out all unnecessary articles. On the other hand, be sure to take plenty of the essential ones, especially socks, underwear and towels etc. Gumboots or Wellingtons may seem rather cumbersome but are a great asset in wet weather.

In my opinion, a case or cases (as the case may be!) are the best, for in them, clothes are most easily kept straight, and this is important when you are staying for a month. When the luggage is packed, see that it is firmly secured of course and also well labelled; also take with you labels for the return journey.

See to it, that your bicycle is in good order before you leave. It will be one of the most useful things you will take. Of course, do not forget a repair outfit and spanners etc., in case they are needed.

Last year we had no pillows and most people made use of a rolled up blanket; in that case it will be an advantage to take a pillowcase to keep the blanket in and to prevent it from becoming "unrolled up." It is much more pleasant to sleep in a sheet than between blankets, so put that down on your list. One will be enough, as it can be doubled or, if you wish to take the trouble, the loose sides can be sewn together so making a "bag" to sleep in.

You will find a watch very useful indeed (last year, one party on the first day worked half an hour too long because they did not know the time – mind you, this only happened on the first day.)

See that all cutlery and crockery is well marked and easily recognisable; it is very useful in that respect to have something which is stamped.

It is very unlikely that, for the entire month, you will have one drop of hot water to wash in. Because of that, take with you soap of good lathering quality (and even then it will be difficult to get a really good wash.) The best place to keep soap is either in a proper case or failing that a little tin, and then it is kept from harming any clothes.

If the weather is like last year's you will get very sunburnt so I should try to obtain some sunburn lotion or cream to take with you.

Include in your luggage some brown paper and string in case you need to send a parcel home, and if you intend sending home any fruit, such as there may be, you will need a good stout box. Besides this, a tin will be needed for sandwiches; last year I

The boys at the Farm Camp attended the Firth Park School in Sheffield

found one to be just suitable, which measured 6"x 5"x 3" and one at least of that size should be brought. Last year, we managed to obtain some bottles of mineral water, but the supply was uncertain and so I should take an empty bottle in which to carry water.

Take plenty of writing paper, envelopes and postcards for you will probably want to write home a good deal. You need not take any stamps, as they are one of the few things that can be bought in the village.

A pack of playing cards is useful for the later part of the evening, but I should not advise taking any other involved games since there is generally too much noise to concentrate deeply. For that reason, if you want to read, magazines are better than books.

In answer to the new recruit's question – How much money shall I need? On the average, ten shillings will be sufficient to cover normal needs – mineral waters, sweets, fruit and stamps; but it is advisable to have more than this in case anything unforeseen happens.

The "regulars" will be looking forward to seeing Careby again, and I am sure newcomers (or goers) will be charmed after making its acquaintance. But a word in the ear of those new recruits – Just see that you do nothing to harm the reputation which last year's team gained for themselves and of which they are very proud – and then all will be well.

P.S. Re-read sentences numbered (1) to (5). Study them carefully; consider there-on and then you cannot say that you were not warned!

Careby revisited 1943 *by Deric King*

This year the Village Hall was used solely for purposes of cooking and feeding with the exception of a few fire watchers who conformed to the general idea as far as sleeping goes, but who differed in that their duty was to keep the fire going - the one in the kitchen. Some of the party slept at the Rectory and the rest at Holywell Hall, in rooms generously placed at our disposal by the Rector and Mr C. C. Hoare.

Everyone was extremely comfortable in both places. The Rectory-ites tended to be rather thankful when the Hall-ites had to cycle one and a half miles in pouring rain. I remember it once started to rain about two minutes after we had left Careby, and within another two minutes water was squelching in our shoes; and that is raining pretty hard! But on a fine and clear morning the run from Holywell to Careby was pure joy and after such a run were we ready for our bread and dripping!

In addition to sleeping accommodation at Holywell Hall we were also able to make use of the Lake and rowing boat. Some imaginative people saw the possibilities of finding out something of what a Commando landing is like. One party was in the boat; the other on land. Weapons were chiefly "conkers". Unfortunately one party suffered a minor casualty that had to be treated at the Hospital. He couldn't have been a Commando!

But we went to Careby to work, and work we did - even harder than last year. Generally the Harvest had been started when we arrived and there was never any shortage of work. An occasional SOS came for labour urgently needed and wherever it was possible we tried to supply the demand. We received the best possible treatment from the people of Careby. Their hospitality was amazing and our thanks are due to them all for their kindness.

In some quarters it seemed that after one year's trial, we were taken somewhat for granted. But whatever our troubles, the Camp was a very happy one. The improved conditions included facilities for a hot bath at least once per week, which was much better than having to find a convenient stream. Although the cooking arrangements were but slightly improved the food on the whole was up to last year's standard and we must again thank most heartily the ladies who, quite voluntarily, came to cook for us.[6]

The Land Army was not seen much in Careby, its place being taken to some extent by Italian prisoners. These arrived each morning in a motor coach just after some of our boys had departed for a distant farm, crowded into a tiny van. We did not grudge the Italians their comfort, though all the same we rather envied them. But, returning to the Land Army, we must be grateful to them, for in 1942 they took over a school at Thorpe-on-the-Hill that had been destined for our camp. Thank you - Land Army.

Brian Hall, second row third from the left who came to Careby at thirteen years old in September 1944 when he was billeted in the Village Hall.
With permission of Brian Hall

6... *These ladies came from Sheffield Domestic College.*

Careby Harvest Camp, 1944 - *D. W.*

Some of the more fortunate were able to make a bit of spending money during the day. These were the potato pickers, who got a bonus of five shillings per ton; but it was arduous work and most of those engaged on it were glad when a change came. Many different types of work were undertaken, including the inevitable "muck-carting" on wet days, and nearly everybody had something to say about those barley awns.

We always felt tired in the morning, but we soon learned to recognise the various reveilles and to estimate the length of time we could safely remain in bed after they had sounded, it sometimes being almost dangerous to do so. For those of us who stayed on an extra week, reveille took the form of a half brick thrown from a great distance on to the roof of the hall by an early riser [7] of the village.

We became very friendly with some Italians who were resident at several farms in the district, and often at night we would congregate on the bridge, talking and singing songs with them. We found them very pleasant sociable people, and they ran a dance almost every evening, which was frequently attended by a number of our boys and cooks.

The services of eight members of the School Staff were a vital part of the organisation – indeed the camp would have been impossible without them – and many a time did the cooking of Mrs Bates win praise when both spirits and supplies were low.

We had a number of visitors. On one occasion Councillor Bingham came over from Sheffield to see us, and on another, representatives of the Kesteven War Agricultural Committee. One Sunday morning two people arrived who had been to the camp in the previous years but had been lured elsewhere. They tried to tempt us (or was it merely to make us envious?) by talks of orchards stretching as far away as one could see, of twelve shillings earned in a six-hour day, and other attractions; but we refused

7... *Mr Barney, who worked as cowman at Careby Manor Farm.*

to be impressed. One day the presence of several policemen on the bridge over the railway aroused curiosity and much speculation; later on the Royal Train went down the line.

A new feature of the camp this year was a semi-official sing-song held just before lights out, which fully compensated for the fact that soon after our arrival the football became unserviceable. The old piano was seldom silent, much to the annoyance of the late-breakfasters, although it was not quite up to its form of thirty years ago - at least, one hopes not. It responded best to the fingers of yet another visitor to the camp, who coaxed a greater volume of sound from that old tin can and the throats of the boys than will be have heard in the village hall for many a year. Once again the punt on Holywell Lake provided amusement, and by the kindness of Major Hoare we were permitted to use his private tennis court.

I don't think anyone was really glad to leave Careby; in fact eight boys just had to stay for an extra week. There was a great celebration on the next to last night, when almost the whole camp went to a Land Army Hostel nearby and played games and sang until after eleven o'clock. Socially I think we had a much better camp than ever before. Thanks are due to many people, but especially to the Rector for the generous way in which he placed his house at our disposal, and took a close interest in all we did.

Excerpts taken from FIRPANIAN...
The magazine of Firth Park School in Sheffield

Careby Parish during WWII

The village of Careby was never directly attacked during World War II but the bridge over the railway line was damaged by machine gun fire during an attack on a train by a German airplane.

Bob Creasey was working in a sugar beet field about half a mile away from the village when he heard an airplane approaching. This wasn't unusual for he often saw and heard RAF planes flying about. Moments later he was startled to see a low flying aircraft with a black Swastika emblazed on the side.

Bob and men with him dived for cover in a nearby spinney. The plane flew north. The German pilot found his target, a train travelling south towards London. As the train rattled towards Careby the pilot opened up on it with his machine gun, strafing the train as it went under the bridge. A soldier travelling on the train was killed.

Bob's aunt, Mrs Thurston who lived in the old toll cottage opposite the school had a close call. She'd been cycling home and when the attack took place she threw herself off her bike to take cover from stray bullets.

Bob was fairly sure the plane was a Junkers 88. A twin-engined Luftwaffe plane, it was one of fifteen thousand built during WWII.

Careby was not a high priority target for the German Luftwaffe but was often under the flight path to several major cities and the surrounding RAF bases.

Young women from Careby cycled up to the hill past Holywell to talk to soldiers of the Home Guard stationed at the entrance to Pettywood Farm, the highest point in the area. The Home Guard manned a beacon in an effort to spot German aircraft. Dozens of beams from beacons lit up the night sky as far as the eye could see. Locals believe it was because of the beacon at Holywell that three bombs dropped nearby.

Two bombs fell at Holywell; one narrowly missed Lodge Farm. The subsequent explosions shook the entire parish. Beds moved. Someone living at Swayfield told his nephew about spotting a German bomber in the moonlight circling Careby before the bombs dropped.

Another time a bomb landed in Docksight Wood. Again, the whole parish was shaken. The massive hole where it exploded is still visible.

Understandably, villagers were worried for their children's safety.

A young lady on ARP duty suggested that the head teacher of the school should contact Charles Creasey. He was a member the Observer Corp. She wanted a trench dug in one of his fields for a school air raid shelter. (Parents from Aunby had declined to send their children to school because of no provision for protection during the air raids).

As well as the Home Guard, the ROC (Royal Observers Corp) had an Observation Post in Clipsham manned by volunteers from the surrounding area. Reports of German aircraft movement were relayed to RAF Langtoft, the nearest Ground Command Intercept (GCI) location, in an effort to give potential targets early warning.

The most significant local Allied Forces activity within the Careby area was RAF Cottesmore, Wittering, North Luffenham, Saltby, North and South Witham, Folkingham, Stretton, Langtoft and Grimsthorpe. All had RAF bases, radar sites, ammunition storage facilities or decoy airfields so activity in the air and on the ground was commonplace in Careby Parish. On a number of occasions planes were forced to make emergency landings in the fields.

In addition to operational activities above and around the village, the RAF did much of their training over the area. Horsa Gliders, towed by Halifaxes practiced overhead. RAF Grimsthorpe was an RAF bomb range and the bombers used the railway line to practice their run in on to the target. Spitfires and Hurricanes targetted them and each other in practice dogfights.

Betty had hung out most of her washing and was almost through feeding the last sheet through the mangle when she heard the dull throb of the Wellington. She quickly wound the last of the sheet through the rollers then hurried outside.

The sun was high. The plane was steadily tracking across the sky to the east towards Witham.

She shaded her eyes.

The sun glinted on a tiny pinprick of another plane high above it. She squinted through her fingers, a Spitfire she guessed, homing in on the Wellington. Another practice dogfight. One of these days, she thought, some pilot will misjudge it.

Hundreds of feet overhead, the pilot of the Spitfire went into an attacking dive.

Betty clapped her hand to her mouth...if he didn't pull away...

'Oh dear God!'

The Spitfire clipped the wing of the Wellington.

Betty could hardly bear to watch as the pilot lost control and his aircraft went spiralling down. Then a plume of smoke billowed up into the sky.

Betty heard later that villagers had rushed up the hill to help the pilot. But it was useless. The aircraft had crashed into woods near Witham-on-the-Hill and the pilot was fatally injured. The Wellington limped back to base.

Whenever planes flew over Careby after that, Betty turned up the radio.

In late 1941 America joined the War and a year later US airmen and pilots were based in RAF North Witham and RAF Folkingham. They turned up in Careby to attend dances held in the village hall. Although popular with the ladies, the Americans were not met with open arms by their British counterparts and local men.

Young lads including Bob Creasey's brother were encouraged by the Hon. Mountjoy Fane to join the Territorial Army and then on to the Leicester Yeomanry. Edgar Halliday who lived in a cottage in the Station Yard joined the RAF. Sadly Edgar was killed in East Germany towards the end of the war. He is buried in Careby churchyard next to his parents.

The son of Commander and Mrs Warr-King who were to come and live at The Old Bakehouse after the war was also killed in Germany whilst fighting for his country.

Careby became home to a number of children evacuated from cities targeted by the Luftwaffe and Mrs Creasey looked after a number of children during the war for varying periods of time. Bob remembers two from Hull in particular, Ron and Trevor Hesp. After the war Trevor returned to Hull but Ron stayed on and eventually married the daughter of the Bourne cemetery keeper.

The Old Bakehouse
With the permission of Margaret Creasey

Although Careby was not too directly affected by the violence, with most of the men away farmers were under pressure to produce food to sustain the nation through the war years. Fortunately they had help from numerous sources in completing this task.

From 1943, Italian prisoners of war, then German then later other Eastern Europeans were held in Britain. As they entered the UK they were screened and as a rule of thumb those individuals deemed a risk were sent further north, whilst those seen as low risk were billeted in the Midlands and in the south of the country. Low risk POWs were used as labour on farms and building sites until returned to their native countries.

Like so many other farmers, Bob's father paid for the use of these prisoners of war. To begin with the Italians and their guards arrived daily by truck, doing jobs like potato picking. In the evening the trucks would come back, pick up the POWs and return them to their billet. The nearest and most likely POW camp the prisoners came from was Camp 106 on Empingham Road in Stamford.

Later in the war Bob's father also employed German POWs. The Germans were immaculate in everything that they did; well turned out, ensuring tools were maintained. Towards the end of the war and beyond, the POWs were housed during the week in an old railway carriage in the field behind Linnet Cottage. Unguarded, they ate their own food and generally went about their business. On weekends and holiday time, trucks arrived and returned them to central camps.

Ukrainian and Hungarian displaced persons also worked on the farms. These people had nothing and generally were not trusted by locals because they had nothing to lose. Some prisoners of war remained in the UK until the late 1940s. One German POW, Ray Volks, kept in touch with Bob's parents for some time after returning to Germany.

The Women's Land Army (WLA) was formed on the outbreak of war to free up their male counterparts. By 1943 the WLA was eighty thousand strong with many of them serving on farms in Lincolnshire. Most of the farmers in the area, including Bob's father, employed Land Girls, as they were known. Throughout the war they were billeted in Hanthorpe Hall near Bourne and continued to work on Lincolnshire farms until their disbandment in the late 1940s.

Most of the farm horses were gradually replaced by machinery during the war years. Grass fields had surrounded Careby but the emphasis on food production caused them to be ploughed to grow crops by order of the Agricultural War Committee.

Living through the war meant restrictions on movement within the village, especially at night. Then after the war was over Careby residents did their best to continue life as normal in the village hall.

Recently a cap badge has been discovered close to the ancient Careby to Holywell lane that in the early part of the 20th century may have continued as a footpath.

The Cap Badge
With the permission of Rupert Elmore

Investigation has revealed that the badge representing the South Lancashire Prince of Wales Volunteers would have been worn by a member of the Eleventh Service Battalion based at Grantham. In 1914 the pioneer battalion, nicknamed St. Helen's Pioneers was drafted around Grantham to build roads and bridges. The wearer of the cap badge may have lived at Careby or Holywell or been involved with a girl there.

In November 1915 the battalion of almost seven hundred men were drafted to France and remained there until World War I was over.

Only six of the soldiers returned alive.

CAREBY VILLAGE HALL

The hugely atmospheric Careby Village Hall looks like a derelict scout hut. Full of history, clad in rusting corrugated iron sheeting painted pale green, ivy creeps through peeling, wooden window frames.

Complete with stage, piano and curtains the village hall was built some time during the 1920s by the Sharpes of Careby Manor on land provided by Charles Creasey. Access was provided through a gate off the Little Bytham road.

Belonging to the village and self-funding the hall was the main venue for activities to raise money for Careby Church. With frequent dances – in the mid-fifties Bill Machin was in charge of square dancing, local bands played and people came from far and wide to pay the entry fee of two and sixpence. Tea, coffee and soft drinks provided refreshment.

Centre of back row, tall girl Cynthia Woodcock, next to her on the right – Mary Wallwin from Manor Farm; Pat Thurston standing next to the figure in the mask. Front row – Stephen Thurston, one of the Haring boys, Elizabeth Barney, Jane Creasey.

One of the earlier recorded events in the village hall was the wedding reception of Tom and Bella Pick. Celia Fenn's mother Margery Bull was bridesmaid and Celia's father was a member of the band who played at the reception.

The Rhythm Boys –
Spring is in the Air!

Aubrey & Rene Edinborough

Aubrey Edinborough, long-standing bellringer for the parish churches and at the time, churchwarden at Little Bytham Church, married Rene Woodcock, a Sunday school teacher and organist at Careby Church. Their wedding was held in April 1958 and Mrs Creasey played the organ. The hall hosted a reception for eighty.

In the 1950s health and safety laws changed and the hall did not comply with new rules so soon it fell into disrepair. In the 1970s Mrs Fane removed the majority of fixtures and fittings.

However on September 9th 2007, the Village Hall Field came alive once more with music, dancing and laughter following the wedding in St Stephen's Church of Louise Cooper and Ian Burris. It was followed by a reception in a beautifully decorated marquee with villagers joining the celebrations.

Next day, the marquee became the venue for the annual Long Lazy Lunch, raising £1,090 for church funds. Margaret and Bob Creasey, along with their usual hard working band of helpers, organised a delicious meal for over ninety diners. Seated around tables, friends and families enjoyed a leisurely and sunny Sunday afternoon.

David Cooper speaking at the wedding of his daughter Louise

CAREBY HILL FORT

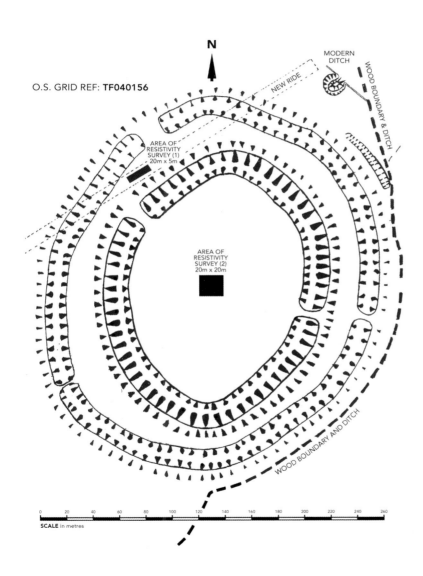

O.S. GRID REF: **TF040156**

N

MODERN DITCH

NEW RIDE

WOOD BOUNDARY & DITCH

AREA OF RESISTIVITY SURVEY (1) 20m x 5m

AREA OF RESISTIVITY SURVEY (2) 20m x 20m

WOOD BOUNDARY AND DITCH

SCALE in metres

0 20 40 60 80 100 120 140 160 180 200 220 240 260

The oldest sign of habitation in the parish lies southeast of Careby Wood: an Iron Age Hill Fort known as Careby Camp. Possibly 4th century BC, enclosing thirteen acres, the earthwork is overgrown but easily visible from the air. The distance between the inner and outer banks is one hundred and thirty feet. The outer bank is very slight and covered in scrub and trees and three feet above the present ground level.

By courtesy of Historic Environment Record, Lincoln
Original drawing by Marian Maguire
Edited by Ian Wilson

CAREBY ROMAN VILLA

The Roman Villa field by the River Glen

An aerial photograph taken in 1984 and lodged with the Historic Environment Record at Lincoln, shows a possible Romano-British Villa close to the river and visible as crop marks less than a mile from Careby Rectory.

(Roman Villa OS Map ref TF028159 {34710,34711}).

1066: Early Days

Careby's fees were allocated to the Wake family who were tenants of Peterborough Abbey.

Hereward the Wake of Bourne, said to be the son of Earl Leofric and Lady Godiva, was uncle to Earl Morcar and his brother Edwin. Hereward had been banished to France by his father for a misdemeanour as a fourteen-year-old. (Recent research has suggested he was a high-ranking Dane who hated the Normans).

When Wake heard the invading Normans had seized his father's estates and slaughtered his brother, Hereward came back and exacted revenge, killing fourteen Normans single-handed. Then he fled to the thickly wooded fens.

In an effort to retrieve his family's estates and save relics and treasures from the Normans, Hereward led a raid on Peterborough Abbey. As payment to the army of the Danish king who helped him he shared the rescued gold. However, afterwards the Danish army deserted him and returned to their homeland.

Harboured by the Abbot at Ely, Hereward gathered peasants for a rebellion against William's new law. They'd fight as foot soldiers with bows and long thin arrows designed to penetrate Norman chain mail.

Meanwhile, Hereward's nephew, Earl Morcar of Northumberland and brother-in-law to King Harold was dispossessed of land at Holywell and Castle Bytham. Before the invasion Morcar and brother Edwin had tried to establish an independent northern kingdom. However, after fighting for King Harold against the Vikings they lost their chance when not adding their forces to assist him at the Battle of Hastings.

With Uncle Hereward hiding in the fens, Morcar and his brother showed half-hearted attempts at rebellion while pretending to show allegiance to the Norman king.

William wasn't fooled. He knew of Morcar's connection with the Wake family and so he planned to build a castle at Castle Bytham to install his brother-in-law Drogo de la Beuvriere as Lord.

Drogo, one of his most trusted soldiers had supplied men, ships and supplies for the King's invasion. He'd already been rewarded with lands in Yorkshire and sixty manors south of the Humber.

He was deeply unpopular. Many fought to retain their lands and the Abbot of Peterborough claimed fifteen acres of Careby land against him.

On the top of the hill Oswin huddled cross-legged against the bank. The wind swept from the north. He loathed watching the long-legged hairy pigs snuffling through the scrub; he'd heard a whisper about Hereward and was keen to know what was going on.

He heard a shout and stood up. Wulfric; running towards him.

'Oswin, I've got something to tell you.' Wulfric doubled over, struggling to catch his breath. 'Saswalo, the Abbot's man, he met Eadwine by the church. You know that Lord Morcar has gone to Ely to help Hereward, don't you?'

Oswin nodded. 'Everyone knows that. So what's Eadwine told you?'

'That Norman invader...'

'The one who thinks he's a king?' Oswin shrugged his shoulders up and down in an effort to get warm.

Wulfric frowned. 'Don't let anyone hear you talk like that. King William to you. Some of his men built a causeway over Ely marshes. Did you hear that?' He laughed. 'It sank. The Normans were picked off by arrows. Hereward did a good job in holding them off. Ryce is with him.'

'I heard that. Who's looking after his land?'

'Never mind about that. Eadwine says Hereward's been betrayed by Abbot

Thurstan.' Wulfric looked over his shoulder as if someone might hear.

'Abbot Thurstan? I heard he was all for Hereward.'

'He was. But the King threatened to raze his abbey to the ground so…'

'Did Wake get away?'

'That's what I've heard. But they'll get him in the end.'

'He's a wily one, that Hereward. They'll have to catch him first.'

'They got Lord Morcar.'

Oswin crossed himself. 'What have they done with him?'

'Apparently he's been sent to Normandy.'

'Lord Morcar's a prisoner?'

'I don't think we'll hear any more about him. God knows what will happen now.' Wulfric stared into the undergrowth. 'How many swine am I supposed to be looking after?'

Domesday 1086

'In "Adewelle" [Careby] Peterborough [Abbey] had and has 5 carucates of land to the geld. [There is] land for 5 ploughs. Now there are 2 ploughs in desmesne; and 10 villans and 2 bordars and 2 sokemen have 3½ ploughs, and 18 acres of meadow. There are 180 acres of woodland pasture and 60 acres of scrubland. TRE worth 60s; now the same; tallage 12s.

In Little Bytham [Bitham] is a Berewick of "Adewelle" 4 carucates of land to the geld. There is land for 4 ploughs. This land is desmesne of Peterborough Abbey. Now 6 villans have there 2 ploughs and 2 oxen. There Saswalo, the Abbot's man, has of this land 2 carucates of land, and in desmesne half a plough; and 3 villans with 1 plough, and 25 acres of meadow, and 100 acres of scrubland. TRE this sokeland was worth 30s, now 20s.'

Domesday began to be compiled in 1080 and provided exact information of the value of each village. Under King William's feudal system, peasants had continued to pay in kind to the lord of the manor for the land granted to them. Each lord was granted lands by the French noblemen, Tenants-in-Chief, in return for service to the King. Every area of land was known as a Knight's Fee. For every Knight's Fee both lords and noblemen were expected to provide horses, arms and equipment as well as offering themselves for forty days annual service to their King.

    After the Conquest, the kingdom had been divided into about sixty thousand parcels of land and bestowed on Norman followers. King William rewarded French noblemen for their help with his invasion by sharing out 55% of the conquered lands. William kept 20% of the country for himself and 25% for the Church. The de Colvilles were awarded Aunby. The family were to reign over Castle Bytham and Careby for eight generations.

Typical cruck house construction, with two closed frames and one open truss

1085 - 1217: MEDIEVAL LIFE IN THE PARISH

Meanwhile ordinary people in the parish got on with their lives, worked hard and tilled the land.

Two Sokemen, who at any time could be called for military service, and ten villeins lived in Careby. Provided for by the lord of the manor, they received two oxen for ploughing, a cow, six sheep and seed for five acres of land.

Required to build their own cruck house or toft, they built it on to a wooden frame with wattle panels plastered with daub: a mixture of mud, straw and manure. Straw added insulation, and when left to dry in the sun the walls became strong. Once assembled, ventilation was provided by a gap in the wall covered by a curtain. Sacks stuffed with straw and small logs as pillows served as beds. Outside the cooking pot hung over the open fire. Cats, dogs and hens roamed. Dirt, smell, fleas and lice were unavoidable. At night animals were shepherded into tofts for protection against wolves and to prevent loss or theft.

The lord of the manor was obliged to provide a rough bench and table and a cooking pot with a few wooden bowls for a communal vegetable stew known as pottage.

Bezentwatyr, (River Glen), was used for transport to Kate's Bridge and beyond. The river also provided a source of disposal for waste.

Springs provided drinking water.

Careby's two bordars were inferior to villeins. Most likely craftsmen, they were forced to work for the lord every Monday and three days a week during harvest. Paying no rent they were allowed five acres to support their family. Provided for in a similar way to villeins, they were responsible for feeding the hounds at the manor kennels and taking turns to watch their lord's cattle and sheep.

Children, if they survived, worked as soon as they were old enough, either clearing stones from the land or chasing birds from growing crops.

Life was extremely organised. Jobs were elected. The Messor oversaw work in the fields. The Hayward was responsible for the hayfields and the Woodward for woodland. An Ale Connor controlled the sale of ale in the village. The Pinder rounded up stray animals and put them in the pinfold and the Beadle maintained law and order. A Tithing Leader was responsible for everyone meeting tithing requirements.

A Steward or Reeve was appointed to control the village if the lord were not present or away fighting. Should he refuse this unpaid job, he was forced to pay a fine.

A tithe barn stored seeds or equipment paid to the church instead of money the peasants didn't have. Careby peasants worked for no reward on forty-six acres of Glebe land.

No one dared break this rule or God would know and punish him.

Always there were fines or rents to pay. To be married: to be buried. Pay to enter into an agreement with a neighbour. Pay to bring a case to court, (at the manor house). A fine for not bringing a case to court: a fine for not being in court. A bereaved family had to pay a heriot tax, the extraction of a peasant's best ox by the lord on his death.

Wealth was viewed as corn or four-legged with horns. Danish invaders had introduced Red Cattle but it was Lincoln Long Wool sheep that predominated in the parish. Stamford was a thriving wool town.

Some land was densely forested with grazing deer and pigs. Arable land running to several hundred acres was divided into strips [8] and ploughed by teams of oxen.

Wheat grown close to habitation was protected against animal invasion. Corn was broadcast by hand with oxen following along behind to cover the seed with

8... *Robert Goodhall purchased Holywell in 1575. The remains of ridge and furrow strips have been identified on land almost opposite Robert's Field at Holywell.*

wooden framed harrows. In autumn oxen pulled a triangular ploughshare with an iron socket at one end for attachment to the wooden plough.

Eighteen valuable acres of meadow at Careby added to twenty-five acres at East (Little) Bytham. Meadowland producing hay was often valued at four or five times as much as arable land. Cut with sickles and when dry forked into carts, it was the men who dragged the hay carts back to Careby. Horses were rare for only knights could afford them and in June oxen were needed for ploughing the fallow field.

Only slightly less valuable than meadowland were the one hundred and eighty acres of woodland pasture called Careby Wood. Valuable not only for pannage but for semi-wild pigs and goats, the wood provided timber for houses, fuel and fencing and the opportunity to hunt deer. Stabilitoines: deer hedges and leaps, were built for stalling deer in flight when hunted.

Life was traditionally governed by the weather…

JANUARY	Mending and making tools; repairing fences.
FEBRUARY	Carting manure and marl; limey clay, for the land.
MARCH	Ploughing and spreading manure.
APRIL	Spring sowing and harrowing.
MAY	Digging ditches; first ploughing of fallow fields left to regain strength.
JUNE	Hay making; second ploughing of fallow field; sheep shearing.
JULY	Hay making; sheep shearing; weeding of crops.
AUGUST	Harvesting.
SEPTEMBER	Threshing, ploughing; pruning fruit trees.
OCTOBER	Last plough of the year.
NOVEMBER	Collecting acorns for pigs - oak trees were common.
DECEMBER	Mending and making tools; killing animals.

If a severe frost killed off the growing crop the impact affected a peasant family for a whole year. Heavy rain in summer was greatly feared because a ruined crop made harvest impossible.

This rural way of life was soon to be overturned. Peasants from Careby and Holywell with Aunby would fight on opposing sides.

MEDIEVAL WEIGHTS & MEASURES

INCH	
FOOT	
ELL	The length of a forearm including the palm of a hand.
SHAFTMENT	Distance covered by extended width of hand and spread thumb.
PERCH	Sixteen and a half feet.
FURLONG	Forty perches, i.e. the length of a furrow, 220 yards.
LEAGUE	Twelve furlongs.
VIRGATE	A square perch.
ACRE	160 Virgates.
HIDE	Amount of land to support a household divided into four virgates.
CARUCATE	120 acres.

CAPACITY

PINT	For liquids.
BUSHEL	A dry measure. (From Latin bussellus meaning basket.)
SESTER	Measure to express renders of honey – three quarters of a gallon.
SESTER	Also used to measure wine, beer, vinegar and soap.
AMBER	Forty-eight sesters of liquid measure.
STICK	Of eels. Stick passed through the gills or stitched together on a cord.
DICKER	Ten leathers or skins.
PAIRS	Of gloves.
SETS	Of horseshoes.
THRAVE	Multiple of two shocks of twelve sheaves.

COINAGE

The silver penny, about the size of an old bronze penny, was thinner and lighter and half the weight. With the King's head on one side and on the reverse a cross and the name of the moneyer or mint, it was undated. Large transactions took place by weight and often pennies were cut in half.

The nearest mint was at Stamford.

MEDIEVAL TERMS

ACCOUCHEUR A man who assisted in childbirth.

APOTHECARY A druggist.

BORDAR Inferior to a villein – associated with cutting down trees, rooting up stumps, digging ditches around a new field using a spade made of wood with an iron rim on the cutting edge. He also tended cows, the dairy, beehives and pigs.

CHANTRY Chapel for chanting masses.

CHIROGRAPH A written or signed document.

DESMESNE (or **DEMEAN**) Home farm attached to the manor.

GELD Tax paid to the crown.

KNIGHT'S FEE One knight's fee had been deemed by King William to be an area of land up to fifteen hundred acres, yielding £20 a year to provide sufficient revenue to support and equip a knight to accompany the King to war.

MEADOW Hay grown solely for winter keep.

MESSUAGE Dwelling with land adjoining.

QUITCLAIM Deed of release - relinquishing claim on property.

SCRUBLAND Land not in cultivation or devastated by raiders.

SOKEMAN A free tenant who paid a low rent to a manorial lord for his toft.

SURGEON A man who treated manually. Often called a barber surgeon, he cut hair and beards and tended wounds often caused by arrows, swords and knives, extracted teeth, performed caesareans and removed gall stones. Many of his patients died.

TALLAGE A toll levied by the Lord on his tenants.

TRE Time of Edward the Confessor.

TOFT A homestead. A house with a garden or field.

VILLEIN Not a free man. Land and possessions belonged to the Lord of the Manor.

YEOMAN A gentleman serving in a royal or noble household who ranked between a sargeant and a groom. After the year 1500 the term applied to a farmer above the grade of a labourer.

1085 - 1216: Set for Trouble

Hereward the Wake was finally dispossessed and imprisoned. His Saxon successor in Careby Parish was Saxwalo.

With Morcar out of the way and the castle at Castle Bytham built as defence against local uprisings, Drogo de Beuvriere was put in charge of construction and installed to keep order. He didn't last long. He accidentally killed his wife, King William's sister.

Drogo, desperate to return to Flanders but with no money to do so boldly requested the King to lend him money. Only after Drogo escaped did the King discover what really happened.

The next tenant-in-chief of the Manor of Bytham was another of William I's relatives, Stephen, Earl of Albemarle. Hearing of Drogo's flight, Stephen begged the King for lands bearing wheat to nurture his baby William, born to his wife Hawise.

Stephen joined the Crusades and Hawise remarried the Earl of Essex, William de Mandeville. He became the next Earl of Albemarle and lord of Castle Bytham, retaining Holywell and Aunby.

For two and a half knight's fees Careby with the two Bythams and Counthorpe was granted to William de Colville of Aunby.

The knighted William de Colville moved into Castle Bytham castle, committed to serving one hundred days a year as service to King Henry II. De Mandeville permitted Adam de Saint Laudo to tenant the vacant Aunby.

Perhaps in thanks for his new possessions, de Colville immediately gifted sixty-seven and a half acres of land to the Knights Templars, religious knights to soon fight the Crusades with King Richard.

By 1190 de Mandeville had died and Henry II forced Hawise to marry yet again.

(It was the custom for the King to give connected widows to rich noblemen because it increased the revenue for the crown.) Hawise's new husband was Frenchman William Fortibus. He became the next Earl of Albemarle.

In 1206 whilst King John was embroiled in foreign wars a rift had begun between the de Mandevilles and William de Colville.

Baron Colville had no wish to support the unpopular, cruel King so he'd paid King John twenty marks[9] instead of serving his knight's fee.

Three years later the King quarrelled with Pope Innocent about whom the Pope had chosen for his new Archbishop. Determined to have his own way, the Pope promptly closed all England's churches for a year. King John didn't care. As a result, the barons, including Careby's de Mandeville who'd sided with the King were excommunicated.

A year later the Pope deposed King John and awarded England to Philip of France. Philip gathered an army ready for invasion but wily John surrendered his crown to the Pope then pleaded for and received the Pope's protection.

So all the lands the Pope had awarded to the French King, John was now in a position to give to the Pope. Philip was requested to disband his forces. All those who opposed King John including Baron William de Colville were excommunicated. As the breach widened between the King and barons fighting for a return to peace and security, de Colville remained consistently opposed to King John.

When de Mandeville died in 1215 he left an eighteen-year-old son also called William. Young William Fortibus became the new Earl at Castle Bytham.

9...   *One mark was valued at roughly 13s 4d or 67p*

At first William did not join the rebellion. But the following year he was one of the twenty-five barons chosen to enforce the signing and observance of the Magna Carta entreating King John to change his ways.

The King had no intention of changing. Although signing the charter he commenced war on his subjects on the 19th December 1216. Hotheaded Earl William Fortibus deserted the barons and joined the King on the ravage of the eastern counties as far as Lincoln.

Fortibus found himself on opposing sides to his neighbour, William de Colville. Fortibus supported dastardly King John; de Colville supported the French and the barons.

The position of the peasants in Careby Parish was extremely precarious. Demanded to be foot soldiers for their lord, Careby's peasants had no option but to support Careby and the Bytham's William de Colville whose family had lived at Aunby for two hundred years.

Aunby and Holywell inhabitants were likewise forced to support Fortibus and King John.

According to 13th century historian Matthew Paris…

> 'John changed from a king to a tyrant… breaking out in the savage cruelty of a wild beast, set out from St Albans to the north. With him amongst others was William Earl of Albemarle. …as he passed along he levelled the cottages of the poor, sent detachments of his army to burn the castles and the mansions of the rich, to carry off all the cattle and plunder what they could lay their hands on. Everybody regardless of age, rank or condition who was found outside a church or cemetery was seized and compelled by various tortures to pay an exorbitant price for his ransom. But it was chiefly against the harmless poor that his wrath vented itself.

...to be in possession of anything was a sufficient cause of death for the inhabitants. Assassins, red with human slaughter, midnight prowlers and incendiaries ran here and there with drawn swords to sweep from the face of the earth, man and beast and everything useful. With knives in their hands they searched villages, houses, cemeteries and churches, desolating all alike. Neither women, infants or infirm old age were spared. Some they suspended by their feet and legs; some by their hands or thumbs, and forced into their eyes salt mixed with vinegar... Others forced into craters or tripods and first placing them over glowing embers, then plunging them into water covered with ice...

The torturers demanded nothing but money which the poor sufferers did not possess. Goods were bought and sold in cemeteries, and not even there without great disturbance and agriculture came to a standstill.'

Returning from the north, John arrived at Lincoln on the 23rd February 1216 and passing through Sleaford the day after he directed his course to Stamford.

Either on his way north or on his way back to Stamford, King John's minions overthrew de Colville's castle at Castle Bytham and returned it with Careby to Fortibus. The King stayed the night at Witham on the Hill; it is not clear whether he was involved in the fall of the castle.

Meanwhile a number of barons, including William de Colville, assembled at Stamford to decide what to do. They invited Louis, son of the French king to take possession of their divided country. Before this could happen King John was suddenly taken ill and died at Newark in October, leaving ten-year-old son Henry to accede to the throne.

Fortibus remained true to the new King and de Colville and the barons sided with the French Louis.

The Battle of Lincoln, fought on 4th June 1217 was a rout for the French. Careby's De Colville was captured and taken prisoner.

News of her husband's captivity soon reached Maud, Lady Colville. She acted quickly and sought the young King's presence. Begging for her husband's release she offered to pay huge sums of money.

De Colville was released and before the year was out King Henry and the French Louis came to an agreement. All prisoners on both sides were to be released without ransom.

Shortly afterwards a royal precept was issued ordering Fortibus, Earl of Albemarle to restore William de Colville to his castle.

This infuriated Fortibus. Why should he be called upon to surrender the fortress to a man he viewed as a traitor?

1221: BESIEGED

Erratic and headstrong Fortibus refused to give up Castle Bytham castle.

The boy-king Henry advised by his Regent the Bishop of Winchester had already begun to alter arrangements for the custody of England's castles. There was little opposition except from Fortibus, who refused to give up all three of his strongholds.

The Archbishop of York excommunicated him. As a result Fortibus barricaded himself into his main castle at Mount Sorrel. The King and his soldiers lay siege. Both Mount Sorrel and then Rockingham were finally overcome.

Fortibus bolted to Bytham where he collected armed men, laid waste the land and tortured people in the surrounding area for anything he could lay his hands on. He pillaged Fotheringhay Castle and fortified his castle at Bytham with the spoils. Then leaving his right hand man Vassallus Foilliis in command he escaped to Yorkshire.

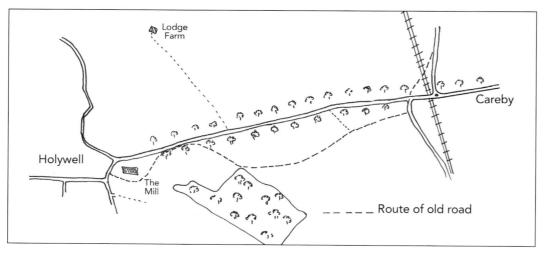

1221. Dry and sunny for early February: a cold, raw day with a brisk wind blowing.

Sokeman Reginald of Careby was the first to see them approach. Somehow, Hugh Pykad had heard the King stayed in Stamford the previous night. Reginald rose early and with his friend Ranulf, sneaked high on Dane Hill on the fringe of Careby Wood. They could easily see the road.

'There they are!'

Snaking their way down the hill past Ouneby, a vast army of men marched towards the ford. At the head of the line, two pack-horses, golden cloths and royal insignias glinting in the sunlight. The horses carried a swaying throne between them.

Reginald shaded his eyes. 'Just look at that! The King's seated on his throne! Henry III. He's just a boy. Wait till I tell Lucy.'

The two men climbed to their feet and shaded their eyes. They stood motionless while the procession passed: knights in chain mail riding fine horses: carts laden with supplies.

'The castle will never withstand this kind of onslaught. I hear Geoffry Wind has gathered some of the locals together. They're going to make a stand. But I don't hold out much hope for them against this army.'

They followed at a discreet distance, the sound of marching feet and the rumble of carts sending a thrill through their veins.

'Where's Lord Colville? Is he with them?'

'Lying low. I heard he might be at Swinstead. Waiting... hoping at any rate, that the castle will be his again soon.'

Two bordars led oxen pulling a cartload of manure. Reginald recognised John and Thomas. They'd pulled to one side to let the onslaught pass and now they dipped their heads as the two men hurried past.

By the time they'd reached Castle Bytham the sun had gone and flakes of snow began to drift amongst the bare branches of the trees. The castle towered above them in all its glory. The sokemen gazed on its moat and walls, battlements rising against the leafless woods behind.

The King had stopped at a safe distance. His knights gathered round.

'Discussing what to do, I should think,' Ranulf whispered.

The battalions had retreated and dispersed to set up camp. A soldier beckoned Reginald over.

'You. Give us a hand.'

Both Reginald and Ranulf helped to unload the carts.

Late in the afternoon, from the north-west; more sounds of marching feet.

'Nottingham's men,' someone said. 'And not before time.'

Reginald straightened to see a vast column followed by carts pulled by oxen loaded with huge lengths of timber.

Ranulf joined him. 'What's on the carts?'

'Mangonels, they tell me. Two of them.'

'Mangonels? Never seen one.'

'Aye. The King's ordered two petrarias as well and hundreds of crossbows, arrows and pikes. They won't stand a chance in there.' The tall thin man nodded towards the castle. 'Better if they surrendered now.'

'Not much chance of that.' Ranulf stretched his aching back. 'I ain't seen no mangonel before.'

The thin man grinned. 'The King's sent for carpenters to assemble them. We've been given charge to wheel the engines into position. Slingers and mechanics will have charge of loading them up.'

'What with?'

'Oh, anything we can lay our hands on. Burning tar; sand if we can find some. Set alight, it gets everywhere.' He hunkered down in the mud, his long shanks folded like bent sticks. 'The beauty of the mangonel is that whatever missile we use, it arcs over the walls.'

'How does that work then?'

'We string rope across the frame and there's a throwing arm that's inserted upright in the middle. Pour tar in the bucket at the end of the arm, set it alight and over she goes.'

'So, stones for petrarias. They batter the walls. Right? You gonna stay and watch?' Ranulf looked at his friend.

Reginald nodded. 'Why not?' They'd be heroes when they returned to Careby and told everyone what they'd seen.

Then the rope arrived: rope of twisted human and animal hair. If the rope broke, twelve hundred feet of it had been ordered from King's Lynn by boat to Deeping and then on to Bytham.

More soldiers tramped from Belvoir Castle.

Darkness came early and Ranulf and Reginald stole back to Careby across the fields.

When they returned next morning with a few willing Careby villagers, wedge-like battalions completely surrounded the castle. Two petrarias and the two mangonels were in position and the soldiers formed in wedges to surround the castle. Equipped with pikes or crossbows, nobody moved. The only sound to be heard was the jangle of horses' bits.

Then someone shouted.

With a roar, the soldiers surged forward. Arrows poured through the air.

Reginald and Ranulf made themselves useful, acting as runners and hauling the heaviest stones they could carry to help load the petrarias.

Five short days of battle. The men operating the mangonels ran out of rope and the King ordered more to arrive with all possible speed, day or night.

Fortibus's men held out for a further five days before the walls were breached. The soldiers rushed forward, brandishing torches. Hungrily, the flames soon reached the keep.

Shouts and jeers as the first bedraggled figure tumbled out. Clad in chain mail, coughs racked his body. He held up his arms as the soldiers surged towards him.

Someone shouted it was Vassallus Foilliis, Fortibus's chief man.

Yelling and whooping, soldiers scrambled towards the breached wall as more spluttering figures showed themselves. Defeated, all were taken prisoner.

The siege ended on the 17th February, the castle a blackened shell. Prisoners were put in chains and conveyed to the Tower of London on carts and later thirteen prisoners were taken to Dover.

Miners from Nottingham were commanded to pull down the castle walls and paid 23s. 8d. for doing so.

William de Colville was re-instated to the manor at Bytham. Every man capable of work was commandeered from Careby and the surrounding villages to restore and rebuild the castle.

Somehow, Fortibus gained the protection of the Archbishop of York who negotiated a free pardon from the King for him and his accomplices.

As some recompense for his treason, Fortibus founded the Dominican Friary at Stamford.

1225 - 1320: Hard Times

The earliest mention of a lord living at Careby was in 1225 when de Colville installed rector William de Gymiles as lord of the manor. He was succeeded by Suspirus his nephew who received all of Careby Manor, the advowson[10] of the church and a tenement at Bytham.

Lord William de Colville, now an old man, was distraught at having to rebuild the castle. He also had to cope with his eldest son Roger bringing him shame.

Short of money, Roger adopted life as a bandit, gathering round him a band of men who lay in wait to rob passers-by. Eventually he fell into a skirmish and was taken prisoner but by some means obtained a pardon for the fine of one mark.

In 1230 when William de Colville died, Henry III committed all de Colville's lands and dwellings to Robert Coffin and William de Dive 'for as long as it pleased the King'.

Roger de Colville disappeared but three years later his brother Robert paid homage to the King for his lands at Castle Bytham and succeeded to the title of Baron of Bytham, claiming lands at Careby.

Meanwhile, Careby villagers continued to struggle to gain property and land. Ranulf de Lunges of Careby and Sybil his wife presented a case at Lincoln Court on the 21st May 1245.

Between Ranulf de Lunges and Sybil his wife - plaintiffs and Baldewyn de Brutcurt, tenant, of two parts of land at Kareby and of 8s of rent in Byhamel (Little Bytham) of the same Baldewyn, whom Agnes, who was the wife of Ralph de Bretcurt, vouched to warrant, of the third part of the 24 acres in Kareby and of 8s in Byhamel.

Plea: Baldewyn has acknowledged the land and rent to be the right of Sybil and

10... *Advowson - a form of property which may be bought, sold or given away and the right or guardianship of a patron to present or nominate a clergyman to a church living.*

for this Ranulf and Sybil have granted to him all the land and rent: to hold to him and his heirs of Ranulf and Sybil forever; rendering therefore yearly 6d at Easter; and doing therefore foreign service of 2 knights fees for all things. Moreover Baldewyn has given him 10 marks of silver. And be it known that Ranulf and Sybil have in the same court received Baldewyn's homage for the said tenement.

Was Baldewyn a Sokeman called for foreign service to the King? Was it the same Sybil, either married or daughter to lord and rector William de Gymiles who presented another case at court over a similar matter in October 1256?

Between Sybil Gymiles, plaintiff and William, son of Ralph de Pokebrok, tenant of 2 messuages and 2 bovates of land in Kareby.
  Plea: William acknowledges the premises to be the rights of Sybil and for this she grants him 1 messuage and land rendering 14d and doing therefore the foreign service which belongs to the messuages and the land.

By 1269 Robert de Colville, knight, was Lord of Bytham and residing at the newly built castle. Careby and Holywell fell under the castle's jurisdiction.

Baron Robert obtained a Royal Charter to hold fairs and weekly markets at Castle Bytham where merchants sold anything from hawks, furs, silks, wine and woad to wool, hides, lead, canvas, grain and livestock.

In Careby, as everywhere else in the land, Ranulf de Careby, William de Careby chaplain, were forced to acquire surnames and documentation to distinguish one man from another.

Careby and Holywell became part of the Lordship at Castle Bytham and a royal possession under the ownership of the Earl of Lancaster, Edmund Plantagenet.

Edmund, the youngest son of Henry III had married Aveline, daughter and heiress of William Fortibus, the latest Earl of Albemarle.

It was agreed to pay Aveline twenty thousand marks for all her possessions, including the advowsons and patronages of the churches in the Lordship and the Knight's Fees of her inheritance – with just a few exceptions.

In 1281 Baron Roger de Colville claimed Free Warren, a privilege granted by Royal Charter of hunting and the taking of any kind of beast, bird or fish from a particular manor. He also claimed Weyf, where he could demand stray cattle or other things lost. Then determined to rule his lands with a firm hand he claimed Infangethef, the right to apprehend robbers on his estate. He also claimed Furcas, the right to set up a gibbet in the form of a letter 'Y'.

Those committed to punishment had their arms tied, carried through the streets to be whipped and often hanged at the end of their journey.

To ensure no local people sinned, Baron de Colville claimed Frank Pledge, a compulsory sharing of responsibility. All men over the age of twelve were joined in groups of approximately ten households under the leadership of one man responsible for giving up anyone suspected of a crime.

Roger de Colville died in 1287. Edmund, his son of three months was placed in guardianship until the age of eighteen when Careby would be granted to him along with other lands for an annual rent to the King of £84.

Coming of age, Edmund married but died ten years later to leave Robert, a son aged ten so the lands at Careby and Ouneby were committed to the custody of Robert de Kendale.

FORGOTTEN PEOPLE

By now wheat production was highly organised with tenants working together to bring in the corn. Primitive corn watermills were constructed on the rivers at Careby and Holywell and Aunby; deemed more reliable than windmills for the flow of water was constant.

Several years of bad harvests between 1290 and 1320 saw the price of wheat doubling and trebling in value. Exports of wool declined and the weaving industry at Stamford suffered.

The hold of the Church on Careby was apparent. In 1290 Cecilia, widow of Gilbert de Montibus of Byhamel gained enfeoffment from Hugh Pykad of Careby of half an acre. Pykad also granted enfeoffment to Reginald le Cou and Lucy his wife, with a court adjacent in Careby. The annual rent was one silver penny, payable to the prior and monks of St Leonard's Priory. Six years later Hugh Pykad granted William Faber a tiny plot adjacent to his property in Careby providing Faber maintained the hedge between them.

Dated 1307, an Edward I silver penny has been found close to Careby. King Edward I ruled from 1272-1307 and the largest coin issued in his reign was the silver penny. Measuring 2cm in diameter, on one side is the facing portrait of the King and on the reverse is a cross within a design and the name of the town where the coin was struck.

Edward I silver penny found on the original Careby to Holywell road
by permission of Rupert Elmore

1310 Ralph Pykad of Careby gives up all rights and claims to his land called Moderwykes to rector William Baiocis.

1311 Robert le Court, heir to Ralph de Court, gives enfeoffment to Henry Adwych, who was the chaplain at Careby, a messuage and a croft with five acres.

1317 24th February, in the will of Ralph le Cou, money and clothes were bequeathed to relatives, also gifts to the bridge at Careby as well as a gift for the bells and belfry of the Church of St Stephen.

1326 a tenant of Holywell, Roger Beler learnt that his villeins were required to work on the Colville desmesne for two days a week and eighteen days in August for the harvest.

1344 Richard Pykad granted to Henry Court of Careby all his tenement in Hundegate. This property lies between the tenement, which once belonged to Richard le Smyth, and a cottage that is the property of Lord Robert de Colville, Lord of Castle Bytham Castle.

Witnesses: Thomas de Baiocis, son of the Rector.

1346 Nicholas of Careby, chaplain, was granted three rods of arable lying by Westmersk, one rod at Nomansland, one and a half rods at Gildhousebusk and half a rod at Scrowes to John, son of Emma, Alice his wife, Robert their son and the heirs of Robert's body, as well as a house in which John and Alice now live.

1347 John Court of Careby is granted enfeoffment of twenty-four and a half acres of arable and half of meadow in Careby field with a mediety of a messuage.

1348 August 2nd William de Baiocis was made Lord and Knight of Careby.

1349 August 2nd Thomas, parson, son and heir of William de Baiocis, made a grant to Robert de Colville, Lord of Bytham of the reversion of the manor and advowson of Careby after the death of de Bayous who now holds it.

1348-9: Visited by the Black Death

De Bayous, De Baiocis and de Bayeaux, the names were variously mentioned as the Rector of Careby at this time. Two thirds of the clergy in Britain, preaching and administering to the sick, died of the plague within a year. Did this happen to Careby's Lord and Rector, William de Baiocis? Was this why he's been depicted in bed with his wife Mabel in Careby Church?

Taught by the Church that illness was a punishment from God for sinful behaviour, no one had an understanding of germs or how diseases spread. Most unlikely that anyone had a bath except when born and when they died, cures involved bleeding or herbs.

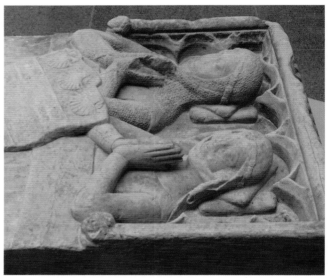

William and Mabel de Baiocis lie in Careby Church
© Tate Photography

Toothache was treated with a candle, the flame burning close to the tooth. People believed that any worms gnawing would fall into the cup of water held close to the mouth. A headache was evil spirits in the head to be treated by a surgeon, usually a butcher or barber who'd cut a hole in the skull to let out the evil.

The cause of the Black Death, according to a French doctor, blamed the coming together of Saturn, Jupiter and Mars in 1345, a sign of wonderful or terrible or violent things to come.

The Black Death originated in the Far East, brought from Europe and the Channel Isles to Britain by a ship carrying black rats infested with fleas. If infected by a flea-bite, the effects on the population were grisly and swift. Rapidly the immune system was overcome and horrible bulbous swellings attacked the lymph glands in the neck, armpits and groin. The glands burst and blood was coughed up from infected lungs. Death was swift – usually within a week. Very few people recovered. The population in this country was estimated at four million and about half the people died, many without the last rites, condemning them to Hell.

Immense fear was generated; friends and relatives were abandoned, farms and villages left deserted. Living conditions were filthy, sewage or rats contaminated water. Cruck houses with straw bedding for livestock housed inside for the winter provided the perfect environment for fleas to breed.

In Stamford, more than one third of the town's inhabitants succumbed, including six clergymen. Close by at Wothorpe the Superior Emma de Pinchbeck died, as well as many nuns.

It is difficult to see how Careby Parish escaped.

The plague made a huge impact; food shortages, grain not harvested; the summer of 1348 so wet any corn was flattened. Untended animals wandered into thickets and ditches or into growing corn. Crops perished in fields. With no flour for bread and untended vegetables, food was scarce. Meat was a rarity, at least for the peasants.

The monk Henry Knighton wrote, *'Many villages and hamlets have now become quite desolate for the people are dead that once inhabited them'*.

Landowners, not receiving rent because their tenants died were forced to lease their land. All prices were low; a horse formerly costing forty shillings could be obtained for fifteen shillings. A fat ox was worth four shillings; a cow twelvepence; a bullock sixpence. Fat sheep were fourpence, sheep threepence, a lamb twopence, and a pig fivepence. A stone of wool could be bought for ninepence.

Very little in the way of rent went to St Leonard's Priory. The rents from their five free tenants – the tenant of Careby Manor being one of them, lowered the rents to one third of their former value. Only two monks were able to survive at the Priory. It was said to be in 'sad distress'.

Pasture, watermills and windmills were let out at a fraction of their value because of the depression.

People turned to the Church. To pacify God they said prayers, sang psalms and filed in processions in the streets to ward off the evil. Nothing worked.

Even the nobility were not spared. The Archbishop of Canterbury died and church authority was undermined. Peasants, miserable and hungry, incensed with anger and resentment, rose up against the church and the clergy. With the decline in church power, eventually culminating in the English Reformation, any survivors of the Black Death were disillusioned by Church inability to deal with or explain the outbreak of plague.

As food prices quadrupled, the lowly peasant had difficulty making ends meet. Fewer workers were required on the land. As a result, the land was returned to pasture for more sheep; they were less labour intensive.

Anyone who survived with a skill was in great demand for work. Those who inherited from deceased relatives became wealthier.

The Black Death ended feudalism. As the weather improved and the country recovered there was more food for those who were left, better clothes, higher wages and more movement towards the town and trade. Throughout the country there was a spate of church embellishments: perhaps a resurgence of faith by those who could afford it, like the de Colvilles.

1363: GLIMMER OF HOPE

Baron Robert de Colville, Commissioner of the Preservation of the Peace in Kesteven, died in 1368. His son Walter succeeded him. Walter's son Robert had died too, so with Walter de Colville the male line came to an end.

After Walter de Colville died Edward III ordered a legal division of the de Colville property. The estate, to include Careby, Holywell and Aunby were divided between the Bassetts and the Gernons who'd married de Colville sisters, Elizabeth and Alice.

Meanwhile, peasants who survived the Black Death believed there was something special about them. God must have protected them, giving them the incentive to improve their lifestyle. Feudal law forbade them to leave their village without the lord of the manor's permission but inevitably they did, seeking higher wages and shorter working hours.

In 1351 the King summoned Parliament to pass a Statute of Labourers to curb these demands. Those who didn't comply were fined or held in the stocks. Some asked for their freedom.

Most stayed.

Richard grabbed his ox and hauled it to the side of the mud-filled track. A rider was galloping towards him and didn't look like slowing down. As the horse drew near Richard could see the Royal insignia of Edward III on the saddle-cloth.

The rider skidded the horse to a halt and shouted down, 'Is this Careby? William de Careby,' he demanded. 'Where does he live? I have a letter from the King.'

Richard hung on to the ox shying away from the restless horse. From the King Edward III? He couldn't wait to return to Careby and find out what was going on. He looked up at the rider. 'You'll find him at Hundegate, my lord.'

'And where's that, you oaf?'

Richard dipped his head before pointing over the fields towards Careby Church. 'By that big house down the hill, sire.'

William de Careby smoothed his hand over the document. He was a clerk, a scholar who could read Latin.

'Go on. Read it out loud. I want to hear it again. I would like to wager Baron Colville has had a hand in this, God bless him.' Robert le Paunton peered over William's shoulder. None of the words made sense to him.

William made himself comfortable on his stool and cleared his throat.

'Dated 15th October 1363.

'King Edward III appoints William de Careby, clerk, and Robert le Paunton, jointly and severally, to choose so many quarrymen and other workmen, as they should deem sufficient to quarry the King's stone in the quarries of Helewell and Careby and to carry it to a place called Catebridge.'

He looked up. 'That's on Carr Dyke at Baston.' A long way to haul stone. He squinted at the document again.

'From Catebridge it is to be conveyed to the Castle at Windsor.'

'There. What do you think of that?'

'It'll be good for both villages.' Robert pursed his lips. 'We should celebrate.'

'There's no time to celebrate. As soon as the ploughing is finished I want every man alerted. Get John Court to spread the word. This is priority. The King's messenger insisted that stone is urgently needed for the new St George's Hall.'

'The new St George's Hall?'

'Yes. Baron Colville spoke to me about it before he passed away. Apparently the King intends to build a new hall at Windsor for the Knights of his new Order of the Garter, whatever that is.'

'Who's going to pay us?'

William de Careby shrugged. 'Someone will.'

'We need more saws.' Henry indicated the pile of broken broad-toothed saws lying rusting in the reeds on the bank of the river.

Dufred, the village smith, scratched his head. 'You'd better get someone to smelt me some more iron then. I haven't got time to do that as well.'

'No. All right. I'll see what I can do. The problem is; our stone is extremely hard to cut.' Henry shrugged. 'Everyone's complaining of blisters. Most of the men have had enough.' He watched a heron skim the treetops. The bird would make a very good supper. 'They don't seem to realise good limestone is hard wearing. It'll still be here long after everyone's dead and gone.'

Dufred waved towards the quarry at the base of Careby hillside. 'Is all the stone loaded yet?'

'Not yet. Robert had to repair one of the barges. Beler's man at Holywell overloads it. John had to cut some more oak planks to plug the hole. But one more trip should do it. At least going by river, it's quicker than hauling over land.'

'What happens when they arrive at Catebridge?'

'Simon Huet and Gilbert Burd take over. You don't know them. The King's men. They supervise the transfer to bigger barges and then the stone goes by river to Windsor.'

State papers of the thirteenth and fourteenth centuries show a number of Lincolnshire limestone quarries under royal control. Careby and Holywell quarries are part of the group of Clipsham's seven quarries first opened by the Romans. Producing rather coarse-grained stone, it varies in colour from pale cream to pale brown or the occasional blue. The stone was used extensively for castles and cathedrals.

Forgotten People

Stone continues to be quarried right up to the present day.

Stone quarrying at Holywell
with permission of Ivor Crowson

1400: Change of Fortune

Throughout the country after the end of feudalism, villagers began to buy or tenant their own land. In Careby, William Smyth and his wife Petronilla were granted a messuage for one silver penny payable to St Leonard's Priory.

In 1379 Thomas, son of John, son of Dufred the smith of Careby was granted an acre of land called Colmanthweye but times remained hard.

Child King Richard II, (effectively his barons), introduced a Poll Tax in 1380 that everyone including poor peasants, were forced to pay in order to support the numerous wars of the times.

The death of Wat Tyler

This tax led to the Peasants' Revolt in 1381. Sixty thousand men, chiefly from East Anglia, descended on London to wreak destruction. Leader Wat Tyler was killed. The peasants were crushed. Many were executed and their demands denied. Soon Parliament gave up trying to control wages paid by landowners and the poll tax was never mentioned again.

New laws were passed affecting all manors. Instead of peasants working the land as remaining bondsmen to the lord they now paid a fee or entry fine when taking up a holding. Becoming freeholders their land was freehold but the old class distinction was not totally abolished. The copyhold deeds continued to be written in Latin.

Forgotten People

Lady Alice de Colville had married a Bassett and her sister Elizabeth a Gernon. Their descendants inherited Careby Manor. In 1382 John Gernon relinquished his share to John Helwell, Knight, James de Kyveton, clerk, and John Parson of Benefield.

Ordinary folk like Careby villager Richard Mason were still being granted enfeoffment. He gained a messuage and croft with one and a half acres of arable. Lying partly between Careby rectory on the east and the holding of John Wadford on the west, it was partly in a field called Martenchyk.

As a consequence of the manorial system dissolving there were many 'gifts', casting the 'givers' in a favourable light.

'Gift by William Makesey of Careby, chaplain, to John Wadford of Careby, of a messuage and 6 acres of arable land and meadow in the town and fields of Careby. The messuage is in Uppegate between a house called Herteshalle on the west and an empty place called Wyndelsore on the east, and abutting the king's highway on the south. One and a half acres are in a place called Newhawe with land of William de Aylyngton on both sides, and abutting on Wytham field on the south. One and a half acres at Honerthorpes with the land of Stephen le Court on the east and abutting on the Redwong on the north. 2 acres are at Calkwelsek, between the land of John Makesey on the west and the land of John Bridde, junior on the east. Half an acre is in Aldecroft, with the land of William Walsham on the west and abutting on a meadow called Godyng on the south. Half an acre is in Crowhille by the land of Thomas Doke on the south and abutting the land of Peter Grenlyng and John Cobbe on the east, and the land of John Cobbe and Thomas Grenlyng on the west.

Witnesses; Richard Mason of Careby, Thomas Doke, Thomas Jonson, John Brydde senior, John Brydde junior, Thomas Grenlyng, Henry Grenlyng of the name and others. 1404'

In 1408 the Canon of Lincoln Cathedral, Robert le Wynnwik, gifted half the manor of Careby and advowson of the church and chantry to Lady Bassett of Bytham and five others.

1410 Gift by Henry Patryk of Anysby (Aunby) and Amicia his wife, to John their son, of a tenement and meadow and pasture land in the town and open fields of Anysby and Careby. The tenement is between a watercourse on the north, the king's road on the east and the tenement of William Patryk on the south. There are also 17 acres of arable and pasture land lying in various places in the fields of Careby. 12 acres lying between Bezentewatyr on the west and Carebymor on the east, and abutting on church land of Careby and on land by Careby Wood, and by Robynbrys on the south. 5 acres lying to the north of the town of Anysby in open fields of Careby between Carebymor on the west and Berwardwelle on the east, and abutting on Holbek on the south, and on various lands of Careby up to the wood. 2 acres lying in the same fields between land of the aforesaid Henry on the west, various lands of Careby on the east, and abutting Berwardwelle on the south and the land of John Margeryson on the north.

Witnesses - William Lesyngam, Simon Belot of Carlby, Thomas son of John of Careby, John Patryk senior of Anysby, William Undyrwod of the same and others. Seals [11]

In 1413 Careby Church and Chantry was gifted to William Mallory, knight. Mallory was a relative of Lady Bassett and very concerned about the deteriorating state of his birthplace, the castle at Castle Bytham.

The Basset line had continued to granddaughter Elizabeth who'd married Richard, Lord Grey of Codnor. Elizabeth received letters from Lord High Treasurer Ralph Cromwell demanding property and part of Careby Wood. As the letters belong in the 'Holywell Collection' containing Careby Manor documents, it is likely she resided at least part of her life at Careby Manor.

Elizabeth died in 1418, still possessing a half share in the manor.

Mallory's connection with Careby didn't last. In 1426, as lord of half the manor of Careby, owning lands and woods as well as the advowson of half the church and half the chancel of St Giles, Mallory was in debt to a gentleman called John Pulter and his associates.

At that time it was the fashion for London gents to buy land in the country. Mallory had borrowed money on the surety of his possessions and failing to repay the loan, Pulter claimed them under the 1353 law of 'statute staple'. (Lincoln was a 'staple' town where the dispute would have been heard at court.)

However, it wasn't long before John Pulter had to make a 'gift' of his acquired assets, including Careby Church to Ralph Lord Cromwell. For this he was paid £125 13s. 4d.

Cromwell managed to keep his post for the following ten years until 1443 and was charged with raising funds to finance young King Henry VI's forays into France. A colourful character, successful diplomat with elegant manners and a powerful landowner, Cromwell fought at Agincourt and was present at the trial and burning of Joan of Arc. As Treasurer he worked hard to recoup debts caused by the high spending on numerous wars.

In November 1442 lands were sold in Careby, Little Bytham, Castle Bytham and Holywell with conditions about Careby Wood previously sold to Henry Grylling. Formerly held by Elizabeth Lady Grey, they were divided into portions. A year later Ralph Cromwell claimed Elizabeth Grey's quarter portion of Careby Church and chantry together with fifty acres of Careby Wood.

In 1443 Cromwell conducted a full-scale investigation into the financial situation in the country and found a deficit of £21,000 with £164,000 in outstanding debts. He had to do something. With widespread concern about public disorder there was a need to find a way out of the impasse of the French war. Bands of notorious criminals were coming openly into market towns. Government finance was struggling. Subsidies, taxes and grants were still not bringing in enough money to meet the full cost of troops and equipment. Henry VI was short of cash, particularly since he'd been very free with grants of land. So as Treasurer, Cromwell made an attempt to recover enfeoffed duchy estates for the King.

Careby had to play its part in giving lands and money to the crown.

For eight years William Mallory, knight, had leased his share of Careby Wood with conditions of cutting and bond in £10 leases to John Grylling. Now he lost his remaining assets of houses, lands and woodland.

All woodland was prized and managed. In Careby Wood large trees were cut down for building houses. The underwood, ash, hazel and willow were coppiced frequently. Cut poles were used for fencing; wattles were constructed for walls and baskets. Bark was stripped for curing meat and tanning leather.

Anyone who took or damaged a tree received a severe punishment but locals could rake out dead wood or pick up fallen timber; hence the saying, 'by hook or by crook' - gathering wood with a shepherd's crook or weeding hook.

Finally, on 27th January 1445, Nicholas Wymbusshe, Thomas Meers, John Soucheverell granted the Manor of Careby to Ralph Lord Cromwell.

During the next few years several lands and tenements in Careby changed hands. John and Alice Westhorpe granted lands and tenements to Henry Grynlyng and two others. William Grylling senior granted a messuage and arable croft in Careby near the rectory to Henry Grylling junior.

The first half of King Edward VI's reign had been characterised by violence and wars but he was a popular king who finally restored law and order.

As fortunes increased, more villagers in Careby began to acquire their own property.

In 1460 Henry Kyng and Anne were granted a messuage in the fields of Careby with the condition to maintain Richard Duk in his lifetime.

Henry Kyng bought lands formerly belonging to John and Jean Suckling. Laurence Gurlyng of Careby bought lands from John Clerk.

In 1480 Richard Holmes and Henry Cobbe of Careby were granted enfeoffment of a messuage and croft. The same year in the will of Reginald Kinge of Careby, a messuage next to Careby Rectory was bequeathed to Agnes (Anne) Bacar, who was formerly the wife of Henry Kinge. As a man of means and influence he left twenty shillings to each of his sisters, three quarters of barley to Peterborough Abbey and 'one half of a quarter' to Careby Church.

1529: CAREBY MILLS

An ancient mill in the folder of Jemima Reynardson's drawings. Lincolnshire Archives H56/2

Villagers relied on their mills. Mills were used for grain grinding, sawing wood and fulling. The grain was threshed from the sheaves and winnowed in the farmyard. It was then sacked up and transported to the mill by pack pony to be weighed and recorded by the tally master. The miller fed it through two hoppers to the millstones.

Unless the miller owned the mill, the lord of the manor who controlled it effectively controlled the population. People had to pay; usually in extra labour to use the mill or they were obliged to give the miller a ten per cent cut.

In Careby, miller William Salford and his wife Margaretta acquired a tenement in 1501. In 1506 he purchased a windmill, (probably by the lane on the hillside) and a cottage in the village. By 1509 he'd bought an acre of land in Little Bytham.

FORGOTTEN PEOPLE

In 1529 son Henry was able to buy a messuage in Hundegate, Careby together with five acres from Mr Dalby of Esynden.

Careby boasted two mills. Old maps of Careby show a waterfall and sluice gates close to the present bridge over the river.

The watermill was leased from Master George Henneage[12] to Edward Nicholson, a miller at West Deeping. Mr Nicholson paid 26s. 8d. per annum for the privilege.

In 1541 George Henneage also leased one acre to miller Thomas Shorthosse at Holywell. Payment was in kind.

The undershot method of milling relied on the use of sluice gates lowered to allow the flow of the stream to fill the millpond.

Edward Nicholson would have started his session, which may have lasted four hours, by raising the outer sluice gate to allow trapped water to flow over the inner gate. The water struck the waterwheel at about axle level. When the level dropped to the top of the inner gate it was raised, turning the wheel into undershot mode.

The miller continued milling until the pond emptied then he refilled it by re-lowering the sluice gates.

If the mill was used for fulling sheep's wool, it was cleansed in water by the continual treading of feet. Then transferred to the millstone it was struck repeatedly by hammers fixed to a wheel.

With the wool industry of Stamford nearby and Holywell women widely known for their embroidery, it is likely that Careby or Holywell mills were used for such a purpose since before the 12th century.

12... *George Henneage, Master of College and almshouses at Tattershall - built by Ralph Lord Cromwell*

Careby Manor

Careby Manor

Careby Manor, said to date from at least the early 17th century, is a Grade II listed building altered between 1800 and 1832. Constructed with squared limestone rubble with squared quoins at the corners of the building, the Collyweston slate roof has raised stone-capped gables and a ridge of ashlar stacks with moulded tops. The east-facing front has a 20th century porch facing the long abandoned street.

In the 1960s, Mr Berger and his family inhabited the manor. His herd of British Friesians grazed the farmland. The cowman lived in the cottage called Maazledene, named after the dairy herd and purchased from Mrs Agatha Fane.

Another worker on the farm, Frank Barney, grew up in Barney's Cottage on Stamford Road and like his father before him spent most of his working life at Manor Farm. Neighbours Vic and Lucy Thurston recalled the prolonged winter of 1963 when Frank regularly brought them a milk churn full of water during the big freeze. Residents on the Stamford Road were without piped water for a month.

Bob Wallwin farmed the manor during and after the war and hosted occasional Meets for the Cottesmore Hunt. He owned a winning racehorse, a point-to-pointer called Careby Boy. The horse was kept in stables at the rear of the manor and villagers were advised when to place a winning bet. However, it's been said that sometimes the horse was fed a handful of yew from the churchyard so it didn't impress the handicapper[13].

When Marshall's Farm was sold in 1951 after the death of Tommy Atkinson, the Wallwins became increasingly tired of their ongoing dispute with the new owner.

Another person who was staying at Marshall's Farm was fond of starting up his little motorbike every evening and driving the short distance for a pint at the Willoughby Arms. As the sound of his bike faded and villagers relaxed behind closed curtains, no one heard footsteps or the slap of hooves echoing past Gardener's Cottage and Granny Ellerby's Rectory Buildings.

Next morning, the new owner of Marshall's Farm went to her garage. Tugging open the doors, she was faced with an exceedingly angry Friesian bull.

Prior to the World War II the Hollingsheads and before that the Sharpe family were long standing farmers at Careby Manor. In the early 19th century farmers and graziers John Berridge and his son tended the manor lands.

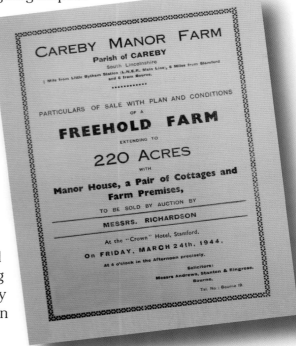

CAREBY MANOR FARM
Parish of CAREBY
South Lincolnshire
½ Mile from Little Bytham Station (L.N.E.R. Main Line), 6 Miles from Stamford
and 6 from Bourne.

PARTICULARS OF SALE WITH PLAN AND CONDITIONS
OF A

FREEHOLD FARM
EXTENDING TO
220 ACRES
WITH
Manor House, a Pair of Cottages and Farm Premises,

TO BE SOLD BY AUCTION BY

MESSRS. RICHARDSON

At the "Crown" Hotel, Stamford,
On FRIDAY, MARCH 24th, 1944,
at 4 o'clock in the Afternoon precisely.

Solicitors:
Messrs Andrews, Stanton & Ringrose,
Bourne.
Tel. No : Bourne 19.

13... *Handicapping - the practice of assigning advantage related to performance through reducing or increasing the weight a horse carries.*

1552: NEWCOMERS

Charles Brandon, Duke of Suffolk
With permission of Grimsthorpe & Drummond Castle Trust

The grip on Careby that had continued through subsequent lords and rectors, Ralph Cromwell and others was soon to be loosened.

In 1515 Henry VIII's sister Mary Tudor married bearded Charles Brandon, Duke of Suffolk. Often sporting a fur-lined coat, tunic embroidered with silver and worn above scarlet hose, Brandon was the recipient of lands that included Careby, conferred on him by his brother-in-law the King.

In the same year Sir John Hussey, knight, late lord of Bytham Castle and now residing at Sleaford, was Comptroller of the Household of the King, and Sheriff of Lincolnshire. Already holding Pickworth Manor, Hussey was granted lands in Careby and he gave the grant of the advowson of church and chantry worth £73 to Henry Hornby, the Master of College at Tattershall.

FORGOTTEN PEOPLE

Careby villagers, still following the national trend, continued to buy their own property. A messuage with fourteen acres was sold for the sum of £6 in 1521. Six years later a tenement and six acres was sold for 56s. 8d. to William Baron, a Careby yeoman. In 1532, perhaps with an inkling of trouble brewing, the prioress of Stamford's St. Leonard's Priory granted a lease of fifty-two years for tythed lands and homesteads in Careby, Holywell and Aunby to Stamford man Henry Lacy, who was to pay the prioress £7 a year.

Henry VIII's first wife had not produced a son and heir so the King applied to the Pope for a divorce. The Pope's refusal incensed him so much that he denounced the Catholic faith. Then in 1537 Henry beheaded faithful Sir John Hussey for High Treason. Possibly under his wife's influence, Hussey had failed to oppose the pro-Catholic uprising.

Charles Brandon, Duke of Suffolk, died suddenly in 1545 and his previous grant of Careby lands passed from Tattershall's Henry Hornby to John Porter, also of Tattershall College.

In 1552, William Porter, son and heir to John Porter sold all interests in Careby to a John Hatcher of Cambridge.

1552 - 1590: A New Era

The sale of Careby Manor to John Hatcher was to begin an almost two hundred year connection between Careby and the scholarly Hatcher family. In common with gentlemen of the time attempting real power and status, John Hatcher bought local property whenever it came available. Already owner of houses in Lyn (King's Lynn) and Cambridge, John Hatcher was soon to exchange land with Thomas Whitehead, a husbandman of Careby. He bought another messuage for £70. For the sum of £163 he obtained part of the advowson of Careby from German Pole of Derby who'd married a descendent of the Bassetts of Castle Bytham. For the sum of £43 6s. 8d. Henry Lacy also sold the Hatcher lands he'd leased from St Leonard's Priory.

In 1560 Queen Mary I granted a license to William Caundissne, (relative and co-heir to the Duke of Suffolk) to alienate Careby Manor from the Church. A Royal Letter also patented a grant issued to John Hatcher for the Chantry lands of Careby.

In the same year William Caundissne sold Careby and Little Bytham Manors, all their lands and thirty houses to John Hatcher and his son Thomas for the sum of 400 marks. [14]

John Hatcher

Born in 1513 – John Hatcher M.D., Professor of Physic, was elected Vice-Chancellor of Cambridge University in 1579. He'd married Alice Greene and they produced at least two sons; Thomas William to be installed at Careby Manor and Sherwood.

Benefactor to King's College and Cambridge University, John Hatcher died in Cambridge in 1587. He outlived his son Thomas by four years.

14... *Approx. £600*

In his will he instructed that his library of two hundred and eighty books be distributed... *'to my nephew Henry Hatcher twentie of my bookes in 8 vo.*

Item. I give to John Hatcher, my sonne's son, 'Omnia Opera Galem'[15] *to be delivered presently after my death.*

Item. I give to Sainte Katherine's Hall thirteene of my best bookes meete for their library at the discretion of Master Livelie (Regious Professor of Hebrew).

Item. I give to the said Master Livelie tenne of my bookes and as many to my sonne Sherwood.

Item. I give to Robert Crudd my servant tenne of my bookes in 8 vo.'

The bequest of ten books to his servant might suggest Crudd was not a domestic retainer but rather an employee who assisted in the course of John Hatcher's profession as Doctor of Physic.

Book ownership indicated the intellectual climate amongst university educated professional classes. Both Thomas and John Hatcher's wills indicate a medical and intellectual circle flourishing at Cambridge University.

Thomas Hatcher

John's eldest son Thomas William Hatcher was born in Cambridge in 1535. Thomas went to Eton and Cambridge, wrote several books and compiled 'A catalogue of all Provosts, Fellows and Scholars of King's College.' These biographies gave glimpses of character and depicted each scholar's coat of arms. Family crests were used for proving credentials like pin numbers today. Considered legal property, they were passed from father to first-born son.

Thomas married Katherine Reade of Wisbech. He mixed in learned circles, was a friend of William Camden, a 16th century writer of historical chronicles with Lord Burghley as a patron.

15... *A medical book*

Katherine bore him six children: John, Thomas who barely survived a year, Alice, Elizabeth, Anne and then in 1578, Henry.

In 1583 Thomas William Hatcher died in Careby aged forty-eight. The cause of death is unknown but plague re-visited Stamford at about this time.

16
*Extract from
Thomas Hatcher's Will*

Sir John Hatcher

Thomas's son John, recipient of Omnia Opera Galem, had been baptised at Careby Church in 1566. He was just seventeen when his father died and twenty-one when inheriting Careby Manor.

Within five years he'd married Margaret Ayscoughe. She bore him nine children in nine years – Thomas and Anne, Mary who died aged four, Elizabeth, a second Mary, Margaret who also didn't survive, Edward, John and Faith.

16... *H 73/24 With the permission of Lincolnshire Archives*

1590 - 1630: REBUILDING CAREBY

Did John Hatcher lease Slatt House and live there with his growing family whilst Careby Manor was rebuilt?

The straight beams of oak still visible today were probably selected from Careby Wood. Builders incorporated the new fashion: inserting dormer windows into the roof. Sash windows, also innovative were added, although some were later blocked to evade the imposed window tax to raise revenue for Charles II.

Clunch was dug from the side of the road and traditionally used for flooring. Disused quarries and small delves are visible close to farms and villages. From them stone has been taken for walls and infilling potholes. Such signs can still be seen in Careby village hall field and the field beyond.

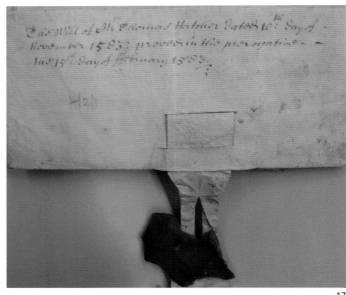

17
1590 - Assignment of a term of years of the lease of "Slatt House" on Hungate Careby. John Apsley of Milbrough co. Sussex to John Hatcher.'

With the introduction of chimneys, kitchens stood at the rear of the chimney base in the hall as the living room was called then. The disappearance of the weekly Castle Bytham market ensured essential bread was baked at home or in the village bakehouse; the dough placed on griddle plates on top of the fire to make small flat loaves.

Brass and pewter pots stocked the manor kitchen, with kettles, cauldrons, frying pans, skillets, platters and silver chargers, spoons and candlesticks. Forks had yet to come to England, fingers and napkins were used instead.

17... H 2/1 With the permission of Lincolnshire Archives

In 1601 Queen Elizabeth I knighted John Hatcher and as a consequence he applied for his own coat of arms.

Then his wife died.

Careby Parish register: *22 November 1601, Sir John Hatcher buried his ladye and Wyffe called Margaret.*

18
Hatcher's Coat of Arms H93/21 With the permission of Lincolnshire Archives

Elizabeth I's reign was a time of great transformation. The country was benefiting from increased wealth, much of it due to silver mined from Peru and Mexico. The expanding commerce was encouraging a new outlook leading to positive energy, pride in achievement and independence.

John Hatcher must have felt this and the strong communal spirit culminating in a great epidemic of rebuilding must have invigorated Careby villagers. As elsewhere in the country new manor houses, farmhouses and cottages were being constructed. Wooden dwellings with thatched roofs had become outdated. By 1604 so many oak trees had been felled countrywide that a government proclamation called a halt to the use of oak to frame windows and doors. Brick or stone must be used instead.

Sleeping on feather beds, laying their heads on comfortable bolsters, the Hatchers ate off tables and stored clothes in chests crafted from heavy oak, carefully mortised and tenoned. It was to be later in the century before walnut and mahogany was imported: inlaid with mother of pearl, veneered or carved, fine furniture was made for those who could afford it.

FORGOTTEN PEOPLE

Plague revisited Stamford in 1604 and wiped out several clergymen and about a third of the town's population. Penniless victims were swiftly transported to outlying areas where there would be less chance of infecting others. Charitable collections were made to help the afflicted poor and for those who disposed of the dead. People infected but better off were ordered to stay inside and put a cross on their doors. Men appointed to tend the afflicted carried a white rod so others could avoid them and anyone coming into contact with an infected person was isolated for six weeks.

Bedding and clothing were burnt and supplies to infected areas left at a point of collection. Burials were conducted under a cloak of darkness. Tradesmen were not allowed to deliver to places that had not been affected and inns were required to take down their signs and not take in travellers. Even domestic animals were confined or destroyed so they didn't stray into infected areas.

With the manor rebuilt, Careby villagers began to improve or rebuild their homes as elsewhere in the country. Following a further account of timber sales from Careby Wood the farmhouse later known as The Elms was constructed.

Villagers; a weaver, blacksmith, carpenters, millers, yeomen and labourers incorporated materials from their old wooden tenements and tofts formerly built of sallow, willow, plum tree and elm.

Most improved cottages consisted of two rooms, some with the roof almost extending to the ground at the side or the rear. Providing a lean-to it served as a scullery or store if provisions weren't already stored in the loft.

Damp proofing didn't exist; cottages rested on horizontally placed oak beams set into the earth. Casement windows replaced pieces of linen dipped in linseed oil; up until now glass had been a luxury few could afford. Furniture was basic; stools or forms surrounding a trestle table. A table that was joyned, round, square or littel, showed the financial status of the owner.

The poor slept on straw pallets or rough mats with a log as a pillow. Sleeping on a flock mattress was considered to be the height of luxury.

The yeoman's house was stocked with tubs and vats for making ale; the vats frequently made of lead. Setting up the frame of a cottage was always time for rejoicing: an excuse for a party and ale tasters elected from the community checked the ale that flowed.

In 1610 at the age of forty-four, Sir John Hatcher received a letter from King James I confirming his position as High Sheriff of Lincoln. Duties included judicial and financial functions, as well as overseeing royal estates and the custody of Lincoln Castle. Taking his duties very seriously, John Hatcher wrote meticulous reports of the prisoners, logging every crime.

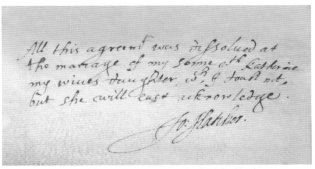

19 *Note attached to the settlement written by Sir John Hatcher*
H 2/19 With the permission of Lincolnshire Archives

A year later he remarried: this time to another member of the Spalding Ayscoughe family. She was Katherine Ayscoughe, a widow. There was a settlement upon their marriage to Thomas Grantham and others.

The settlement was dissolved when on 14th October 1617 John's eldest son Thomas, aged twenty-six also married Katherine Ayscoughe, the daughter of his father's new wife.

Father and son gained a strong foothold in Lincolnshire society.

Careby Manor was almost complete. In 1631 a number of wainscots (fine oak for panelling) were transported from Lyn. Possibly the oak came by river to Catebridge and was then hauled on a wagon to Wytham and down the hillside into Careby.

John Hatcher stroked his neatly trimmed beard. How many fruit trees would they need? Sufficient to provide for the family and all the servants: fruit to sell to the villagers; the rest they'd send to market. John shrugged his neck against the broad lace collar Katherine insisted he wore. Stiff with yellow starch it rubbed against his grey curls.

'What do you think Thomas? I thought plum trees could be planted over there.' John indicated towards the south. 'How many trees do you think we'll need?'

Thomas raised his arms and stretched, the full sleeves of his linen doublet fashionably slashed and embroidered. Ribbons fastened the doublet to the top of his breeches and the tension they caused reminded him to have them replaced with stretchy laces.

The area before them had been levelled, the bare earth glistening in the sunshine. Thomas was acutely aware of mud clogging his boot heels. He wished he'd remembered to step into clogs.

Concealing impatience he said slowly, 'I should leave that sort of thing to our steward. Isn't that what you pay Nathan for?'

John shot his son an irritated glance. 'You should take more interest. This will all be yours one day.'

'Yes, Father.' After a pause he added, 'then if I can make one suggestion?'

John adjusted the buckle on the knee of his breeches. 'Go on,' he said finally.

'The ground is uneven here. I think we should instruct the mason to build stone steps to the new orchard.'

Beneath his full moustache, John's mouth curved into the beginnings of a smile. He nodded. 'Grand idea. I'll see to it.' He unrolled the furl of paper he carried.

'Thomas, I want you to look at this. Should we plant the plum trees here?' He stabbed at the plan with a gnarled finger. 'That would leave room for apricots and cherry trees. Then over here...' He traced with his finger again, 'I think... nectarines and peaches? What do you think?'

'Yes, Father. Excellent idea.'

'The Hall at Apethorpe has stock.' John fixed Thomas with a penetrating stare. 'I want you to ride over there and pick out the healthiest trees you can find. I've already ordered plum, apple and pear trees from Greatford.'

As Thomas walked away he heard his father call out, 'and we'll need to guard against coneys. I've heard some have escaped from the Warren.'

Sir John had been granted Free Warren. This meant he received the privilege conveyed by King James I promising to hold him harmless for killing game within a stipulated area.

Carefully guarded against poachers, rabbits known as coneys were introduced by the Normans from Spain, Portugal and Gibraltar. The coneys were farmed in artificial warrens or coney garths for the sale of their fur and meat. Evidence of the warrens belonging to the Manor is still visible on the site of the old quarry east of the River Glen.

1590 - 1640: The Farm

The Hatcher accounts indicate a prosperous household with the farm run as a commercial concern.

With government exerting pressure on landowners to provide more corn because of the increase in population, the two-field system was common. Land was fertilised by leaving one field fallow for a year and applying manure, vegetable waste, clay or marl to improve it.

Arable land became so exhausted that landowners were compelled to leave more land aside. Because of shortage of land, flocks were allowed to graze this fallow field and cattle were tethered around the edges of cornfields. In Careby grass was grown for hay but pasture shortage meant Thomas Hatcher was forced to graze animals at Pinchbeck, Baston and Bourne Fens.

Several other powerful families resident in the neighbourhood: the Goodhalls at Holywell, the Berties at Grimsthorpe, the Hackets at Creeton and the Harringtons and Johnsons at Witham were led to a policy of selective enclosure. In the economic climate expenses had risen with little opportunity to raise rents on long leases from copyholders leasing their land for life.

Money had to come from somewhere so John Hatcher copied his neighbours, particularly the Earl of Lindsey at Grimsthorpe who enclosed his land to increase his number of sheep.

John Hatcher converted arable to pasture but for this he was fined. When presented to the enclosure commissioners for allowing four farmhouses to fall into decay and also converting eighty acres of arable into pasture, he complained: 'I'm no common feeder or seller of beeves and muttons nor common grazier, I've been unable to keep enough animals to feed the household without hiring other pasture and so I decided to enclose and convert.'

John Hatcher crossed his legs under the desk, the heels of his new shoes with their elaborate mulberry-coloured rosettes scuffing the mat on the floor.

Rain battered the window. He stood up and drew the shutters together, the hinges groaning as he pulled them across.

Sitting down reluctantly he sighed and opened his notebook. In the light of the candle stuttering at his elbow, he dipped his quill into the inkwell. At the head of the page he carefully penned the year; 1625, before working out the percentage of crops from his seventy-four and a half acres under arable. Carefully, he wrote a list...

- *Barley 34%*
- *Oats 12%*
- *Peas 36%*
- *Wheat/Rye 17¹/₂%*
- *Fallow 10%*

By the time the manor house was finished father and son had increased their arable to ninety acres. Thomas suggested they grow more lentils at the expense of oats.

After a marked decline in keeping animals between 1590 and 1630, perhaps because of time taken up with rebuilding the manor, the number of animals at Careby Manor increased after enclosure. The Hatchers bought some Grimsthorpe land on the north side of the Wytham road for their flock of one thousand sheep. More fragments of land were acquired away from Careby including Aunby's sheep walks and land in Little Bytham.

Sheep became their main interest, wool earning them between £150 and £200 a year. Usually the fleeces were sold to Mr Reynolds of Colchester but one year the wool was transported to Suffolk, another to Oundle.

Every May, John or Thomas travelled widely to attend every market of importance to buy sheep, cattle and horses. Horses were increasingly employed as draught animals, not only to draw the plough but also to pull the larger wagons introduced by the Dutch in the mid-16th century. Oxen: male castrated cattle, were still used to pull a plough in the heavy clay-like land found between Careby and Holywell.

In June the Hatchers travelled to Rothwell to buy coach horses. With the introduction of Dutch carriages coach horses were becoming popular with those who could afford them. The Hatchers visited Corby (Corby Glen) in August to buy and sell dairy cattle. In September Waltham was attended for steers, cows and calves. Sheep and oxen were bought and sold at Stamford.

As the years passed it fell to Thomas to travel and visit the markets at Stow Green, Spilsby, Grantham, Market Harborough and Melton Mowbray. In 1629 he travelled all the way to Derbyshire to buy a young bull.

Their few dairy cattle were unable to supply the needs of the village so butter and cheese were brought in, a habit the Hatchers kept up for twenty years. Stamford supplied groceries, hemp and onions from the Fens, cloth, buttons and a child's saddle. Tea, coffee, pineapple and bananas became available in the country for the first time. Every September Peterborough Fair supplied hops for ale making. Imported wine was transported to Careby from Boston by river, along with olives, fish, salt and groceries not available locally.

Bartholomew Davies described as a servant, was dispatched to London twice a year to negotiate legal business. He also purchased suits, bought socks for the children as well as spices, currants, raisins, prunes and sugar for the kitchen.

Fish were farmed for the table. The River Glen, perhaps still named Bezentewatyr was dammed to create eel and fishponds close to the mill.

Thomas Hathcliffe of Ravendale granted a swan mark to Thomas Hatcher and sold it to him together with some swans. Swans were regarded as Royal birds and a privilege from the Crown to be granted a swan mark and be allowed to keep them. A swan herder marked the skin of the cygnets' beaks to match the mark on the parent birds.

Venison was produced from Careby Manor's sixty-one acre deer park. Parks where roe, fallow or red deer roamed were usually enclosed by a wall or massive earthen bank and topped by a stout fence with a ditch dug on the inner perimeter to limit take off, keeping deer in and poachers out. Strict laws introduced by William I prevented those working on the land to interfere with wild boar and deer.

Stone walls encircled Careby's deer park.

THE FUNERAL

One day, stillness fell over the village.

No sound from outside, no shouts from the labourers in the yard next door, no cries from children playing on Hundegate. The bright sun was shut out. But even with the drapes firmly drawn, the frail figure of Katherine could easily be seen lying on her back, the tissue thin skin on her face waxy-white. Slowly and for the last time, her fingers slipped from the old man's hand.

'She's gone Father.' Faith looked up from the other side of the bed, tears filling her eyes. She'd never known her real mother, step-mother Katherine had brought her up as her own.

Sir John leaned forward and gently kissed his wife on her forehead. Then he painfully straightened and turned to hobble stiffly to the door. He raised his rheumy eyes to his daughter-in-law who was clinging to Faith.

Katherine let go and with a keening cry dropped to her knees at the bedside.

Sir John cleared his throat. He croaked, 'your mother is at rest now. I'll send word to Thomas and tell him. And I'll summon a searcher to pronounce...'

'Death.' Katherine turned and lifted her tear-stained face to stare at Faith. 'Does someone really have to come to pronounce my mother's death?'

'I'm afraid so. Shall we tell Martha to come and help us wash and prepare Mother?'

Katherine dipped her head. Then in between sobs she said, 'You'd better tell the servants to cover all windows and mirrors.'

'I'll put all our jewellery away.' Faith inched towards the door. 'You stay here on watch. I expect you'd like to spend time with your mother alone.'

The windows and mirrors were draped with hessian cloths and even bowls of water were covered to distract the spirits of the dead. The toll of Careby Church bells echoed as a stream of visitors arrived to watch over the body. Friends, family, Rector John Sheffield and his chaplain crept into Careby House, treading carefully up the stairs amidst the servants' keening cries and clapping hands, their way of expressing protest against death. Everyone in the house wore mourning clothes of non-shiny fabrics to deter any returning spirits.

Lady Katherine Hatcher was carefully laid in a shroud, her hands crossed on her pelvis.

Wrapped in the linen, the women knotted the shroud at her head and her feet. On 13th August 1637 a solemn procession followed the bier, walking the short distance from the porch of the new manor house and southwards down the street. To the sound of the bell tolling the seventy-seven years of Lady Katherine's life, Sir John led the procession, flanked by Thomas and his wife Katherine and younger son John. They turned behind the rectory and haltingly made their way to Careby Church porch.

Sir John had ordered his finest pair of black horses to be decked with black ostrich plumes. He'd hired a bier from Stamford and guards bearing torches trundled at the sides of the coffin draped in black velvet.

Guards were employed to stop any theft of the hired candlesticks illuminating both the bier and jewellery assigned to the body.

The church was brimming with mourners. Some stood outside. Once the cortege arrived and became settled inside the candle-lit church, an edifying sermon began. Then prayers and masses were said to aid Lady Katherine in purgatory.

Afterwards: the wake. With much drinking of alcohol, mourners danced and played games in the manor gardens.

FORGOTTEN PEOPLE

Sir John survived his wife by three years, dying in 1640 aged seventy-four.

His surviving children were Thomas, John aged thirty-seven and married to Eleanor. His youngest daughter Faith was soon to marry Robert Meeres. William, born in 1613 had emigrated to Virginia, America in 1632 with his wife Mary Sarah Smith and baby son Edward.

There is some contention regarding William's parents. One source claims William was the child of Sir John's younger brother Henry and his wife Elizabeth (Livingstone).

1641-8: BLOODY CIVIL WAR

When Sir John Hatcher died, eldest son Thomas was forty-nine. A well-respected member of the landed gentry, Thomas was a close friend of Edward Rossiter who later became a colonel in Cromwell's army.

Thomas was an ardent Parliamentarian and one of two Members of Parliament representing Stamford. James I had alienated his subjects and his son Charles I inherited the same disregard for democratic government. Being a Member of Parliament was not without difficulty.

Scotland had risen up against the King's religious policies and defeated his army but the political crisis in England continued and Charles was forced to call Parliament. It wasn't long before the King marched rashly into Parliament to arrest a group of his opponents. He failed. They'd already fled.

The King also introduced drainage schemes for the Fens. People including Thomas Hatcher who represented them feared the schemes would negatively affect the livelihood of thousands of people. As a Member of Parliament and a private landowner he voiced his concerns. The Earl of Lindsey who held Grimsthorpe (and later died fighting for Charles I) was one of those drainage contractors commissioned by the King.

Sheep and cattle farmers, fishermen, wildfowlers, yeomen who harvested reeds and sedge for thatch were all likely to be adversely affected by the drainage schemes. Thus the King's plans played a role in bringing a large part of Eastern England into Parliament's cause against him.

With the country divided, in 1641 King Charles I demanded an oath of loyalty from everyone in the land. The oath to be signed read:

'Contrary to the same Doctrine and according to the duty of my Alliance, his Majesties Royal Person, Honour and Estate, as alsoe the Power and Privileges of

Parliament, the lawful Rights and Liberties of the Subjects, and any person that maketh this Protestation, in whatsoever he shall do in the lawful Pursuance of the same; and to my power, and as farr as lawfully I maye, I will appose and by all good ways and means endeavor to bring to condign Punishment all such as shall, either by Force, Practice Councils, Plots, Conspiracies, or otherwise do any thing to the contrary of any Thing in this Present Protestation contained: and further; that I shall, in all just and honourable ways, endeavor to preserve the union and peace betwixt the Three Kingdoms of England Scotland and Ireland; and neither Hope, Feare, nor other Respect shall Relinquish this Promise, Vow, Protestation.'

Rectors, churchwardens and overseers of the poor were commanded to appear before the Justice of the Peace in each Hundred. They were bidden to return to their parishes and witness the taking of the Protestation Oath by all males over the age of eighteen. The names of those who refused were noted and assumed to be Catholics!

On the right is the list of names of those men who signed in Careby. This copy of the Protestation document is reproduced here with the permission of The House of Lords, where the original is held. †

A year later with the country in chaos, King Charles gathered his supporters and raised the Royal Standard; a

† *John Lenton (10th name) was Thomas Hatcher's servant.*

call to arms against the Parliamentary forces. The country was thrust into war.

Villagers fought villagers; families became divided. As a Parliamentarian, Thomas Hatcher found himself sandwiched between Royalists: the Berties of Grimsthorpe and Uffington and the Noels of Exton Hall. Stamford's second Member of Parliament was a Royalist. The Cecils at Burghley, later to be besieged by the Royalists were Parliamentarians.

Thomas Hatcher was commissioned as Captain Hatcher in the Parliamentary Army under the command of the Earl of Essex. Entreated to raise a Company of Foot from the Stamford area, Thomas received a letter of protection delivered to his London house in James in the Field.

Thomas was then charged to raise a troop of sixty horses. Soon to be promoted to Captain of Troop of Horse, he was also given the post of Quartermaster for the regiment, responsible for food, clothing and equipment. Other members of his family were drawn into the war. Thomas's uncle, Henry Hatcher, became a lieutenant serving under Captain Anthony Mildmay.

Each regiment comprised one thousand horse soldiers besides officers and seven hundred foot soldiers. This included the quartermaster, provost marshal, chaplain, surgeon, carriage master, a commissary to distribute victuals, a purveyor-general of munitions, master gunner, fireworker and petardier, bridgemaster and a battery master.

Stamford and the surrounding area became the scene of many skirmishes and battles between Royalists and

Musket Balls and Dagger Guard
With the permission of Rupert Elmore

Parliamentarians. In Careby evidence of conflict has been discovered in the shape of two musket balls and a copper alloy dagger guard with a rectangular space to take the tang (point) of the dagger.

In the spring of 1643 Thomas was brought before the court at Grantham Assizes and along with several others charged with High Treason for having supported the Parliamentary side. He was given full protection for all his property by Parliament after he'd been attainted.[20]

The Royalists and the Parliamentarians continued to be divided. In August 1643 Parliament sent Thomas Hatcher as a commissioner to Scotland together with Sir Henry Vane, Sir William Armyne and Henry Darley to seek an alliance between Parliament and the Scots. Two clergymen, one a Presbyterian, accompanied them.

The alliance was sealed with a military league and religious covenant - Solemn League and Covenant. The hope was to unite the churches of Scotland and England under a Presbyterian system of church government.

The following January the Army of the Covenant marched into England against the Royalists under the command of the Marquess of Newcastle.

Thomas Hatcher had replaced the King as Governor of Boston and he together with other Parliamentarians, had agreed that taxes must be raised to pay for the maintenance of horse and foot troops against the Royalists.

The county of Lincolnshire was expected to find £812 10s. by October 3rd and thereafter weekly for the following three months. Thomas Hatcher was named as one of Lincolnshire's sixty-seven committee members responsible for nominating collectors. Any collectors neglecting to pay were penalised by treble payment followed by prison or sequestering their estate.

Almost immediately Lincolnshire joined Norfolk, Suffolk, Essex, Cambridge,

20... *Attainted – The loss of civil rights after being convicted of High Treason against the King.*

Hertford and Huntingdon for the mutual defence of each other against the Popish Army in the north.

The early part of the war went well for the Royalists under the outstanding cavalry commander King Charles' nephew, Prince Rupert of the Rhine.

On July 1st 1644 Prince Rupert outmanoeuvred the Parliamentarians and relieved the City of York. The city had been defended by the Marquess of Newcastle against the combined forces of the Scottish Covenanters under the Earl of Leven. Lord Fairfax and the Earl of Manchester commanded the English Parliamentarians.

Battle of Marston Moor – 2nd July 1644

On one side:		*On the other:*	
22,000	Parliamentarians & Scots	17,000	Royalists
Comprising:		*Comprising:*	
7,000	Horse Soldiers	6,000	Horse Soldiers
500+	Dragoons		
15,000	Foot	11,000	Foot
30-40	Guns (cannon)	14	Guns

Thomas Hatcher shrugged on his new buff coat. The thick leather was sewn so that the skirts would cover his thighs, protecting his legs from the slash of sword cuts. Over the top he placed his body armour: back and breastplates and a helmet that had cost him a further twenty shillings. From Stamford his wife Katherine had purchased more wide yellow silk for the army's obligatory sash;

no one could mistake him for anyone else but a Parliamentarian.

As a thunderstorm ripped open the heavy belly of the sky, Thomas inserted the toe of his boot into the stirrup and swung into the saddle. Adjusting his sword, he tightened the cord round his wrist; he couldn't afford to lose his weapon.

Alarmed by the lightning, his horse spun round. To the east, York spires rose into the steely sky. All around him, their vast army of soldiers, helmets glistening, pikes raised, standing on an expanse of wild meadow.

'Colonel Hatcher. My Lord Newcastle arrived at midday with a group of Gentlemen Volunteers.'

'Thank you. Do you know what he plans?'

' He's strongly opposed to a pitched battle. He's convinced that German Prince to hold off. All the men are tired and Lord Newcastle insists on waiting for reinforcements. None of their men have been paid. I don't think they're keen to fight. They're deserting. Some have returned to ransack York.'

Soaked to the skin from the rain, the messenger squelched away.

The Royalists occupied low-lying moor behind a deep drainage ditch, an effective obstacle for a cavalry charge. From a distance during the day, Thomas had witnessed Prince Rupert's soldiers seize a rabbit warren to the west of the cornfields. From there it looked like they might infiltrate the Parliamentary position.

Thomas also watched the Regiment of Ironsides. Under command of Lieutenant-General Oliver Cromwell they'd driven them off and occupied the ground. Brief cannon fire heralded minor skirmishes but neither side attacked. At four o'clock, another contingent of Newcastle's men arrived from York and the Royalist army began to take up their positions.

The Scots and Parliament's infantry occupied Marston Hill between the villages of Long Marston and Tockwith. Other soldiers were concealed from view and artillery fire, allowing them to attack from a close distance.

Word had gone round. Lord Leven was keen to attack. He'd convinced Lord Fairfax and the Earl of Manchester that now was their chance. The Prince intended to delay his challenge until next day and the disorganised Royalists were settling down for the night.

Thomas could feel a tightening in his chest. At last there'd be action. His horse moved beneath him. All the horses swung their quarters into the wind and stamped their feet.

His troop was impatient for battle. Francis Ayscoughe, Cornet, (second Lieutenant), rode at his side. Parliament lost York yesterday but when Prince Rupert issued the challenge this morning the Scottish Covenanters, joined by thousands of Presbyterian English voices, sang psalms all day, eager for the fight. Now the roar of twenty-two thousand voices swelled, oblivious to thunder, rain and wind. Damp banners proclaiming God was on their side fluttered above them.

The Lord Is My Shepherd swelled in Thomas's ears, the words forming on his lips. God was on their side. He signalled for his men to close ranks. He knew the procedure. Three thousand cavalry divided into two lines. Deployed in eleven divisions of three or four troops together with six hundred musketeers concealed between them. They'd fire as they advanced and disrupt attacking cavalry.

In the centre, rain beating into their faces, the thud of hoof-beats muffled by the swelling chant of the cavalry, Thomas Hatcher led his troop at a steady trot to charge across the ditch. Swords brandished, they hacked and slashed at their foes.

Amid screams of the wounded, the clash of the infantry's pikes, the thud of fallen horses, loud whinnying and the crack of musket fire, they scattered the surprised Royalists like the mud flying all around them. In the gathering dusk, lightning lit up the moor. Men from both sides sprawled on the ground, some still clutching their swords or muskets; rain washing blood off white faces.

Rupert's right wing was routed and in the confusion Thomas heard that he'd fled towards a bean field.

On the left wing, aided by the Scots, Cromwell's regiment quickly defeated the Royalists under command of Lord Byron. Byron panicked; instead of commanding his troops to stand their ground behind the ditch, he ordered a hasty counter-charge that prevented his own field guns and musketeers from firing without the risk of hitting his own men.

Cromwell was slightly wounded in his neck by a musket ball.

Lord Fairfax and his right wing of horse and foot scrambled across the ditch and secured three field guns, losing men to musket fire as the Royalists picked off several units.

Under cover of darkness a horseman skidded to a halt alongside Thomas Hatcher.

'Message from the Earl of Manchester, my lord. All of Lincolnshire's infantry is to make a stand and push forward. Cromwell is recovered. He says he will lead his troop to the rear of Rupert's stragglers. You're to go with him.'

Thomas took a deep breath and dug into his reserves, the pain from a sword thrust forgotten. He nodded at Francis Ayscoughe to go with him then wheeled round on his horse and raised his arm. His men shortened their reins and nudged their horses into formation.

Nightfall. Under the rising moon fugitives from both sides covered the countryside for miles around, many of them still being mowed down. Thomas wondered how many came from Lincolnshire. He might even know them.

A messenger from Ireland riding in search of Prince Rupert wrote:

'In this horrible distraction did I coast the country; here meeting with a shoal of Scots crying out, Weys us, we are all undone'; and so full of lamentation and mourning, as if their day of doom had overtaken them, and from which they knew not whither to fly; and anon I met with a ragged troop reduced to four and a Cornet; by and by with a little foot officer without hat, band, sword or indeed anything but feet and so much tongue as would serve to enquire the way to the next garrisons, which (to say the truth) were well filled with stragglers on both sides within a few hours, though they lay distant from the place of the fight 20 or 30 miles.' [21]

Parliamentarians & Scots	Royalists
Casualties	*Casualties*
300 killed	4,000 killed
	1,500 were taken prisoner

Parliament had been alarmed at the loss of Leicester. Lord Fairfax was instructed to engage the main army so in June 1645 at the Battle of Naseby, together with the newly promoted Cromwell to Lieutenant General, the Parliamentarians attacked the Royalist outpost. Cromwell's wing with six and a half regiments of cavalry rode on the right. Thomas Hatcher's Troop of Horse was late arriving for battle and his regiment was assigned to the extreme right flank.

In the battle that followed both the King and Prince Rupert were ridden off the field. The King was eventually handed over by the Scots to the English Parliament. In 1648 Charles I was imprisoned in Carisbrooke Castle and effectively the Civil War seemed over.

21... *Mr Arthur Trevor to the Marquess of Ormonde, quoted in Young (1970)*

1648: POLITICS, POLITICS

Charles escaped from Carisbrooke Castle, leading to a second Civil War. By the time the King was recaptured, most of the army leaders realised they could no longer trust him. In November, Parliament sent him a list of grievances, a Remonstrance and a long list of demands. They hoped for negotiation with the intention of restoring Charles to his throne without power, dissipating the control of the Army.

When the King's answers were far short of what was hoped for the House of Commons capitulated, eventually declaring them acceptable.

The leaders of Cromwell's New Model Army realised that Parliament, controlled by the Presbyterian faction, had been too ready to come to an agreement with the King. Colonel Pride, a brewer before he joined the Model Army had an idea.

On December 6th 1648 Thomas Hatcher left his London house, crossed St James' Park and strode to Westminster Hall. He was expecting trouble. Tired of fighting, he was in agreement that Presbyterian MPs should work for a negotiated settlement with the King who should be restored to his throne. Thomas had voted to that effect.

His throat tightened when he saw soldiers patrolling the streets. He faltered on seeing Colonel Pride's Regiment of Foot occupying the approaches to the House of Commons. Already he'd seen Colonel Rich's Regiment of Horse clattering into Palace Yard at Westminster Hall.

Stationed on the top of the steps leading into the House of Commons stood Colonel Pride. Thomas Hatcher threw his head back and straightened his shoulders. He was a moderate. Nothing to be ashamed of. He began to climb the steps.

Colonel Pride brandished his list. 'Name?'

'Thomas Hatcher Sir.'

Pride scanned the paper for those members hostile to the intentions of the senior members of the Model Army. Called the Grandees, they wished to try King Charles I for High Treason. Pride nodded at the waiting soldiers. 'Arrest this man.'

Before Thomas could protest his arms were pressed against his sides and he found himself marched to the Queen's Court. There he was thrust against Edward Ayscoughe.

'Katherine warned this would happen,' Ayscoughe said softly. 'What are you going to say to her?'

Thomas shook his head. 'I'm not an extremist. I stand for all the good people of Stamford. I don't want to see a Republic.'

'We could lose our lands.'

'There's that too.'

'You won't help your constituents if you are locked up.'

'No.'

The court was crowded with MPs. Almost eighty had been arrested. They were taken to one of three public houses next to the Palace of Westminster, named Heaven, Purgatory and Hell. Hell was chosen for their imprisonment. Next day all the arrested MPs were moved to two inns close to the Strand.

Six days later the first of the prisoners was allowed home. By the 20th December Thomas had been released.

Charles I was executed and this resulted in a republic being declared. Oliver Cromwell conducted an invasion of Ireland, the third civil war. He designated himself as Lord Protector with the objectives to form a stable form of government and spiritual and moral reform.

FORGOTTEN PEOPLE

Perhaps having had enough of war, John and Thomas Hatcher gained a pass to cross from Gravesend to France with their servants John Lenton of Careby and Joseph Williamson. Thomas settled Careby Manor on his younger brother John but this state of affairs didn't last. John died in 1652.

For the next five years Thomas Hatcher represented Lincolnshire in Parliament.

His only surviving child, John Hatcher the fourth, married Elizabeth Anderson. Ten children followed; two did not survive. Following family tradition John was commissioned as Captain of a militia troop of horse in the regiment of Thomas's friend, Colonel Edward Rossiter.

Charles II was invited back from exile to assume the throne and commissioned Thomas Hatcher as Deputy Lieutenant to the Earl of Lindsey at Grimsthorpe. Continuing to retain an interest in Careby Manor, Thomas bought additional Aunby sheepwalks for £1,110.18s. in 1672 while son John followed the family tradition and became Sheriff of Lincolnshire.

John Birch-Reynardson made sense of what happened next. From a number of letters he discovered a vacancy had occurred in the representation of Stamford in 1676.

Against his father Thomas's advice, but after consultation with friends, John Hatcher was persuaded to stand. Frances Wingfield who had represented Stamford in the Restoration Parliament and Sir Thomas Meres, cousin and MP for Lincoln, offered their support.

John Birch-Reynardson wrote:

In 1676 a vacancy occurred in the representation of Stamford owing to the appointment of William Montague to a Judgeship and after much consultation with friends John Hatcher determined to come forward in the interests of the Country party under the leadership of Lord Shaftesbury. He had two influential friends in Frances Wingfield and Sir Thomas Meres; the former having sat for Stamford in the Restoration Parliament, was well acquainted with the leading politicians of the borough; and that old parliamentary hand Sir T. Meres M.P. for Lincoln and of the Court party, knew everybody and was able to give his cousin John Hatcher discreet advice as to the best way to gain influential assistance. Anxious thoughts were turned, at once, to the family at Burghley: it was hoped that the old Lord, John 4th Earl, would at any rate be neutral, that the young Lord would be an open friend and that the goodwill of the Dowager, a keen politician, and of her brother, Lord Bridgewater could be secured: their relative and rival Anne Cecil, Lady Stamford with her grandson the Earl of Stamford must also be approached, though their interest in the borough may not be much valued. All did not go well for long.

A strong rival soon appeared in the field in Henry Noel, 2nd son of Viscount Campden, of Exton: and worse than all, on testing the Burghley feeling it was found that Lord Exeter's henchman, a certain William Thursby, had been promised his support, and was to be brought forward in that interest. (This William Thursby, who must, I think, have been deputy recorder of Stamford, made a fortune in the law, was afterwards chief justice of Ely, in the reign of Will III and sat for the borough of Northampton, in which county he had bought various estates.)

Under these circumstances, John Hatcher, a man of peace, retired from the contest. His cousin, Sir Thomas Meres, found vent for his anger by hurling the contemptuous term "Apple Roaster" at the head of William Thursby, describing him thereby as a man who roasted a constituency for his master's eating. As time went on, however, it was found that W. Thursby was not such an efficient cook as had been supposed, and seemed likely to allow the house of Exton to triumph over that of Burghley. He was instructed to withdraw, and overtures were made by Lord Exeter, with offer of his support to John Hatcher, which after due reflection were declined. [22]

When John Hatcher wrote to Lord Burghley withdrawing from the contest he asked for peace to be restored to 'ye poure miserable divided towne of Stamford.'

Henry Noel was returned for Stamford without opposition on 27th Feb. 1676.

John Hatcher survived his father by two and a half years and was buried at Careby on 1st January 1679.

The same year Careby was one of three thousand three hundred returns contributing to the rebuilding of St Paul's Cathedral.

John's widow Elizabeth became left with the responsibility of a number of children, Anne aged twenty, Elizabeth, eighteen, Thomas, seventeen; Catherine aged fifteen, who was to marry local man Osborn Fish. Fourteen-year-old Henry was later to marry Elizabeth Delaval but died when he was twenty-four. Twelve-year-old Jacomina grew up to be a spinster. With Mary and Charles not surviving the youngest were seven-year-old John who eventually married Frances Plume and Christiana aged six who was to move to Dorset after marrying Edward Farmer.

22... *H97/19 with the permission of Lincolnshire Archives*

People were entering an age when an appetite for pleasure and novelty was developed. The middle class was emerging. Ladies wore tight-bodiced, long feminine dresses. Men wore wigs, jacket and breeches or full-skirted frock coats. They did their best to 'keep up', to be seen enjoying their wealth. It was the age of marble fireplaces, Chippendale furniture and flamboyant lacquered furniture to match flamboyant dress. It was also the fashion for a man to choose a rich widow for his wife.

Until Thomas the eldest was deemed old enough to run affairs, John Turner was appointed to receive the rents of the Manor of Careby on behalf of his sisters Anne, Elizabeth and Catherine. Each later received marriage settlements of £2,000.

Then John Lenton, Colonel Thomas Hatcher's faithful servant died. In the 1685 will of Careby resident Edmund Greenbury, his sister Martha, sister Ann, Steven Emsby of Careby, Widow Lorn, **Widow Lenton**, Elizabeth Ross of Stamford, Benjamin Sculthorpe, Thomas Lorn of Careby, Harborne Wallis of Careby and John Times of Careby were named as beneficiaries.

Young Thomas Hatcher, now in charge of the manor received a locksmith's bill in 1688. It arrived with two keys for The Park gate. Samuel Reynardson, soon to be the new owner of Holywell Hall wrote later on discovering the bill in his possession, *'This paper serves as evidence Careby Park has used to be locked up.'*

1754: Everything Comes to an End

By 1689 Careby, Aunby and Little Bytham Manors had been redistributed between the family. After the deaths of both Colonel Thomas and his son, John, young son Thomas and his wife Grace had been awarded one share of the estate. The Right Hon. William Herbert of Grafton Park was awarded a second and Edward Payne and Jonathan Gorselow-Snow; husbands of Thomas's two elder sisters, and John's daughter-in-law Francis Hatcher were bequeathed the third share between them.

Rents from tenants were considerable. The rents from Thomas's share were put aside for the huge impending marriage settlements of his sisters.

Thomas's marriage to Grace Harbord failed. Suddenly money became important. £250 for her maintenance was to be paid annually and a similar sum to any future wife. He went on to marry Sir Edward Hussey's daughter Jane.

By 1705 Thomas was in serious debt, forced to raise a mortgage of £5,500. As was the custom the money was raised through a private Act of Parliament that decreed that by sale or mortgage of some part of Thomas's estate, and for the better execution of his marriage settlement, Sir Edward Hussey of Caythorpe, Granada Pigot, Robert Fisher, Richard Middlemore of Grantham and William Trollop were given the responsibility to raise the money to pay off the debt.

The Act listed property to be sold or mortgaged. 'The Manor of Careby and Little Bytham, with the appurtenances, messuages, farms, cottages, mills, arable lands, meadows, pastures, feedings, woods, underwoods, rents, reversions, services, lands, tenements and hereditaments belonging to the manor of Careby and Little Bytham or accepted, reputed, taken, used, occupied and enjoyed as part, parcel or member thereof, situate, lying and being in Careby and Little Bytham, Ednam, and in or called Awnby. And all that the advowson, donation, patronage, and right of presentation of and unto the rectory, parsonage and parish church of Careby with the appurtenances; and all that the manor and Lordship of Little Bytham, with all the right and appurtenances thereof of Little Bytham, Castle Bytham and Creeton.

The manor of Careby, listed as 'Careby House' was listed with outhouses, buildings, yards, gardens and orchards, the Park, the Warren, the ground called the Pitts, Careby Wood, two fields called Little Hills and Spurbridge; the Quarry meadow, and the farms called Cawlton's, Waddington's and Snart's. Parcels of ground called the Home Leas, Lord's Meadow, Crooks, the Mill Field, Quarry Field, Dog Kennel Close, Fryery Close, Shipwright's Close, Cross Hills, Lister Willowford Meadow, Partee Meadow, Little Staunton's Close, Spurbridge Meadow, Stocken's Furze-Close Meadow, Furze Close and all the Manor of Awnby.'

Thirty-two creditors were finally paid, including £1,100 to Richard Marriott, £1,581.5s. to his sister Jacomina Hatcher; £1,700 to Charles Eryon, John Rogers and Richard Walbridge. Thomas repaid his brother John £107 and brother-in-law Osborn Fish £100. Other creditors included Edward Sympson, the family woollen draper; Thomas Baldwin, vintner and Thomas Hartman, corn chandler.

Thomas Hatcher continued to endeavour to 'keep up'. In the same year, he joined Lord Exeter's Honourable Order of Little Bedlam. The club, reconvened in 1705 for pleasure, academic and scientific reasons, was based at Burghley House. Each member was named after an animal; Earl Exeter was Lyon, Thomas Hatcher was Bear.

At their own expense all members had their portraits painted by leading portrait painter, German artist Godfrey Knellor. Each painting adorned the walls of Burghley House until either the member left or died. Then it was returned to the family.

Nine years later at the age of fifty-four Thomas Hatcher died. His second wife Jane lived on at Careby House, dying at the age of eighty on June 3rd 1735.

During Jane Hatcher's lifetime much of the estate continued to be tenanted. In 1724 Thomas Payne recovered his fifth of the manor from tenant John Skillingfleet. In 1727, a bargain and sale of manors at Careby and Little Bytham were held in compliance with the trust set up to pay Thomas Hatcher's debts.

After Jane Hatcher died a 'Survey of the Manor of Careby and Aunby', was commissioned by those who by now had a share in the estate. They were the Right Hon. Marquis of Lindsey, the Hon. Col. Ballenden, Thomas Payne, (widower of Elizabeth Hatcher who had died); Hatcher Ffish who was the son of Catherine and Osborn Fish of Little Bytham and Charles Snow, son of Anne Hatcher and Miss Jacomina Farmer, Christiana's daughter.

Thomas Hatcher's debts of £5,500 – list of creditors
H109/31 With permission of Lincolnshire Archives

The 1735/6 Survey includes a list of tenants and farms in Careby.

The cover and page 1 of the Careby Survey, 1736

H64/3 With permission of Lincolnshire Archives

137

Totalls of the Severall Farms

The Demean Lands .... 295 acres
The Park, Lord's Meadow, Dry Close,
Upper Fryery, Nether Fryery, Quarry Pits, The Warren

The Mannor House with Gardens, Courts and Yards.
The Bowling Green, the New Orchard, Walnut Tree piece. .... 5 acres

John Winchby - Snart's ground, Black Piece, Lounds Close .... 7 acres

Mr Colton's Farm - Great Ground, Cold Oake Close, Tare Ground,
Little Hill, The Holme, Corn Close and Pingle adjoining .... 232 acres

Hatcher Fish Esq - Old Pasture, north part, east part, west part.
Upper part of Tare Wood field, Tare Wood Field, Calves Close,
Calves Close Meadow .... 138 acres

The Rev Mr Fish - Careby Close .... 19 acres

Mr Hurst - Dog Kennel Close, Rail Meadow, Quarry Field .... 36 acres

Widow Waddington - The Marsh, Pancake Close, Great Ground 85 acres

Mr Troop - Warren Close .... 2 acres

Richard Lounds - Dry close .... 13 acres

Alexander Pitts - Alexander Pitts' House & homestead, Crop hill, Crop hill Meadow .... 19 acres

Francis Ward - Lale Revets Close .... 6 acres

Mr Turnhill - Long Close .... 48 acres

Mr Exton - Furz Close Furz Close Meadow .... 52 acres

Edward Preston - East, North and South Part of the Lings .... 57 acres

Thomas Hale - Brakey Close .... 11 acres

Edward Nicks - Nicks Close .... 17 acres

James Ormond - Gunby's Close .... 8 acres

Thomas Cousins - Cousin's Close .... 3 acres

Geo Simpson - Three Pound Close .... 4 acres

Mr Claypoole - Near Wood Field, Tare Dry Close .... 74 acres

Thomas Durham - Bliss's Close, Windmill Close .... 36 acres

William Preston - Brakey Close .... 12 acres

William Parker - New Leys .... 18 acres

Mr Boyall - *Great New Leys & one other part the same.*

Glade Shooting upon Great New Leys North to Brakey Close, south Careby Meer East William Preston - west. Seven Leys Shooting - upon Witham Cony grey east To Mr Allisons Glebe west Great New Leys North, Nathan Ginsell South .... *30 acres*

Jonathan Rudkin, John Bury, John Oldham - *Little Dean Hill, Great Dean Hill* .... *71 acres*

Mr Rudkin - *Spurbridge field* .... *5 acres*

Mr Bury - *Tare Little Hill, Great Spurbridge Meadow,*

Aunby Farmers - *Parly Meadow* .... *5 acres*

Land in Aunby
Slipe - Mr Bury .... *8 acres*
Stocking - John Oldham .... *4 acres*
Little Holme, Great Holme - Mr Claypoole .... *6 acres*
The Wood - Demean .... *131 acres*
Macklem Dare - Mr Exton .... *8 acres*

Totall of all the Farms in Careby .... *1,427 acres*
Land in Aunby .... *581 acres*
Total .... *approx 2009 acres*

Sir John Cust
H56/5 With permission of
Lincolnshire Archives

By 1745, Sir John Cust, Speaker of the House of Commons whose daughter Anne was later to marry Jacob Reynardson of Holywell Hall, together with William Welby, were allowed to dispose of one tenth of Careby estate.

The same year Henry Vernon sold one tenth of Careby estate to Samuel Reynardson, the new owner of Holywell. It appears Vernon continued as tenant. Then in 1754:

William Montgomery, Gentleman demandeth against John Staples gentleman. The moriety of one fifth part of the Manors of Careby, Little Bytham and Awnby with the appurtenances and the moriety of one fifth part of thirty messuages, one water corn mill, three dove houses, one thousand seven hundred acres of land and fforty acres of meadow - seven hundred acres of pasture, one hundred and sixty acres of wood and ffour hundred acres of Ffurze and heath with the appurtenances in Careby, Little Bytham, Castle Bytham, Awnby, Edenham, Creton and Wytham and also the advowson of the church of Careby 19th October 1754 demandent John Staples, tenant.
Henry Vernon and wife and Edmond Wilson, vouchees.

Careby Estate was divided and the manor house, lands and village were sold to Sam Reynardson. Warren Farm and land to become Marshall's Farm was sold to Lord Ancaster of the adjacent Grimsthorpe estate.

From Cheshire quarter sessions - Settlement Examination 7 Oct 1743 John Burton born in Careby said his father John Burton had a considerable estate at Careby. The son was given a vagrancy pass apprehended as a vagabond and was to be conveyed to the house of correction at Middlewich then on to Carbey in the county of Lincoln.

So who was John Burton?

1849: The Railway

Careby used to be well known for train spotting, particularly at weekends, with the added attraction of the old brick railway bridge. It drew many spotters with photographic equipment, but since electrification and the new high bridge they have found elsewhere to watch trains.

In 1985 the Village Hall field became unrecognisable. Four Portakabins, plant machinery and a rapidly assembled Bailey bridge covered the grass.

The Bailey Bridge
With the permission of
Margaret Creasey

Late one winter Saturday evening curious villagers gathered in the darkness. The Bailey bridge was mounted on rollers and a fence removed for heavy plant machinery to roll the bridge across the B1176 then across the railway line. The bridge nudged the front garden of Corner Cottage before being positioned into place.

For the next two months traffic and villagers clattered over the temporary structure until the original bridge was demolished. Then with heavy machinery the contractors bulldozed the brickwork piers on to sleepers laid across the rails of the east coast main line.

About eight-thirty next morning Dave Cooper of Careby was driving his men home from an exhausting Saturday night shift on the railway at Woodwalton. Their lorry was waved down by one of the contractors standing on the Bailey bridge. He was very concerned they'd damaged the rail on the fast line. He wanted Dave's men to help. Immediately.

◀ *Watercolour of*
Mallard on her
record breaking
run by Phil Belbin
(1925-1993)
NRM Collection

Dave's men, exhausted and wanting their beds were not prepared to spend another couple of hours removing rubble. They were driven home.

Dave returned to Careby and surveyed the damage. He telephoned his supervisor who asked him to stay and do whatever was required to make the line safe.

In two hours the demolition contractors had cleared the rubble away. Twenty yards of track were unclipped and with the help of the contractors, Dave eased the rail back into place. By lunchtime he'd clipped the rail down and informed the supervisor who came out to inspect the work.

The fast line was crucial to locomotive speed records. Just four years later in September 1989 at Careby on a test run, a Class 91 heading south broke the British locomotive speed record at one hundred and sixty-two mph.

Clearing the rubble from the demolished bridge
With the permission of Aubrey and Celia Fenn

On a previous service between Leeds and King's Cross the guard made the announcement whilst descending Stoke Bank that this was the location where Mallard reached its world record speed going downhill.

The guard said, 'this morning the train went down the bank at one hundred and forty mph. This means Electra is the fastest locomotive in Britain.'

On July 3rd 1938 Careby was at the heart of a British speed record for a steam locomotive. A dynamometer car had already been hitched up to test the brakes; the Westinghouse team from Chippenham was inside. They'd made previous brake-testing on Sunday runs but hauled by different A4s from Mallard. If they'd been observant they might have noticed that this A4 had a Kylchap double chimney, and the driver spoke with a broad Doncastrian accent instead of the usual Cockney twang.

There was a good reason for this change of crew. Engine driver Joseph Duddington was well known for fast running. He grinned at his young fireman, Tommy Bray. 'Hope you're ready for this.'

Tommy knew exactly what Joe meant. He tightened his grip on his shovel.

Sam Jenkins on the footplate leaned close to glance at the speedometer. Nigel Gresley, Mallard's designer, had urged them to have a crack at the record under secrecy of high-speed 'brake tests'. Braking was the last thing on the crew's mind.

'Come on. Shovel in more coal, quick as you can.' Joe growled.

Tommy bent over his shovel, thinking as he stoked. They could do it. There'd been a bit of a problem; overheating, but Joe knew of the warning stink bomb of aniseed in the middle 'big end'. The phial would boil and break if the engine did overheat and they'd be warned by the smell.

If they couldn't do it no one would. Mallard, Gresley's masterpiece of a streamlined A4 Pacific had large, six foot eight driving wheels that meant maximum revolutions per minute.

Tommy glanced out. They'd gone through Grantham at walking pace because of engineering possession and the engine, pulling six empty coaches and a dynamometer car was accelerating up to Stoke summit with a comforting roar.

Duddington put the regulator in the roof and the acceleration was incredible. Stoke Box flashed by.

'Up to eighty-five.' Sam tightened his lips. 'That brake testing team are in for some ride.' He'd suggested they get a taxi back to Peterborough from Barkston but they'd declined.

Joe's face gleamed. 'I'm going to give the old girl her head.'

'She's new.' Tommy knew that this engine was five months old but sufficiently broken-in to run freely. 'Don't go blowing her up.'

'She's jumping to life like a wild thing. Look at this. Hundred and eight… nine…ten…hundred and sixteen. We can do even better than this.'

Approaching Little Bytham, Joe pushed the regulator further open. The engine rattled over five sets of crossing and points. He frowned. That might slow them down.

Sam leaned out. Cinders flew through the air to bounce on the roofs of cottages close to the line. The station flashed by. 'What's the speedo say?' The wind snatched the words from his mouth.

'One hundred and twenty-three miles per hour. Gotta nurse her a bit …'

Tommy lurched towards the speedometer as they tore under Careby Bridge. 'Bloody Hell. Hundred and twenty-six miles an hour…'

Mallard flashed by the mile-post south of the bridge. Joe let out a whoop of joy. 'Over one hundred and twenty-six! Can you believe it? We did it. We did it. We've beaten the record.'

Tommy knew that the record was a hundred and twenty-four miles per hour, made in Germany two years before. He sniffed the air. 'Can you smell it?'

'What?' Joe smiled knowingly.

'We're going to be in trouble.' The smell of aniseed permeated the cab.

Joe Duddington closed the regulator.

The speed record sign at Aunby, and on the right the commemorative plaque carried by Mallard. With the permission of Walter Smith

Sam Jenkins rubbed his hands together. 'Worth it though wasn't it? Not every day we break a record.'

Mallard, an LNER 4-6-2 locomotive No 4468 broke the speed record on the railway line passing Careby. A sign on the railway embankment near Aunby marks the event. Mallard was hauling two hundred and forty tons and achieved the highest speed for a steam locomotive of one hundred and twenty six mph over four hundred and forty yards. The engine was damaged and she limped on to Peterborough where another engine took over, (one of her predecessors, an Ivatt Atlantic) and Mallard travelled back to Doncaster for repair. She was working again in normal service within a fortnight.

On the same stretch of line in 1934, engine driver Bill Spireshaft had rushed Papyrus past local boys in the school playground at one hundred and eight miles an hour, beating the Flying Scotsman's one hundred mph record.

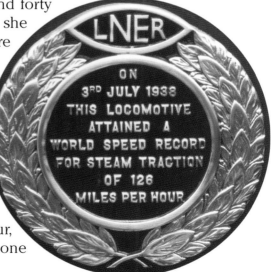

The station and goods yard at Little Bytham looking north

In 1849 the industrial revolution touched Careby Parish. Work started on building the next section of the Great Northern Railway line and Little Bytham Station.

The arrival of the railway meant an end to coaching. Trains became the main means of transport in and out of the parish. The railway yard close to Little Bytham grew to be an extremely busy place with grain, sugar beet, vegetables and animals produced locally transported by train to Peterborough and sold on.

Railway contractors purchased timber for sleepers and sand from Grimsthorpe estate and navvies were brought in for the construction of two sets of railway lines.

William Pope, landlord of the Reynardsons Arms had died aged forty-four in 1845. His wife Elizabeth became landlady and the inn became home to several navvies. In 1851 seventeen-year-old James Simmons and fifteen-year-old James Newton lodged there. They were joined by four others including fourteen-year-old Daniel Austin who made bricks for the railway at Little Bytham brickworks. William Freestone, his wife and six children living at Freestone's Cottage next to Careby Rectory garden, crammed in five railway workers.

Four more navvies lodged with stonemason John Holmes and his family at the Old Bakehouse on the far side of the river. Another four men lived with the Drurys, and two men with Thomas Wilford. Railway contractor John Downs, employer of twenty-six men lived with his wife in a Careby cottage.

Navvies not so fortunate lived in encampments beside the track. As single young men they'd come to England from Ireland during the potato famine of 1840 to find work. Dressed in long trousers, shirts under dark waistcoats they wore peaked caps and sported bushy beards.

So named after canal navigators, navvies were disliked and feared by the local population. Often drunk and violent they tramped across the country in gangs. With no compensation for death or injury they achieved major feats of engineering equipped with little more than gunpowder, picks and shovels and horse drawn wagons. Lashing long wooden poles together to form precarious scaffolding, they built countless bridges over the lines.

Conditions were appalling. The men were permanently soaked through rain or snow with no means of getting dry. They suffered the effects from inhaling fumes when digging out tunnels. Food was poor. Water was often polluted. Many deaths and injuries resulted. Perhaps because of these conditions the wages were a surprisingly high thirty shillings a week.

Then in 1852 the direct main line from Kings Cross to Doncaster and beyond was finally opened.

Close to Little Bytham the GNR Company bought over five acres of land near to the Careby Glebe for £335 10s. Reverend John Birch-Reynardson sold the land and to facilitate this he'd previously exchanged land in Addlethorpe with his brother Charles at Holywell Hall.

The arrival of the railway in Careby precipitated a new road from Careby to Holywell built under the supervision of the rector and his brother. Then an avenue of chestnut trees was planted, stretching from the centre of the village all the way to Holywell.

The Stamford road was re-routed to zigzag over the new brick bridge instead of going straight on to Little Bytham.

Charles Birch-Reynardson in his book 'Down the Road' wrote:

> 'Grandpa said trains were the invention of the devil. Travelling by train at forty mph takes ten hours to get to Scotland against forty-eight hours by stagecoach but Grandpa prefers coaches and feels they are safer...

John Birch-Reynardson's chestnut avenue.

'…*You are comfortable in your corner. Your 'Times' is, luckily for you, fairly clear as to print this morning, which by the way is not an everyday occurrence, your pipe draws well, your tobacco is good. Your thoughts turn to the pace you are going and how merrily you slip along; you pass through the country as if you were riding a whirlwind; you pass villages and churches and houses and fields and fences and can hardly distinguish them; your only object is to get over the ground. You are on your way to Edinburgh and you are on the "Rusher".*

'*The tea-kettle with its steam, has taken the place of four bright bays; the grimy engine driver and stoker have taken the place of the coachman; the guard or conductor in his blue coat and foreign looking cap has taken the place of the guard in red, with his glazed hat and cockade: and the long mellow horn of former days is now replaced by a shrill and certainly not to be called mellow whistle. The railway carriage, it is true, is a large commodious affair, with its comfortable padded seats, windows that fit tight, a lamp in the roof to turn darkness into light in the tunnels through which the train passes as it speeds on its headlong way through the bowels of the earth.*

A comfortable foot-warmer of tin or zinc filled with hot water warms the feet of the old ladies and gentlemen.

How different is all this from former days, when the stage coach, with its four in and twelve out, or the mail, with its four in and three outside, exclusive of the coachman and the guard, started upon its journey of perhaps three or four hundred miles at eight o'clock at night or six in the morning. The snow is on the ground, the wind blowing piercingly cold, for it also freezes hard, the stars shining.'

It was no accident that Little Bytham Station was sited as close as possible to the junction of the Witham-on-the-Hill road. Archibald Kennedy, son of Grimsthorpe's agent Lewis Kennedy, fought for and negotiated its position. Up until the building of the Great Northern Railway, Grimsthorpe had to import its coal via the River Welland. The coal was carried to Bourne on the River Glen or collected from Cate's Bridge so the position of the station was of great importance to Lord Willoughby.

Once the site was agreed upon, Lord Willoughby agreed to build a public house where local farmers, carters and their horses could gain refreshment. Stables were built at the rear of this public house.

Painting of The Willoughby Arms by Geoff Forman With the permission of Jonathan and Mrs Forman

It was a waiting area for Lord Willoughby, his family and friends and was called The Steam Plough. Built in 1853, the first landlord was Mr Hiddon followed by John Johnson from Brandon in Suffolk.

There can't be many historic houses that had their own full-size railway lines operating across the estates. Between 1855 and 1873 the Edenham Branch Railway ran for four miles from its junction with the Great Northern Railway at Little Bytham, first spanning Careby parish boundary before running towards Edenham close to Grimsthorpe Castle.

As one of Lincolnshire's most unusual and short-lived private railways, it was built at the expense of Peter Robert Willoughby, twenty-second Baron Willoughby de Eresby. It carried goods and livestock and passenger trains that ran daily in each direction at fares ranging from fourpence to ninepence.

Lord Willoughby had been ready for the opening of Little Bytham Station in 1852, which was then a simple two-platform affair. He'd built a new road to transport coal from the railway across the estate using steam road traction. However, it soon became clear that this road was only suitable for horse-drawn vehicles. The decision was made to convert the road into a tramway and pave it with stone and timber to provide a smoother and stronger load-bearing surface.

The Little Bytham end had been laid with wooden blocks for the tramway but the gradients into the West Glen valley approaching the station were too steep. Major earthworks would be required to lessen the gradients.

Iron rails were ordered from South Wales and it was hoped they'd arrive in time to enable the men to use locomotive power to help shift the earth to build up the valley by nine feet. All the gravel laid at the Careby end was to be shifted to the Edenham end but without rails the job was impossible. Despite Grimsthorpe Bailiff Scott wanting to speed things up, bad weather and late arrival of the rails meant that the railway was not ready in time for the newly converted Ophir engine. Daniel Gooch, the eminent railway engineer, had been entrusted with her conversion at Swindon.

Cottages in the Station Yard
With the permission of Isobel Draper

The engine that arrived without wheels was finally conveyed from Little Bytham Station on a wagon drawn by four horses to Edenham because the embankment at Careby was still unfinished.

It must have been a great nuisance to transport coal from the station up the Witham road to the coach road before joining the newly built railway a mile into The Park. But this was what had to be done. When the engine's wheels arrived, trials began with Ophir and a few wagons hauled coal.

Locals were sceptical of success but Lord Willoughby remained confident. He ordered a double cottage for the engine driver and his mate to be built opposite the Steam Plough Inn.

The greatest challenge still lay on the boundary of Careby Parish. Plans had been drawn for the line to be built on an embankment behind the public house then across the West Glen river and up the hill past Warren Farm.

No simple task for men with only picks, shovels, horses and carts to assist them. Bricks were carted from the brickyard at Edenham to build the bridge over the river. Wooden blocks were set into gravel for the wheels of the steam traction engine 'Ophir' to run on. Two wagons were ordered.

Wooden blocks laid on the steep sections over the Glen valley assisted the engine up gradients but by March 1855 the decision was made to convert the tramway into a proper railway. The Careby end had been laid with wooden blocks on gradients one in twenty-seven, too severe and steep for a conventional railway.

'Major earthworks were required to achieve a workable gradient for the new railway on the approaches to the bridge over the River West Glen; the contract was awarded to a Mr Culshaw. It was necessary to raise the level of the embankment at the bridge by nine feet, for which much of the earth would be obtained by deepening further the cutting over the hill between the Witham Road and Hale House. The higher embankment had a wider base, which made it necessary to widen the bridge over the river. This was done by building a second arch alongside the first, on the north side, tying the two together with iron tie bars to prevent any

settlement under the weight of the extra embanked material. It was then possible to shift the line of the track a few feet and so achieve a more even radius curve towards the Station Yard. The new works largely obscured the original road, but a small section of this can still be detected, running downhill on the inner side curve near the Willoughby Arms.' [23]

In January 1856 the weather was bad and work over the Glen valley made poor progress. By April one hundred and forty yards of embankment was still to be formed.

By the summer one hundred and twenty men were working on the railway and accommodated at local inns and farms. Forty men stayed at The Steam Plough in what must have been very cramped dormitory living.

The line finally opened in July and Havilah, a second engine painted blue arrived just in time.

Lord Willoughby's next goal was a passenger service to Edenham but the inspector rated the line as highly dangerous and it took three more inspections before he was satisfied.

He wrote:

The line is not suitable for passenger traffic. It should have longtitudinal sleepers throughout, with cross transoms and tie bolts at proper intervals, or the rails should rest on transverse sleepers not more than three feet apart, since the rails are exceedingly light. The intermediate blocks may be allowed to remain. The line should be carefully ballasted and properly packed. The rail joints must be properly secured. A platform and station building and distant signal are required at Little Bytham. The points are of a pattern not now used; they are not safe and have to be changed. Gates are required for the road at Little Bytham, and a gatekeeper. [23]

23... *'Lord Willoughby's Railway' by R E Pearson and J G Ruddock.*

Eventually, in agreement with the highway surveyor of Careby Parish and for a yearly payment of £5, locos were allowed to cross the Careby road.

On July 22nd 1857 the line was approved for passengers subject to three conditions. Only one engine on the track at a time; no engine to exceed twelve tons and the fifteen mph speed limit must be kept with eight mph on the curves. There had been a derailment when the engine Havilah had been driven furiously and toppled down a bank.

A year later there was a brisk trade in coal and general freight. Passengers were increasing, particularly on Grantham and Stamford market days. But soon, the opening of the GNR line from Essendine to Bourne would cause a dramatic slump in use.

Then Lord Willoughby became ill and died in 1865 at the age of nearly eighty-three, two days after he'd agreed the sale of his railway and engines to the Bourne and Saxby promoters. In 1866 this scheme was withdrawn from Parliament and passenger traffic stopped.

The new young Lord gave the train drivers three months notice to leave their Careby cottages. The Trustees of the estate reinstated the men at Edenham.

The last recorded access payment of £5 to cross the Careby road was in February 1872. A year later the line was abandoned, probably after an incident when runaway wagons killed the towing horse.

In 1890 a sale was organised when quantities of rail, goods wagons, a turntable and other items were auctioned in Little Bytham yard. Next to the Steam Plough the track was broken up to make way for an extended garden. The engine shed and stable in the station yard remained in use by GNR.

The level crossing was abandoned. It was discovered in 1970 when new sewer excavations revealed the crossing beneath six inches of road metal.

The railway embankment marking Careby Parish boundary has become a retreat for deer and wildlife flitting between the hawthorn trees. It also stands as a monument to the industrial revolution and Lord Willoughby's vision.

At the beginning of the 20th century the double track main line to and from Kings Cross was so busy that hold-ups were becoming commonplace, so the Great Northern Railway undertook a scheme to add two additional tracks on certain stretches – including the line through Careby and Little Bytham. This involved demolishing the original station and building a new one with two island platforms. The platforms were reached by a footbridge from the new booking office, which is now the only reminder of the station's existence.

Deer on the abandoned railway embankment

The station booking office

A busy line – and a busy signal box, with signalman Robert Swinton on duty.
With the permission of his daughter, Isobel Draper

157

1861: Careby School

Careby School was closed in December 1959 and for a time the building accommodated a Branch County Library. The school was eventually sold as a private dwelling to Mr and Mrs Len Wood. Hugh and Ann Marshall, Fred and Gloria Gascoyne preceded Michelle and Alan York who have lived there since 1999.

Michelle and Alan spent two years converting the buildings into a beautifully appointed four bed-roomed house, retaining many of the original features including all the doors, graceful vaulted roofs and the lamps outside. An attractive garden covers the front playground. Michelle says, 'We hardly notice the trains, are very happy here and hope to spend many more years in Careby.'

Careby School Log Book reveals fascinating glimpses into the past. Visits by nurses, the clergy and dignitaries are recorded by the head teacher as are periods of bad weather, waves of disease or pupils absent for harvest. *All quotes from the Log Book are with the permission of Lincolnshire Archives, ref SR109.*

> **'October 2nd 1950**
> *Richard Barbary, qualified Teacher Regd. No. 19/12338 take permanent charge of this school from today. My wife Sarah Blanche Maria Barbary also takes up appointment as Infant Mistress being a qualified teacher Regd. No. 19/15224.'*

Richard and Sarah Barbary moved into the schoolhouse several weeks after the beginning of term. Enid Creasey who'd taken over for a few days when teacher Mr Cook became ill warned the children to be on their best behaviour.

Careby School Log Book

The bell ceased tolling in the pretty belfry high on the roof, the signal for children to stop playing. A sharp blast on a whistle. The children froze. John nudged his brother as they lined up, nodding at two strangers standing close together in the playground.

Both in their mid-forties, Mrs Barbary, very tall, wearing glasses and hair drawn back in a bun. Her husband, much shorter with dark hair, also wearing glasses.

A steam train rumbled in the cutting, smoke drifting in the misty air.

Mr Barbary's voice, soft and kind: 'I don't want to hear anyone talking. Infants, go in first with Mrs Barbary.'

There was a hush as the children filed into the cloakroom, hung up their coats and changed their shoes.

Cornish-born Richard Barbary was like a new broom. He reorganised the school milk delivery but the milkman fell out with him and at first refused to deliver the milk. Then in less than three weeks Mr Barbary insisted the Council empty the lavatory buckets once a week. By October 23rd *the lavatory buckets are being emptied and removed weekly from today!'*

After new sanitary pails came from Harrison and Dunn in Stamford...

The boy pulled his sleeve over his hand and reached over the school wall to the railway embankment.

'Go on. Get that big'un,' his friend urged.

'You do it then. I can't reach.'

The taller boy reached down and pulled hard. He straightened, waving a long vicious stinging nettle.

The others sniggered as they gathered round the back of the girls' dunny.

'Wait for that one to go in.' A fat boy nodded towards a nine-year-old girl with plaits.

They crouched down, inserting the tip of the nettle in the hole at the back of the dunny.

'Ow.' A loud wail followed by a scream. A red-faced girl came rushing into the playground, hands clutching her bottom.

Then on Sunday, November 5th 1950

'Richard, someone's at the door. Can you get it for me dear?' Sarah picked up another potato and began peeling.

Richard Barbary put down his newspaper, stepped into the tiny hall and pulled open the door. Standing in the front garden was a man he didn't recognise.

'Mr Barbary?' The stranger drew his brows together and held out his hand. 'Mr Turner. Little Bytham School. I won't come in. Don't want to disturb you. Just passing. Wanted to introduce myself and to say…'

'I'm very pleased to meet you…'

'Who is it, Richard?' Sarah Barbary appeared behind her husband. She wiped her fingers on her apron and stretched out her hand. 'Do come in to the front room,' she said in her soft Cornish accent.

'Thank you. I mustn't stop. I just wanted to tell you that we have two confirmed cases of poliomyelitis at my school.'

'Oh no.' Sarah's eyes grew large and she clutched Richard's hand.

'Yes. I must tell you that if any of your pupils live in Little Bytham they must be excluded from your school.'

The next day, four children turned up as usual from Little Bytham. They were excluded. Almost immediately the Headmaster coped with another scare. A family in Careby contracted scarlet fever but later it was diagnosed as tonsillitis. Over Christmas children were struck down with chicken pox. In spite of these early setbacks less than a year later a Diocesan inspector visited the school and wrote:

> *'In view of the short time the present staff have had with the children, their conscientiousness and thorough work is deserving of real praise. I hope that it can and will be linked up in every way with the life of the parish church and the parish.'*

The Headmaster was keen to provide extra-curricular activities.

Mr Barbary led the way out of the cloakroom and past the dividing wall towards his back door. The boys jostled into the kitchen.

'Cor,' Robin said as soon as he stepped inside.

'Let's see,' David pushed the others aside.

Around the edge of the lino was a railway track. The boys followed it out of the kitchen, across the hall and into the front room. Starting forward to inspect the trains they clustered round as Mr Barbary flicked a switch next to a battery. A train began to move.

Boys lined up in pairs in the playground; tools brought from home over their shoulders.

'When you get over the railway bridge, I want you to turn in and wait by Joe Buxton's shop,' instructed Mr Barbary. 'A horse is being shod so everyone must be very quiet.'

The headmaster shepherded the boys past the horse and stone buildings housing Tom Pick's pigs then through the gate to the plot of land leased from farmer Charles Creasey where neatly tended vegetable plots were divided by grassy paths.

Each child tended a plot ten feet by ten. Planting seeds, weeding and tending vegetables until the end of term, the results of the childrens' labours culminated in a prize for the most productive plot.

A needlework teacher came once a week and taught the girls. Boys were bussed to the Willoughby Gallery at Corby Glen for woodwork with Mr Blaber. At Christmas Robin Wallwin dressed up as Santa Claus. Nativity plays and concerts took place in the Village Hall.

In 1952 the school was closed for children to visit Peterborough Showground to see Princess Elizabeth. Two weeks later Careby children produced a display of Sword and Morris Dancing at The Rectory.

Careby School pantomime in the Village Hall, 1959

Mrs Fane stood on the terrace directing helpers setting up tables. Her daughter Daphne and Granny Ellerby assisted. White cloths fluttered in the breeze as they were pinned on tables with brightly coloured bunting. Boxes of second-hand books arrived to be laid out and priced according to value and condition. Stalls for cakes, vegetables, jams and pickles lined the garden and teas were served at small tables. Games of bagatelle, skittles and a bran tub for the children to dip into kept everyone amused until it was time to bowl for the pig that had been wheeled down to the rectory in a crate.

A year later Robin Wallwin bought a television and invited villagers to Careby Manor to watch Princess Elizabeth being crowned. The children watched the ceremony at Central Cinema in Stamford when on June 24th Mr Clapton's bus pulled up outside the school. Mr and Mrs Barbary sat at the front and joined in with songs all the way to Stamford.

Such happiness didn't last. 1955 started badly. Several children were ill. The School Log Book penned by Mr Barbary records:

24th January - *Head teacher off sick.*

25th January - *Mr. Barbary still absent. Mrs Barbary took charge.*

26th January - *Head still absent. Mrs Barbary absent ill, Miss Enid Creasey took charge. Mrs S B M Barbary died at 3pm this afternoon.*

27-28th January - *School closed*

31st January - *School closed for funeral.*

4th April - *Dr Golby, the Director of Education from Lincoln called. He wished me the best of everything.*

6th April - *The children made a presentation of a fountain pen on my leaving. I, Richard Barbary leave this school with great regret and sorrow today.*

Mrs Wilson with her daughter Ann moved into the schoolhouse then a succession of teachers followed, including Mr Cheal.

Careby School pupils with head Mr Cheal in the mid 1950s...

1	Not known	**12**	Not known	**23**	Yvonne Rose
2	Mr Cheal, teacher	**13**	Bobby Britton	**24**	Janet Pick
3	Mavis Birch	**14**	Not known	**25**	Not known
4	R. Hall	**15**	Robin Clarke	**26**	Sally Wallwin ??
5	Pete Jones	**16**	Not known	**27**	Not known
6	Pete Woodcock	**17**	Not known	**28**	Daphne Woodcock
7	Brenda Rose	**18**	Isobel Swinton	**29**	Not known
8	Barbara Rose	**19**	Not known	**30**	David Allam
9	Elsie Prentice	**20**	Mary Prentice	**31**	Michael Birch
10	Gladys Swinton, teacher	**21**	John Woodcock	**32**	Alfie Bartram
11	Valerie Setchell	**22**	Mary Allam	**33**	Not known

During school hours one pupil became chief dog walker for teacher Miss R who drove from Grantham every morning with her dog. The girl's father wrote to the Education Authority to complain.

Another girl said, 'Miss R was a little fat woman with glasses who terrified me by pulling up my skirt and smacking me hard on my bottom.' But whatever the misdemeanour, she was redeemed when given the role of the Virgin Mary in the school nativity play.

In September 1958 Margaret Mablethorpe of Grantham was appointed new Headmistress. She travelled to Little Bytham by train but left the following summer. Eventually Nora Elvin took charge of the five children left on roll. The last visit was to Little Bytham School to see newly hatched chicks in the brooder.

On the 28th December the school furniture was removed. Careby School officially closed.

Careby School Christmas Party...

Left to right, back row:

Mrs McPherson, Granny Ellerby with one of Mrs Brewster's children; Mrs Lambing from Gardener's Cottage, Eva Medwell - Mrs Brewster's sister; Rev Piercy; teacher Mrs Mablethorpe; Mrs Brewster and child from Dog Kennel Cottage; and Lucy Thurston from Stamford Road.

Front row left to right:

Stephen Thurston; Peter Lambing; Pat Thurston; Richard Brewster; Jane Medwell of the Willoughby Arms.

SMALL BEGINNINGS

In 1861 the census recorded several children in the village as scholars. It is likely the children came from land-owning families and received private tuition. The arrival of the railway and available nearby waste land was all the spur that was needed to build a school in Careby.

A former toll cottage was earmarked for the schoolhouse. Well-connected and on several local committees, Reverend John Birch-Reynardson was instrumental in the planning and building of the school. Initially catering for sixty children, the school was a detached building with two gable ends.

The schoolroom measured 27x18x15ft and was built of reddish brick. Large windows of frosted glass allowing plentiful light ensured concentration for pupils. The austere interior with a picture of Queen Victoria and an embroidered text on one wall shadowed a globe, the Bible and a few books laid out on the mistress's desk.

Ann Thornton was the first mistress. Children faced her perched in rising tiers of hard wooden benches that had iron supports attaching the seats to the desks. Boys filed from the front entrance, girls from the rear and they sat mute in segregated rows. An open fire flickered in the tiny grate.

Children didn't attend if the weather was wet, cold or snowy. There was nowhere to dry their clothes. Chilblains were common. Truancy was a problem, particularly with the boys. From the age of eight they cleared fields of stones, helped with haymaking, picked potatoes and peas and gathered in the corn. With their tiny wage supplementing family income, the new law for children to attend school was often ignored by parents.

Making their own by-laws, charging fees, School Boards were elected by local ratepayers. Pupils at Careby were charged twopence a week but some families couldn't afford that.

Chanting multiplication tables and poems or copying from a blackboard propped on a wooden easel, children learned from the Bible, morals, reading and copywriting. The youngest were provided with slates for paper was too expensive for mistakes. The children were expected to wipe their slates clean at the end of each lesson with a sponge or rag brought from home but many spat on their slates and wiped them with their sleeves.

As the children grew in ability, they were allotted a pen. Monitors doled out inkwells at the start of the day and children learnt beautiful copperplate writing. Needlework was introduced at a very young age for most girls were destined to go into service.

THE SCHOOL
CAREBY.

An early photograph of Careby School – too dangerous to stand where the children are today!

Boys wore peaked caps with trousers cut below the knee, white collared shirts and a dark coloured jacket or waistcoat. Girls were dressed in large floppy berets or wide brimmed hats above coats or pinafores over calf length dresses.

Button-booted Aunby pupils walked to Careby clutching a hot potato for lunch. More children trudged from Holywell.

When the school bell rang at twelve midday, Careby children hurried home. Through the back door into the scullery to wash at the sink then into the rush-matted living room to eat. Simmering on the stove might be stew flavoured with sage and coloured with Oxo. Vegetables often lay on a corner of the table; long shiny carrots and radishes. Potatoes with earth welded to their skins sat alongside pea-pods and long stringy beans.

Slipping on to plain wooden chairs, the children ate at the table with warmth at their backs. The fire was kept going all year for cooking, drying the washing and boiling the black kettle for hot water. On either side of the fireplace cupboards were stacked with crockery.

On the first page of the Log Book written in pen and ink by Reverend John Birch-Reynardson…

> 'Dec 17 1875 - Mr Clifton Collins called in the afternoon and inspected the Careby School and on January 13th 1876 the following report was made. "The children in the school are neat and orderly those presented for examination passed in reading and writing but the arithmetic was very weak - a log book Portfolio Admission Register and Circular school cash book are required and it is very desirable that a boarded floor should be laid down. Miss Preston will shortly secure her certificate under article 59..."'

Teachers like Miss Preston had gained experience by acting as monitors first. From the age of nine they graduated to pupil teacher until receiving a certificate of qualification. Younger pupil teachers assisted in controlling the class.

The children were trained to do good. Discipline was enforced; frequently with a cane of bamboo, rattan or birch. If a child had difficulty learning at the same speed as the others he was pilloried and made to stand in the corner wearing a dunce's cap. At Careby, boys were caned across their bottoms for rude conduct, leaving the playground without permission, sulkiness, answering back, throwing ink pellets, truanting and being late.

Girls were caned across their hands or bare legs.

Miss Preston wrote:

'FC was very rude with one of the little girls and punished for doing so.'

'JA JC HL punished for throwing stones.'

Miss Preston, lips tight and eyes like needles, drew herself to her full height. 'John Allsopp! Come out to the front of the class.'

A small boy, not yet eight years old, unfolded himself from the bench and slithered to the end of the row. Reluctantly he began to walk down the steps of the tiered desks. Fifty pairs of eyes followed his progress towards the front of the class.

No one moved. No sound could be heard except for the scrape of John's boots on the floor.

In front of the desk stood a single chair.

'Bend over.' Miss Preston held the cane in both hands, flexing it slightly as she approached the boy.

The child lay across the chair and at the back of the class came a small sound of sobbing.

'Sorry Miss. Sorry...' John's apology turned into a long drawn out wail as the cane came down hard on his bottom. He endured five more strokes before being sent back to his seat.

Miss Preston's eyes drilled into J.C. 'Next.'

Then more caning:

> 'Several children rude and disobedient - they were well punished.
>
> WL and HT were very rude and impertinent to their teacher.
>
> Two boys were punished for getting onto the railway bridge'.

Caning on the hands, not the writing hand, was more painful, three to six strokes were usual on the fingers. If the hand was withdrawn, extra strokes rained down. Often a caning would be reinforced with home punishment. Wise children kept quiet.

The following year the school leaving age was fixed at ten years. Pressure was exerted for all children to attend school.

> 'Sent for absentees. Several absent.
>
> 14 April 1876 - Good Friday - No school, a very heavy fall of snow such a storm as never was known for these many years.
>
> April 24 - Had the police to see if any boys was absent to go to work, they were several.
>
> 1877 March 3 - Policeman visited school to see if there were any complaints. (None).'

School Manager Reverend John Birch-Reynardson and his wife Sophie ran the school and kept a close eye on the teacher, the products of the children's labours finding their way into the Rectory. After one inspection, the Rector gave three children, including Fanny Charity, a shilling for passing the Inspector's examination in all three subjects.

'Mrs Reynardson and Miss Wynyard (her sister) *visited and gave a spelling Bee, sang songs and inspected the needlework and knitting and pronounced themselves pleased and the next day more wool arrived for knitting.*

1877…

'Jan 11 The following day Sophie Reynardson visited, heard the children sing and promised to bring some sugar plums for some of the little boys to count.

On February 12th most children were away from sickness, only 19 present. On the 22nd the school was closed for eight weeks due to measles and scarlet fever.

April 25th - Most of the children got better and able to attend school again.

May 4 - 6 yards of calico sent to school to be made up into shirts and chemises.

May 19th Mary Camm left school and gone to service.'

Mary was twelve. According to the 1891 census, Mary Camm aged 25 was living at 28 St Mary's Street in Stamford and was employed as a servant for the Rector of St Mary's.

In October, the day after his wife Sophie was ill - *Reverend Reynardson found fault with some of the children's head of hair so untidy he thought of bringing a pair of scissors to cut it next time he came.'*
The Rector must have been continually conscious of Inspector Clifton Collins' presence. An entry in the Log Book: *'Their parents ar left and got work elseware.'* The faults have been struck out and corrected.

1878 was marred by sickness and closures. It was a constant battle to keep boys in school. At harvest the school closed so children could help on the farms. In winter boys went bush beating on Holywell estate. These distractions caused poor results, especially in arithmetic.

Schools' Inspector Mr Clifton Collins reappeared on January 11th 1878.

> '...the children are neat and orderly. Few well read and write very fairly but are still backward in arithmetic though there is some slight improvement in this subject since last year. Separate class registers should be kept for boys and girls. The letters in the Portfolio should be filed and numbered in the order of their receipt. The singing must improve. Much more decided progress in Arithmetic will be looked for next year.'

Emphasis on homemaking and sewing continued for girls. They were taught skills about running a household. Boys still truanted and laboured on the land. Some parents were unable or unwilling to contribute the weekly twopence fee.

Mr Collins returned on December 23rd:

> 'The children are remarkably neat and tidy; their needlework is good: their reading and writing are creditable but the Arithmetic is unsatisfactory throughout the school. The infant class requires more careful instruction in elementary subjects. The grant is reduced one tenth for faults of instruction, particularly arithmetic.'

Then fierce Miss Preston left the school. On the 18th April 1879 Caroline Davis took charge. She was twenty-three years old and originated from South Luffenham. She lived in the schoolhouse with a fourteen-year-old servant girl named Elizabeth Tomblin from Barrowden.

Having gained a 2nd class certificate at Lincoln College, Caroline found the fifty-one children extremely backward. Within the week, Sophie Reynardson arrived to assist with reading. At the end of the month a dozen Royal Readers arrived.

Caroline wrote on her first day, *'Commenced duties on Monday morning and Reverend J B Reynardson and his wife kindly paid visits on Monday and Thursday afternoons and supplied the school with books, pens and pencils.*

Finding the children exceedingly backward in every subject especially arithmetic.'

Within three weeks she'd written: *'the great fault is, the children are put into higher standards than they ought to be, consequently their work will always be considered bad.'*

Reverend Reynardson was calling almost daily to test the children in mental arithmetic.

Caroline wasn't inclined to use the cane as much as her predecessor. *'I was obliged to speak strongly to John Charity and Herbert Postle for using vulgar language.'*

John Charity continued to be a problem and was spoken to by the Rector.

By the summer standards had improved and at the beginning of August the children were rewarded by attendance at the Village Feast.

'67 children partook of a very nice tea on the lawns of the Rectory Gardens: after which games and races were indulged in and the children sang a few songs. At 8 o'clock they all separated having spent an enjoyable day.'

Lessons continued until the middle of September *'when five boys were punished for pelting down apples over the garden wall, and then going over the wall to fetch them. After which I gave a lesson on "Stealing" to the whole school which I hope will do good.'*

*Painting of Careby
School by Geoff Forman
With the permission of
Jonathan and Mrs Forman*

*'Week ending Friday 17th October 1879 – Opened school after vacation of four
weeks. The harvest not nearly finished, consequently the attendance is very poor.*

*During the vacation very great improvement has been made – that is a
classroom for the infants, the playground enlarged and a new office* (the toilets)
built for the girls.'

The infant classroom measured 24x15x15ft. Built in pale yellow brick from
Little Bytham brickworks the classroom had smaller windows, and was
sandwiched between the existing school and the schoolhouse. Its east-facing
window was bricked up. A bell tower perched on the roof and a brass bell
summoned the children to school. A folding screen divided the classrooms.
Now the school could accommodate up to eighty children.

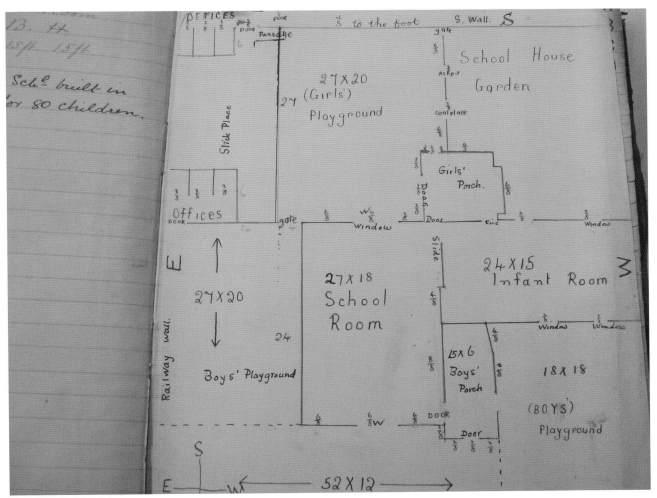

Plan of Careby School classrooms

On the second week of term: *'the stove in the new room finished on Friday.'*

But a week later, disaster: *'the classroom was unbearable for the smoke and school was cancelled.'*

Then: *'Mrs Reynardson spoke to me about the tree in the playground having been chopped. I tried all possible means to discover the culprit but did not succeed.'*

Caroline had been in bed ill (effects of smoke inhalation?) so had no idea who lopped the branches. Her sister Anne had been left in charge.

Emphasis was placed on scripture, hymns and singing. A good number of children passed these examinations. The following year the inspector wrote: *'the teaching did not seem to have reached quite the whole class but a fair proportion answered well enough to give proof of careful teaching, especially...'*

Standard II		Standard III	
Ellen Holmes	*Lucy Daff*	*Bertha Scott*	*Ellen Horne*
Rose King	*William Hall*	*Bessie Horne*	*Amy Biggs*
Agnes Scott	*Constance Burton*	*Thomas Pick*	*Edith Drury*
David Barratt	*Charlotte Biggs*	*Mary Barratt*	

On January 27th 1887, another inspector's report:

'The discipline, tone and general appearance of the school are excellent. The general results in Standard Subjects are creditable; but writing spelling and notation of the 2nd standard and arithmetic of the 4th standard are weak points and mental arithmetic needs attention.'

In 1890 Sophie Birch-Reynardson who had done so much for the children, passed away.

The following year school fees were abolished and the leaving age raised to eleven years. In preparation for the next school inspection the head teacher wrote her intended syllabus in the Log Book. Although History and Geography and Physical Exercise (Drill) are not listed, there was a wide range of subjects…

> Object Lessons, Poetry including Longfellow, Southey and Scott; reading from Royal Readers and Westminster Readers; Dictation, Composition, Letter Writing, Grammar - Parsing and Analysis, Sentences, Recitation and Punctuation; Arithmetic; Vulgar and Decimal Fractions, Bills for Parcels, Reduction, Compound Multiplication and Division. Drawing and Beadwork, Geometrical Copies; Embroidery, Pricking, Paper Plaiting; Music - Scales and Singing.

Clifton Collins was succeeded by Mr. Thorold who arrived on March 2nd 1896.

> *'This school maintains its character for excellent work. The children are evidently taught with much care and they respond very well on their part. The teachers of both divisions are to be congratulated on a good examination. Tone and discipline excellent and a very good school.'*

Three years later the school leaving age was raised to twelve years. The school received £8 in aid for the increase of salaries. The Education Act of 1902 abolished School Boards and replaced them with Local Education Authorities.

In 1904 fifty-five pupils were registered. Reverend Baseley and curate Reverend Pearse paid frequent visits, standing in for the now very elderly rector.

Forgotten People

Mrs Ellen Baseley was Headmistress at the beginning of World War I but a year later Florence Haden-Scott took charge and found the school in a neglected state. She also remarked: *'the school furniture needed attention and there were no locks on the cupboards.'* With forty-two children on roll, the Assistant was Miss Annie Pearce and the monitor Elsie Hall. Elsie must have been a sickly girl for the Log Book records her many absences.

It couldn't have been easy for Florence Haden-Scott. Towards the end of the war the winters were severe with freezing temperatures and prolonged snow. Coal was in short supply.

In May 1914 John Birch-Reynardson died. Four years later: *'Reverend Callender visited the school at 11.45 and interrupted the work of the school by entering into an argument with the Head Mistress.'*

The School Log records in unfamiliar handwriting:

'The Head Teacher had to be absent from duties during some part of the day owing to indisposition – and only came in at intervals to see that work was progressing as usual and for registration.

July 31st 1918 – I resign charge of this school today – Florence Haden-Scott.'

Reverend Callender was a stickler for high standards. In January 1919 he visited the school again: *'Leslie Arnold is absent. He is 11 years of age and very dull and is illegally employed by Mr C Creasey who is moreover one of the school managers.'*

The new teacher continued the battle for better conditions. *'The temperature in the schoolroom was 43 degrees and the room very damp, no wonder the*

24...   *SR 109 - All Log Book entries with permission of Lincolnshire Archives.*

children go down with colds. The heating arrangements really are inadequate unless the fires are lighted very early.'

Then in April: *'No fires because we have run out of coal – both classrooms extremely cold.'*

In 1925 mumps, chicken pox and whooping cough followed an impetigo outbreak. The school closed until further notice. When it re-opened on November 27th the school dentist visited.

'Mr Egan, School Dental Surgeon, visited today. He saw 33 children and operated on 11 extractions, scraping and stopping.'

The next day: *'Secular work began at 9.15 and terminated at 11.15 to enable children to attend Memorial Service to Queen Alexandria held in the Church. This procedure was taken by the wish of the Education Committee. Poor attendance today owing to snowy conditions of the weather.'* [24]

By 1938 school numbers had dwindled to eighteen and once again a single teacher struggled to teach all ages. War broke out and on September 11th school reopened after an extra week's closure. Five London evacuees made up school numbers. A week later two more arrived.

In July 1940 fourteen evacuees came to stay at Holywell Hall. Before and during the war Major Hoare, who also ran the local Home Guard, was leasing the Hall from Mrs Fane. Many evacuees attended Careby School, pushing pupil numbers to forty-one. Another teacher was required, especially as the evacuees stayed on at school for all but two weeks of the summer holiday. A couple proved so unruly that they were transferred to a hostel in Bourne.

Less than three years later teachers Mr and Mrs Barbary had arrived.

St Stephen's Church

St Stephen's Church is tucked away at the end of the village in peaceful and gentle surroundings. The church is fortunate in having an enthusiastic Parochial Church Council. Despite the small number of parishioners considerable sums of money have been raised for the maintenance of the church, including generous assistance from the Bythams with Careby Hunter Trials and more recently Grimsthorpe sponsored rides.

Another memorable event was the Evening of Fine Music.

One bright Sunday afternoon at the end of April 2007, a bus driver found his way to Careby. He reversed the bus all the way down the street and about 45 Oakham School musicians tumbled out by the lych gate to rehearse for the concert. Loaded with instruments of all shapes and sizes together with music stands and amplifiers, they manfully struggled with them all the way down the church path.

After rehearsing, the musicians demolished their supper while their potential audience accumulated in the sunshine and enjoyed a glass of wine and glorious buffet supper.

In a church full to capacity, the Chamber Choir sang a wonderfully varied programme. Stabat Mater was sensitively rendered. There were contemporary songs announced by the conductor Peter Davis and the first half finished with evocative harmony and a stunning 'Sit Down You're Rocking The Boat'.

In the interval the Chancel was rearranged to accommodate the Big Band, directed by Steve Foster. They swung into action with foot tapping numbers by Duke Ellington and Al Jolson and fine solos by many members of the band. At one point the trombonists paraded their tunes out through the churchyard and back into the church, serenading members of the audience. Two vocal soloists added hugely to our enjoyment and 'Mr Bojangles' was requested as an encore.

Glenside News

In the same year Careby PCC planned the restoration of the medieval cope. This amazing piece of embroidered work began life in the early 16th century as a vestment worn by the priest during Mass. Somehow the cope survived the Reformation, defying both the ravages of the King's men and later, Cromwell's soldiers.

After the restoration of the Monarchy with the succession of Charles II the cope came to light again. Cut up, it was turned into a Frontal, an embroidered cloth hanging in front of the altar. Decorated with embroidered seraphs with the lovely Assumption in the centre, the background is glorious red silk velvet.

The Frontal was framed and hung on the wall in the church with a copy of the Yorkshire Post dated September 3rd 1937 placed behind the backing.

In 2007 the Council for Care of the Churches gave a generous grant and the Cope/Altar Frontal was taken to Burghley House to be restored by Sheila Landi and her team. Inevitably the cope had suffered from damp, insect infestation and dirt.

Careby Church Cope

Proving to be exacting and time consuming the cope aroused great interest among experts, one of who was sure it was made in the same (English) workshop as a cope now in a Gallery of Textiles and Costume, Italy.

Again on display in Careby Church, the cope was dedicated and thanks given for its restoration on November 16th 2007.

Painting of the Lych Gate by Marjorie Bradshaw

Jeff Midwood, former Parish Chairman, conceived CHAMP: Careby with Holywell and Aunby Millennium Project. A lych gate was to be built at the entrance to St Stephen's to celebrate the Millenium.

Prince Galitzine of Holywell Hall generously donated £2,500, while Careby resident Jo Wood organised 'Fund a Slate', and extra funds were raised from a car treasure hunt, a raffle and from cakes sold at Stamford Market.

Wilf Stead and Roy Grundy excavated the footings and stonemason David Espin built the walls with Dave Bryant assisting. Aubrey Fenn crafted both roof and entry gates with oak provided by Dick Tinsley of Holywell. Burghley House's blacksmith wrought the ironwork. An automatic light censor in the red cedar roof illuminated the church path.

On Saturday 19th August 2000 a Parish Picnic followed the opening ceremony with games and races, a bouncy castle and an opportunity to visit the flower festival in the Church. In glorious sunshine Geoff Forman's vintage fair organ entertained parishioners on the paddock beside the church.

Dick Tinsley

A Stamford Mercury reporter quoted a resident: *'it has all been marvellous. I have lived here for over seventy years and I don't ever remember a village party like this. We have something to be proud of in the lych gate, which should last until the next millennium.'*

A few weeks later the Bishop of Lincoln was invited to position a time capsule under the paving of the lychgate. It contained a copy of the Sunday Times, the Rutland & Stamford Mercury and a supermarket receipt.

Floods

In 1998 after torrential rain, water rose inside the church to a depth of three feet. Overnight the river subsided and the challenge of cleaning the worst of the damage was left to industrial cleaners. Parishioners rescued the kneelers before restoring the church to its former glory.

The Bishop of Lincoln

On a pillar inside the church:

'Water in this Church 19 inches deep on the 7 day of aug in the year 1922 and 22 inches in the vestry. Also ten years later in 1932.'

184

The river had also burst its banks in 1957. Daphne Fane was rescued from her home at Little Paddocks.

Restoration

In 1992 it was recommended the church bells should be carefully dismantled and re-hung. The oak bell framing dated 1693 was clearly unsafe and was to be demolished. A new floor must be installed in the bell tower and the decayed sills of the belfry louvres cut out and replaced. The tower had to be repointed.

Together with other restoration the final cost was estimated at £30,000.

The church's beautiful Victorian ceiling was to be treated for beetle infestation.

Re-hanging the Church bells

Described by Pevsner as a Victorian wooden tierceron-vault with all ribs performing three-dimensional curves, the ceiling was designed and executed by a boat builder in the 19th century. Several hundred pounds must have been spent and it is believed unique in this country.

Two or three decades previously the ceiling had been surveyed. The inspection was carried out from normal means of access, from ladders. The timbers of the chancel had been examined at the ends of all beams but the ends of other roof timbers had not been inspected.

So Rentokil was contacted and a ladder placed in readiness for a proper inspection. Then churchwarden Bob Creasey was urged by the Rentokil representative to climb the ladder and take a look.

At each end of the vast ceiling a tiny trapdoor almost invisible was let into the vaulted ceiling. Bob poked his head through the opening and swung his torch. Any beetle infestation in the ceiling was momentarily forgotten. The trap door had obviously been missed at earlier inspections.

The original six-inch beams had been eaten away to leave only one inch. Some beams were so infested they didn't reach the wall supports. Thoughts rushed to the recently packed church celebrating midnight mass.

The congregation had worshipped under a virtually unsupported roof.

The advice given was to close the church. However the chancel roof was sound so the nave was partitioned off and services held in the chancel.

Proceeds from the Flower Festival of 1984 were put towards the cost of repair and the estimated sum of £52,000 was raised. An English Heritage grant provided £31,000 and charities accounted for a further £11,000. The remaining £10,000 was raised from local events where people came together to preserve this lovely church.

Work began fourteen months later. The old roof was removed and signs of burning on the walls of the tower were evident together with traces of at least one other roof.

The women huddled together; the hems of their gowns and wooden clogs heavy with mud. Gathered close to the manor, they sought safety in numbers because their men were out in the fields with oxen ploughing the top field.

The drum of hoofbeats galloping past Berwardwelle in Uppegate was such an unusual sound that villagers had burst on to the street. Six strangers, breast-plated and brandishing swords swept past by and clattered past the rectory towards the church.

Richard Wright had warned this might happen. He'd heard what had happened in Stamford, how the King's men tore down rood screens in the churches and set them alight.

Beatrice couldn't believe such a thing would occur in Careby. Thomas had visited the church this morning, lighting and placing a candle on the ledge below the rood screen and praying for the soul of his father. The priest had chanted Mass for him.

Beatrice clutched Elizabeth's arm. Smoke was curling behind the bare arms of the trees. The strangers galloped back up the street. The women stepped off the road to let them pass and a gust of wind lifting their starched caps.

When the hoofbeats faded Elizabeth pointed. 'Look, the roof! It's on fire.'

The women clutched at each other. Close to the tower the thatched roof of the church was ablaze.

'Call the men! Fire! Fire!' The women scattered, dashing into their houses for wooden pails.

By the time the men had rushed off the hillside to help, the church was well alight. In spattered hose and loose fitting tunics they stood in a line from the river, choking and gasping in the smoke. Churchwarden Richard Inglishe was organising the passing of buckets. William Symson stood by, clutching his cope and wringing his hands.

The women gathered and worried for the safety of their houses. Thatched with straw, wattle and daub walls, they were all they had to live in.

But the wind blew from the west and sparks fell into the river.

Closing Ring

The Reverend Stanley Hoar *(left)* and Mildred Phillipson of Castle Bytham arranged for St Stephen's rare closing ring to be restored in 1976/7. Sent to the Department of Archaeology at the University of Leeds, the layers of paint were treated with Nitromors. Rust was removed mechanically with a needle and vibrotool before the cleaned metal was immersed in a bath of sodium carbonate solution.

Rare because of the thoroughness of Victorian restoration, Careby's closing ring on the entry door of the church was estimated to be from the last quarter of the 12th century. Architectural evidence suggests the closing ring was originally made for the Romanesque south doorway but after the nave was rebuilt, a larger door was made and the closing ring transferred to the new door. The door surface was hollowed to accommodate the back plate of the handle and the ring secured to the door by a centrally located pin.

The plate showed no evidence of excessive wear. The ring was not intended as a door-knocker but a sanctuary knocker; in times gone by an accused man clung to the knocker and shouted, 'Sanctuary'. Once admitted, he was allowed to stay in the church until receiving a fair trial.

All three portions, oval ring, pin and plate were decorated.

Careby Church Closing Ring

Figures of dragons were applied to the surface of the ring. Each dragon was attached to the ring by a rivet at the centre of its body. The left-hand dragon had a curving neck and a slightly curled tail; the dragon on the right had a straight neck and tightly curled tail.

The pin was formed from a single piece of iron hammered round the ring to swivel freely in the loop. The loop is rectangular where it held the ring and decorated with a face of almond-shaped eyes, bulbous cheeks, prominent nose, deep mouth and a bearded chin.

The back plate is circular, slightly hollowed with a raised rim and decorated with three windows and three flowers. The 'windows' are four punched rectangles, each surmounted by a circle: the 'flowers', one rectangle with three circles.

The man eased his foot off the accelerator as the lane narrowed and led downhill. No traffic, poor lighting. Only the moon illuminated the church.

He coasted over the narrow river bridge, turned round in a gateway and drove back to swerve close to the wall. Killing the engine, he listened. Already there was a tight feeling in his chest. He adjusted the balaclava until only his lips and eyes showed. His breath came in short gasps to form a damp patch on the rough wool close to his nostrils. It always grabbed him like this - the tension.

Screwing his body out of the car, he pocketed his keys, zipped his jacket on to his sparse frame, and gazed at the church hunching alone in the darkness. The tower rose like a clenched fist against the navy blue sky. In the churchyard overhanging branches clashed angrily in the wind and an owl swooped, its screech eerie in the night.

Hairs rose on the back of his neck; his wife would have interpreted the ghostly whiteness of the bird as some kind of warning. He shook off the thought and with a swift glance up the street, slipped on to the church path. Fumbling in a pocket for a thin pair of gloves, he tiptoed across the gravel on to the grass and glanced to his right. Across a wide sweeping lawn the windows of the rectory stared back, tall, black and angular.

He grinned: the anticipation, the waiting, all had been worth it. Even the possibility of being caught upped his excitement.

He hadn't expected the church to be locked and it wasn't. He shone the pencil light of his torch on the knocker and stifled a laugh. St Stephen's Knocker they called it. Well, it would be Steve's knocker from now on.

The porch faced south so he was shielded from the road. He stared at the knocker again; this was what he'd come for. He'd read about it in the newspaper and if it was as rare as everyone seemed to think, he had to have it didn't he?

It was a matter of seconds to clip the pin holding the closing ring in place and then the cold iron was clasped safe in his hand. He flashed the beam of his torch over the lizards before stuffing it in his pocket.

He stood for a moment. Should he remove the iron back plate from the door as well? It would take longer - and there was the sound of a dog barking from across the river, deep and menacing.

He grimaced: quit while you're ahead old son.

St Stephen's Knocker was indeed stolen. The next day two ladies visited the church and found the door ajar. Immediately they noticed the closing ring was missing.

The University of Leeds was contacted and from photographs a copy was made.

The reproduction Closing Ring and original Backplate

Architecture

Careby Church was almost certainly constructed of timber and thatch under the supervision of a Saxon Thane. A Saxon cross fifty-eight inches high together with two very small stone coffins are presently stored behind the south door. The rounded shape of the shaft and the smooth rounded stone knob at the centre of the cross is reminiscent of a wooden original of a pre-Conquest date.

The 12th century chancel is Norman with a priest's doorway and one original north window. Outside it is easy to see chancel and tower at opposite ends of the church built in a similar style with thin limestone rubble.

> *"The Norman north arcade has been cut through an earlier wall, whose side - alternate western quoin still survives, with the west wall of the later aisle built straight against it. The antiquity of the site is attested by the sections of Pre-Conquest."* [25]

The nave has traditional squared hewn blocks and is mostly of Perpendicular[26] architecture. (A ready supply of stone was probably transported down river from the quarry a few hundred yards distant.)

The west tower dates from the early 13th century with a belfry staircase built into the thickness of the walls. Two bells hang in the bell tower and the low pyramid roof gives the tower a French appearance.

Early English, the porch was added in the late 12th or early 13th century. The windows are also of Perpendicular style as are the beautiful row of arcades.

The misericorde, (Latin for Loving Kindness), is positioned by the doorway to St Giles' Chantry. When lifted, it presents a higher seat on which the priest may rest during long periods of standing.

25... *H. M. Taylor - Anglo-Saxon Architecture (Cambridge 1965) vol 2 page 716*
26... *Perpendicular – any time up to 1500*

The stained glass in some windows has been dated between 1275 and 1300. This coincides with the period showing a late 13th century heart set in the west wall of the north-facing chantry; thought to be brought from the ancient chapel at Aunby in the 19th century. Two hands hold the heart with a shield bearing the arms of the Wake family. The arms are repeated in the early stained glass in the north window of the chantry.

It was the custom for wealthy people to endow chantries for the purpose of easing their souls into after life by the process of prayer, thereby implying the existence of Purgatory. However, the Protestants couldn't find such proof in the Bible so chantry use was abolished in 1537 at the same time as the Dissolution of the monasteries.

The chantry on the north side of the church was named after St Giles. A 7th century saint who lived life as a hermit, St Giles became the patron of cripples and said to perform miracles.

The chantry screen has early English bases with both door and wall decorated with a splendid leaf band carved at a later period. Inside, mounted on the wall is a memorial to the Hatcher family, owners of Careby and Little Bytham Manors from the sixteenth to the mid-eighteenth centuries.

From the Beginning...

In Saxon times church tithes were compulsory. Once collected they were divided between the priest, the village, support for the poor and the upkeep of the church.

Like many churches in the locality, Careby Church was part of the lands of St Peter's Abbey of Burgh (Peterborough). The Abbey claimed dues for labour services, ploughing, reaping, hay making, carriage duties, repair of the lord's hall and mill, a food rent and an ecclesiastical tithe. Tithes amounted to one tenth of produce that came from or was nourished by the earth. Traditionally, it was a form of payment by the community to the lay rector.

The church was seen as a piece of property and mark of status. It was also the focus of the community, a meeting place, a market place and a constant moral anchor. Morality tales were painted on the lime-washed walls.

Succeeding Peterborough Abbey's Abbot Leofric who'd fought for Harold at Hastings then died within a fortnight; newly installed Abbot Brand sought to recover lands for his churches from the Norman invaders.

Courts were set up to decide the fate of Careby Church and several others but it was ruled that the final decision must come from King William.

The new King had yet to grasp Olde English so hadn't made up his mind as to who should have what. He'd already awarded lands to French noblemen who'd helped him invade Britain. In the meantime Abbot Brand sought confirmation of Peterborough Abbey's lands from Edgar Aethling, whom he believed should have been King. When William found out, Abbot Brand had to pay very heavily to retrieve the manors and churches in Lincolnshire.

William took control of rebuilding English churches and installed Norman priests as an easy way of controlling the people. The priest became lord of the manor too, displacing the thanes who had expected to be tenants for life.

In Careby the Norman influence was reflected in the names of its priests. In 1225, lord of the manor William de Gymiles was rector until 1257 when he bequeathed part of the manor and advowson of the church to his nephew, Suspirus de Bayus. In 1277 William de Baiocis officiated as rector and lord of the manor.

FORGOTTEN PEOPLE

Those with sufficient funds and wishing to please God and increase their chances of salvation continued to contribute to religious causes. Richard de Franceys gave a grant for the sustentation of light at the altar of the Blessed Virgin Mary in Careby Church. Twopence was to be paid annually to the hospital of St John de Acres. (One of six religious hospitals in Stamford at the time.)

Careby came under the auspices of St Leonard's Priory, a small Benedictine monastery in Stamford with a cell of two Durham monks surviving on a poor income. In 1291 the monastery's value was £28, a considerable sum of money but not enough for the Priory to prosper. Hugh Pykard of Careby paid one silver penny to St Leonard's Priory, his fee for leasing houses with a court adjacent to Reginald le Cou.

Somehow, Careby Church continued to benefit. In 1310 Ralph Pykard of Careby gave up all rights and claims to his land called Moderwykes to priest William Baiocis. A year later, Robert le Court, heir to Ralph de Court, gave enfeoffment[27] to Henry Adwych (chaplain), of a messuage and a croft with five acres.

William de Baiocis died in 1349 when the Black Death raged in Stamford. He'd

The William de Baiocis monument returns from the Tate Gallery

arranged that Careby Manor and the advowson of Careby would revert to the De Colvilles at Castle Bytham after the death of his son Thomas. The same year Thomas became the new lord of Careby. William de Baiocis lies in bed with his wife Mabel on the south side of the church. The monument, carved from a single slab of stone was exhibited at the Tate Gallery in London in 2002.

27... *Enfeoffment - Under the feudal system, the deed by which a person was given land in exchange for a pledge of service.*

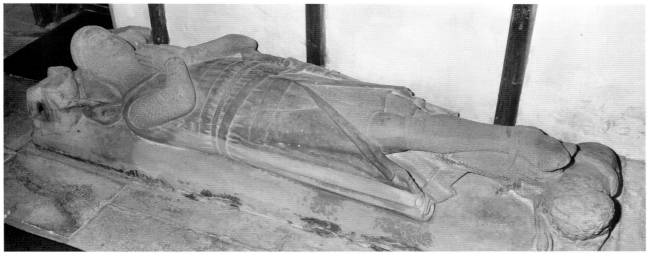

The unidentified single knight in the chancel of Careby Church

Also lying in the chancel is a single knight in chain mail. Although unidentified, he is thought to belong to the same period. Possibly brought from the demolished chapel at Aunby, the knight may be William de Colville who lived in the mansion at Aunby before becoming Castle Bytham's lord.

William de Baiocis' le cure[28] was Ralph le Cure of Careby. In Ralph's will of February 24th 1317, he left money and clothes to relatives, gifts to the bridge at Careby, as well as a gift for the bells and belfry of the Church of St Stephen.

Such a practice was commonplace; in medieval England the Church dominated people's lives - they grew up to believe the only way to Heaven was if the Catholic Church let them. The Church held great power, owned much of the land, charging for baptisms, marriages and burials, leaving peasants always poor. If the poor didn't pay their tithes they feared going to Hell.

28... *Le Cure – parish priest*

The rich showing rank and hierarchy, gave to the Church but expected favours in return:

> *Enforcement by Robert le Wright of East Bytham (Little Bytham) of Ralph and his son of a perch of meadow land in East Bytham meadow and lying between that held bondage by Robert, son of John and that belonging to the chantry altar BVM in Careby church. He is to pay yearly to the altar lights of the BVM in East Bytham church 18 silver pennies and 4d to celebrate four masses for the souls of Robert and Beatrice his wife.*
> *Sunday 13th June 1339* [29]

This ostentatious almsgiving caused resentment amongst the poor and led those without chattels to steal from the church. At the close of Easter, German Clerk of Barnack stole a chalice worth twenty shillings from Greatford Church. He was arrested at Careby and released to the Bishop of Lincoln. There is no record of what the Bishop did to him.

Each day the rector and others joining them sat in the chancel to celebrate Mass. When the rector was not praying he might educate local children, for few people in medieval society were literate. Wearing the distinctive long tunic and mantle long abandoned by the population since the 5th century but retained by the clergy for sacred purposes, this cope or cloak was highly coloured. Different copes were worn to celebrate different religious occasions. Perhaps the Careby Cope was embroidered at Holywell, (Bredestorp) for in medieval times their women were highly renowned for fine embroidery.
    Deemed a great honour to work on the church, skilled workmen belonged

29... *H102/10 With the permission of Lincolnshire Archives*
BVM – Blessed Virgin Mary

to a guild with craftsmen taking in apprentices for money. If any twelve-year-old boy was lucky enough to be apprenticed and live with a mason he finished his apprenticeship fourteen years later. During that time he was neither to marry nor drink alcohol. Once his apprenticeship was over he became a journeyman: paid and eventually amassing enough money to start his own business.

The Dissolution of the Monasteries

In the early 16th century during Henry VIII's reign, any religious house with an income of less than £200 a year was closed and demolished for building materials or reclaimed as an Anglican Church. Thomas Cromwell was responsible for the dissolution of the monasteries and his men closed St Leonard's Priory.

No church escaped the looters and by 1547 every rood screen in the land had been toppled and burned and the use of every chantry suppressed.

The rood screen with a representation of the crucifixion, bounded on one side by the Virgin Mary and on the other by St John, either hung over the chancel or was suspended from a beam. Below the rood another beam provided a ledge for candles to be lit and placed by individuals praying for the souls of the dead.

The King declared this practice illegal. Instead, emphasis was laid upon a simple life. Many holy days and saints' days were banned, wall paintings were concealed by lime wash and services in Latin ceased. Henry put himself at the head of this new Church and introduced and had printed the English Bible and a copy was deposited in every parish in his kingdom.

There were uprisings: Lincolnshire being at the heart of them. Sir John Hussey, who had a share in Careby Manor, was beheaded for treason.

Careby Parishioners

Following the Civil War civil officials were appointed to record marriages, births and burials. When church power was restored with the accession of Charles II, one of the earliest burials recorded at Careby was:

> **1685 - Thomas Lenton**[30] *buryed March 28th*
>
> *Rev Sculthorpe Rector*
> *John Snart, Churchwarden*

Reverend Sculthorpe rented land at Holywell. The proposed main house may now be known as either Hollow Cottage or the original Bridge Villa (Home Farm).

The details are amongst the particulars of sale drawn up by the bankrupt Goodhalls of Holywell Hall in 1728:

> *In tenure of John Scullthorpe*
> *Together with a Large Barn and Stable standing upon*
> *Stone Pitt Close. Main house to be built to the same.*
>
> *The Great Seed Close* .... *Rent*
> *Lobbingly Moor Meadow* *£26*

The parish register first records the presence of the Hatchers in 1566, when John, son of Thomas Hatcher was baptised.

30... *Faithful servant to Sir John Hatcher*

On the floor of the church is a flat stone showing Thomas's burial site, inscribed:

Sepulchrum hujus familiae ex impensis Thomas Hatcheri armigeri Anno Domini 1714.

Underneath lies the body of Thomas Hatcher Esq descended from the ancient family of Hatcher, for many generations Lords of this Mannour. He was born November iiid MDCLX and died September the vith MDCCXIV. He had two wives but no issue. The first was Grace, daughter of Wm Harboard Esq. The second was Jane, daughter of Sir Charles Hussey of Caythorpe in this county, who surviving him in memory of her indulgent husband, erected this monument. Anno Dom MDCCXXX1.

Here is also interred the body of Jane, relict of said Thomas Hatcher who departed this life June 3rd 1735 in the 80th year of her age.

Also recorded inside the church:

26 Aug 1720 *John Hatcher Esq.*

22 May 1721 *Mrs Frances Hatcher wife of late John Hatcher. She being buryed in linen[31], fifty shillings were distributed to the poor.*

March 11th 1732 *Mrs Hatcher gave a silver patten for the more decent administration of ye bread, with this inscription - ex dono Jane Hatcher Wid MDCCXX11*

Jane Hatcher widow of Thomas Hatcher Esq. Gave a Communion Flaggon to ye Parish church of Careby in ye County of Lincoln for more decent administration of ye Holy Sacrament this 17th day of July 1732 markt at bottom with this inscription - Jane Hatcher Vid dedit Ad MDCCXXX11

Item. At the same time Mrs Hatcher have a large linen cloth and a large napkin for a cover for the Communion table.

31... *Acts of Parliament designed to protect the domestic wool industry required all bodies to be buried in wool. Presumably the family paid the penalty of five pounds for not doing so.*

Register for Careby 1722

Robert son of Alexander and Ann Pitts was born January 10th and baptised the same day.

Ann, wife of Alexander Pitts was buryed January 25th

Robert, son of Alexander Pitts was buryed January 27th

> *William Cawthorne - Rector,*
>
> *John Waddington - Churchwarden*

In 1732 William Cawthorne died.

Burials

Richard Lawnde   William Cawthorne Rector   April 30th

> *Culpepper Butcher - Rector*
>
> *John Waddington - Churchwarden*

There were only two of them.

'Here, let me.' Will carefully inserted the flat blade of the pickaxe under the rim of the stone.

'Be careful. Don't go leaving traces.' The second man knelt on the stone floor near to the chancel and held the lamp. He was nervous; the flicker of light might be seen through the windows. He wished Will would hurry.

'It's coming up. Grab this end.' Will whistled through his teeth as he worked. Between them they heaved the stone slab to one side.

'John, give us a bit o' light.' Will took the lamp, lowered it into the vault and peered in. Coffins lined the walls. 'Here. Hold this.' He passed the lamp back to John. 'I'm going down.'

A soft thump as he landed. 'Pass me the pickaxe.'

'What are you going to do?'

'What do you think?'

'But you can't smash the lead... What...what about the bodies inside?'

'They won't know. I thought you were up for this. Come on. Hurry up.'

John held the lamp low and averted his gaze. The thuds as the pickaxe swung, reverberated against the walls of the vault like gunshots.

'Here. Grab hold of this silver, there's quite a haul.'

Silver plates and flaggons piled up on the church floor.

'Right. That's it. All done. Pull me up. I've no wish to linger.'

They resealed the floor and when John held up the lamp it was impossible to see where they'd been.

The Hardwicke Marriage Act of 1754 prohibited marriages to be performed anywhere except in the Church of England, Jewish synagogues and Quaker meeting houses. Parish rectors read marriage banns for three consecutive weeks before the wedding and recorded marriages on separate forms as illustrated below. Previously, the legal age for marriage had been fourteen for a boy and twelve for a girl.

Careby Register 1763

Abraham Partridge. Labourer, and Elizabeth Hammerton - spinster, married by banns 25th November

> *Wm Gale - Rector* (who'd gained a BA at Cambridge)
>
> *Edward Pawlett - Churchwarden*

In the 19th century more information was required:

Copy of Parish Register of Careby in the County of Lincoln

Alderman
Elisabeth - daughter of Henry and Alice . . . . *baptised April 3rd 1803*
Cunnington
John, son of Thomas and Susannah . . . . *baptised July 14th 1803*
Wilkinson
Lucy daughter of Henry and Mary Elizabeth . . . . *baptised Sept 3rd 1803*
Wilkinson
Sarah Susan daughter of Henry and Mary Elizabeth . . . *baptised Dec 2nd 1804*
Cunnington
William son of Thomas and Susannah . . . . *baptised March 10th 1805*
Withers
James son of Thomas and Nancy . . . . *baptised March 8th 1807*
Partridge
Elizabeth, daughter of Abraham and Mary . . . . *baptised June 7th 1807*

Burials

Alderman Elisabeth daughter of Henry and Alice . . . . *July 10th 1803*
Harcourt Thomas . . . . *January 4th 1804*
Skeath Priscilla. . . . . *October 3rd 1805*

     Thomas Foster - Rector[32]
     Wm White - Churchwarden

32... *Thomas Foster was a magistrate and rector at Careby and Ryhall from 1772 until he died in 1826.*

In 1813 a separate baptism and burial register showing columns for specific information was required.

1838... Baptisms

March 7 . . Emma, daughter of Thomas and Eleanor Willford (clerk and grazier)

April 19 . . . . John, son of John and Ann Berridge (Farmer and grazier)

July 1st . . . . . . Samuel, son of Francis and Sarah Belton (Mason and cottager)

October 21 . . . . George, son of John and Elizabeth Skeath (Pauper)

November 25 . . . . Jabez, illegitimate son of Anne Ormond (servant)

Reverend Deverell

Reverend Deverell donated a large painting of Salvator Mundi[33] that hangs above the altar. He also presented the church with a fine toned organ.

A Shock

Extensive 19th century renovation of the church was arranged and paid for by Reverend John Birch-Reynardson. In 1856, according to the Stamford and Rutland Mercury of October 1935, in the course of reparation to the chancel floor, a slab was about to be taken up by stonemason John Holmes under the direction of the Rector. But before they could proceed, a portion of the floor disappeared with a loud report. Both the Rector and John Holmes leapt to their feet and rushed to the other end of the church. They stared at each other in alarm.

'However, they eventually returned and surveyed the abyss with wonderment. The debris had fallen into the chamber of death. The vault that had been closed

---

33... *Salvator Mundi or Saviour of the world is a subject in iconography depicting Christ with his right hand raised in blessing and his left hand holding an orb surmounted by a cross.*

for many years being now exposed to view, the opportunity was seized for examining the coffins deposited there. Several of the corpses, which had been encased in lead, had been removed from the compartments in which they had been placed at the interments, being set upright against a wall. The mutilated appearance of these coffins, together with their positions proved a sacrilege had been perpetrated. The lead had apparently been perforated with a pickaxe, and the tradition respecting the vault containing treasures was probably the cause of the sacrilegious act.'

The newspaper article also suggested that the church originally possessed a steeple but that this fell on the roof of the north aisle and completely destroyed it. The present leaning of the tower in a northeasterly direction may support this theory.

The interior of St Stephen's, Careby – looking east

The Reverend John Birch-Reynardson had the tower restored and large sums of money were spent on beautifying the remainder of the church. The walls were scraped and painted and the organ loft removed to expose an arch leading to the bell tower. John Holmes carved a new stone pulpit, reading desk and stone altar rails.

Born in Little Bytham in 1839, John Holmes lived in the terrace of cottages opposite the village hall field. He later moved to The Old Bakehouse on the far side of the river.

At the west end of the church the Rector designed the rich colours of the window as well as the east window above the altar. Taken from drawings of

The window in St Stephen's dedicated to Sarah Jones

subjects with the help of his sister Emma Lucy, they include the Transfiguration, the Ascension, Christ in Glory, Christ blessing little children, the Flight into Egypt, Christ instructing his Disciples, the Stoning of Stephen, the Crucifixion and the Visit of the Virgin Mary to the Tomb after Christ was risen.

The sanctuary tiling behind the altar is dedicated to members of the Birch-Reynardson family.

Another window is dedicated to the memory of Sarah Jones (Anne Yorke's chambermaid from Erddig). Sarah, dearly loved nursemaid known affectionately as Lalla became most important to the Reynardson children. Apart from a short return to her native Wrexham where she flirted with the idea of marriage to one or two schoolmasters she lived as nursemaid, confidante, housekeeper and retired nanny at Holywell Hall.

Rectors and Chaplains of Careby

William Gale	1763
Thomas Foster	1772-1826
John Robert Deverell	1828-1844
John Birch Reynardson	1844-1914
Reginald Pearce Assistant and curate to JBR	1900-1911
Frazer Allen	1911-1914
Reverend Pierce	1914
A. Early Ayre	1914-1917
Reginald Callender	1917-1920
Rev Clowes (Little Bytham)	1921-1923
Charles Cleaver	1923-1935
E.C. Smith	1936-1945
W. Richardson	1946-1947
Rev Bainbridge	1947
Rev Butler	1949-1950
Rev Hooson	1949-1951
Rev Bullis	1950
Rev Summers (Thurlby)	1951
Reverend Piercy (Braceborough)	1954-1959
Rev Howell (Greatford)	1962-1964
Rev PE Bush	1969-1971
Stanley Hoar	1972-1989
Brian Bennett	1989-2004
Jo Saunders	2004-2009
Sue Evans	2010

MRS FANE & THE BIRCH-REYNARDSONS

Agatha Isabel Acland-Hood, granddaughter of Colonel Charles Birch-Reynardson married Major Hon. Mountjoy John Charles Wedderburn Fane in 1926. Their son became Lt. Commander Antony Reynardson-Fane RN. Daughter Daphne came to live in Careby.

Mrs Fane's brother Charlie, a Midshipman on HMS Invincible had been killed in 1916 at the Battle of Jutland. A memorial to him is in Holywell Church and his name is on the roll of honour alongside eleven other men of Holywell who gave their lives in the Great War. Arthur Ailwyn, a second brother, lived only one month and was buried in Careby churchyard in 1900.

So as sole heir Agatha Fane inherited Holywell and most of Careby Parish.

Agatha Fane
National Portrait Gallery

Before and during WWII Mrs Fane leased the Hall to Major Hoare, a banker who some said was as fierce as her own reputation. Mrs Fane and her husband, when he was not away fighting, moved to Aunby Manor with their family. In 1952 they bought Careby Rectory and Daphne moved to Little Paddocks on the far side of the River Glen.

At first Holywell Hall was leased to the Lockwood family. Then they bought the property. Aunby was sold.

An early aviator, Mrs Fane used to keep her aeroplane at Pickworth. Staff at the Hall nicknamed her Buzz from her habit of buzzing the Hall when returning from a flight to let them know she was back. An early ambition was to win a horse race, a car race and an aeroplane race in the same year. Although achieving victories at Cottesmore Point-to-Point and scoring second when car racing at Brooklands in Surrey, she was never allowed to race solo in an international air race. She was famed for shooting parties on the estate and acted as a Justice of the Peace.

Mrs Fane died in 1993. Ten years later her daughter Daphne also died. Daphne was a familiar figure in Careby, a hard-working member of the Red Cross, often encouraging children to visit her dogs and donkeys at Little Paddocks.

Mrs Fane's grandfather Colonel Charles Birch-Reynardson was a noted yachtsman. He married Emma Maria Stracey in 1875 who bore him two daughters, Miriam Anne, born in 1876, and Alice Mary, born in 1877.

In 1901 the Colonel was a retired army officer living at the Hall with his wife and a number of servants. Alice Mary was still living at home. Agatha's mother Miriam Anne had married Arthur Acland-Hood, a major in the Rifle Brigade.

Holywell was a thriving community. At that time twelve live-in servants included butler Joseph Archer; Sarah Jane Fisher the housekeeper; Susan Alice Matthew the cook. John Alfred and George Benjamin Taylor were footmen and Hartsel Goodyear and Edith Marian Stokey were both lady's maids.

Nineteen-year-old Anne Elizabeth, Constance Coombes and Christian Cameron were housemaids. Rosalie Swann was the kitchen maid and Jane Elizabeth Stalker the cutlery maid. George Henry Bloodworth was employed as odd job man and William Thompson and Charles Nichols were grooms living over the stables. They often crept across the courtyard archway and climbed through a window into the servants' quarters.

North of the Hall Gardener's Cottage housed long-standing head gardener Arthur Postle, his wife and six children. In Coachman's Cottage Edwin Todd lived with his wife and three daughters.

Another long serving employee, soon to retire, was Robert Baron from a long-standing Careby family. He lived with his wife Yaka and their servant from Pickworth at Bridge Villa. Now known as Home Farm, it became home to the highly regarded farm bailiff in the 1860s.

Blacksmith's Cottage housed Norfolk blacksmith William Jackson and his family. At Turner's Lodge, now Lodge Farm, horseman William Chamberlain lived with his wife and nephew. The two Mill Houses accommodated farm foreman John Stanton and his family, boarding two waggoners, Joseph Wass and Philip Tracey. Next door, corn miller James Meredith and his wife and son boarded Holywell's carpenter Amos Stinson Templeman.

Three Pettywood Cottages off the Clipsham Road housed shepherd Owen with his wife and five children, the Pell and Cox families. The Camms lived in Sharman's Cottages; Henry Camm was the domestic gardener and the Sharmans were farmers living at Sharman's Lodge. Carpenter's Lodge accommodated the Pearson family.

Colonel Charles Birch-Reynardson died of pneumonia on 8th November 1919 at the age of seventy-three. He'd been staying at the home of his late sister's family at Hopetown House in Scotland. His body was returned by train and buried in Careby churchyard.

Stamford Mercury reported he'd been a local Justice of the Peace although not seen on the bench for many years because of his affliction – the effects of an accident whilst playing polo in India.

Emma Maria, his widow, moved to London but later returned to live at Witham-on-the-Hill. In 1944 she died aged ninety-three and is also buried at Careby.

AUNBY WITH HOLYWELL

Traditional Water Mill
H56/2 With the permission
of Lincolnshire Archives

All that remains of Aunby is the manor, one or two farmhouses and associated cottages. Some provide holiday accommodation; there are fishing lakes and an old mill. The mill was built around 1850 and modelled on the successful mill at Holywell. But the flow of water was poor, the millpond took three days to fill and when released the flow was exhausted after three hours.

Brothers Malcolm and David Wood bought Aunby Manor from the Westminster Pension Fund in 1957. When Malcolm married Janet in 1962 they moved into the cold and draughty manor. A year later after enduring the long freeze when they had to pipe water from Spurr Bridge, they moved out but continued to farm the land.

Malcolm's mother Mary enjoyed the lake, fishing for trout and rowing the boat that came with the property. She planted daffodils on the banks that still bloom in the spring.

As a memorial to his grandmother, Robert Wood has created the Mary Wood Fisheries from the original lake that has been in existence for at least one hundred and fifty years. Meadow View lake was created in 2003.

Farm cottages opposite the manor remained derelict for many years. Locals remember that after the war Italian POWs who'd served time at Marshall's Farm lived there with two pretty dark-haired daughters who often cycled back to Careby.

The cottage close to the ford on the main road used to be two cottages; homes to Mrs Birch and and next door, Mr and Mrs Templeman; their lorry kept in a lean-to in the field at the end of the Aunby lane.

In 1926 Dallas Money, a farm labourer working near Sleaford was given the task of driving a flock of sheep to Aunby. After several days on the road he arrived and liked it so much he was given a job on the farm. He stayed for many years.

One hot afternoon when the farmer was away, Dallas spotted some farmhands hovering near the barn.

'Dallas, give us a hand will you?'

One farmhand was removing hinges from the barn door. Dallas strolled over, thumbs casually hooked behind his braces.

'Come on. Look lively. Grab hold of this.' Jack made room for him to help lift the door. They lowered it to the ground.

'Where we taking it?'

'To the river of course! Dan's had this idea to dam the river and make a swimming pool.'

'Will it work?'

'Let's see. Are you in?'

'Of course I'm in.'

Dallas told Malcolm Wood that they got into a lot of trouble when the Boss found out. 'He was as mad as hell.'

1066 - 1672: Ouneby

In Saxon times Aunby was called Bergestorp.

The mention of Philip de Colville in the Roll of Battle Abbey confirms that this large and influential family invaded England with William the Conqueror and settled at Bergestorp.

Thomas, Philip, Geoffry, Robert, Ralph and Richard witnessed three deeds of gift made to the nuns of St Michael in Stamford, confirming this was a large family.

Soon renamed Ouneby, Ouneby manor house continued to be the focus of the village due to the emergence of feudalism – land held on condition of some kind of service. De Colville had to promise military service to nobleman Drogo de Beuvriere who'd been installed at Castle Bytham by his brother-in-law William I. In turn de Colville's peasants had to promise him service.

In the 11th century manor houses were built on a similar but smaller scale to castles. Vast oak beams were set into stone foundations. Evidence shows that Ouneby was stone built. Contained inside an inner gate, the manor would have had a handsome main hall for meetings and dining equipped with trestle tables. A solar also serving as a private sitting room was where the family slept. The latrine or garderobe was located inside the manor. Well lit with torches, it was fitted with a stone or wooden bench with a number of holes. Smell was kept at bay with double doors and with no glass in the window. The kitchen, often with a tiled floor, would have had a furnace and two ovens and be connected to the pantry. The Buttery adjoining dispensed ale. Outside were henhouses, a granary and a dairy. At Aunby there was a chapel and burial ground.

Beyond the inner gate, a house for servants, a stable for the lord's horse and two barns for wheat and oats. Manors of this period were enclosed by a ditch or moat, high wall or hedge to keep out invading armies, wolves, deer and wild boar. Outside the enclosure there'd be another good-sized barn, a stable for cows, another for oxen and a pigsty.

Life centred on the manor, the chapel and farmland. De Colville held economic and legal power, including the maintenance of a regular court held in the great hall.

The peasants had very little and ate a simple monotonous diet. Coarse bread, cheese and onion for breakfast; grain mixed with hot water and vegetables, and if available, strips of meat or fish mixed in and eaten in the evening.

Domesday records…
Berewick of Bergestorp is in Bitham of four carucates of land subject to Danegeld. This land is the desmene of St Peter of Burgh. There is land for 7 ploughs. It is the Sokeland of the same Manor and 2 bovates are inland. 25 Sokemen have 6¹/₂ ploughs there and there are 70 acres of meadow and 6 acres of scrubland.

In the reign of Henry I (1100-1135) the manor of Ouneby belonged to the Earl of Albemarle and was reunited with Holywell and Castle Bytham. The Monastery of Peterborough owned within Ouneby, four hundred acres of land. In 1250, clerk John de Auneby was granted enfeoffment of the church lands.

'Enfeoffment by Richard Bunchelot, burgess of Stamford, of John de Auneby, Clerk, son of Benedict de Auneby, all the lands which he has of the enfeoffment of the master of the hospital of St Thomas the Martyr by the bridge at Stamford and which lie in two separate cultures in Careby fields. Rent a silver penny at the feast of St Thomas the Martyr at Christmas.'[34]

When Walter de Colville succeeded to Castle Bytham in the 13th century the Hundred Rolls record that tenant Adam de St Laudo was in possession of the

34… *H101/33B With the permission of Lincolnshire Archives*

manor of Ouneby with its appurtenances for the service of half a knight's fee. In 1606 Thomas Harrington of South Witham sold Aunby to William Bodenden of Ryhall. The sale included all lands and meadows; two hundred acres of land and heath and feeding pastures called Sheep-Gate. Ten years later the highly prized sheep grazing was sold to Thomas, Earl of Exeter of Burghley for £1,400.

In the 19th century the Reverend John Wild found a document giving particulars of Aunby in 1626.

> *'Whereas the village of Aunby was first constituted from ye ancient use of Pasture for sheep, Beasts, and a warren of Coneyes, with a shepherd's and warrener's lodge onely thereon, to bee broken up for corne, and used in tillage and building of houses fitt for husbandry and other necessaries there convenient...'*

During Earl Exeter's ownership several local men were taken to court. In 1627 John Tapp was accused of treading down grass. A year later at Lincoln Assizes William Haddon was accused of chasing sheep with dogs. Thomas and Jeffrey Holmes, Osea Johnson and Robert Bull were accused of taking stones and digging soil from Aunby Heath.

By 1639 Earl Exeter had sold Aunby sheepwalks to the Earl of Stamford and three London gents for £1500. Then in 1653 John Balguy of Stamford bought the sheepwalks with two London gents, paying £1300 to Robert Harrington.

In 1672 Careby's John Hatcher bought the sheepwalks for £1119. 18s. Uniting Aunby with Careby, he paid £442 11s to Mr. Morley, £280 to Mr Lee and £397 7s to John Balguy.

Aunby land remained in the Hatcher family until purchased by Agatha's Fane's great-great-great-great grandfather, Sam Reynardson of Holywell Hall, in the 18th century.

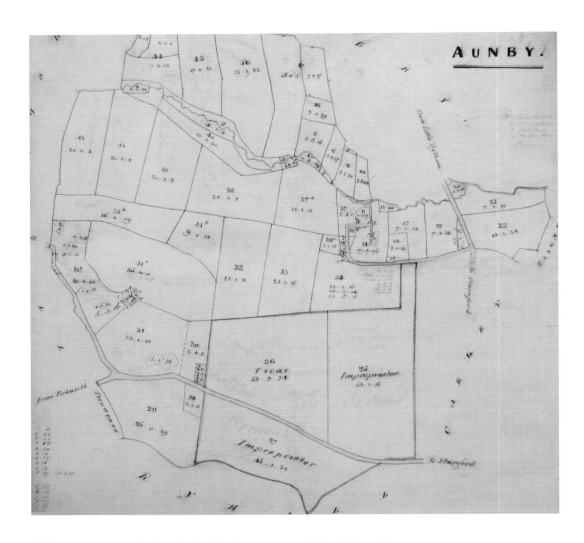

Map of Aunby – *H 103A/5 With the permission of Lincolnshire Archives*

CASTLE DYKE

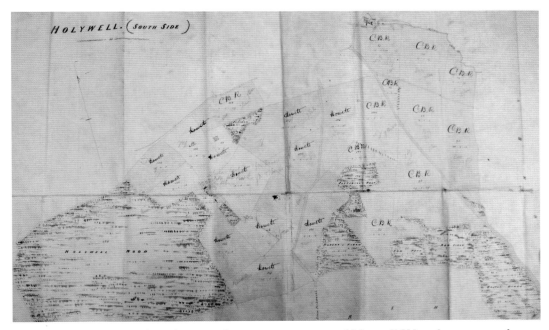

Castle Dyke, situated at the southeastern corner of Newell Wood, covers a large area. The listed monument is a moated island on a thickly wooded site. Enclosed by an embanked ditch that creates an outer enclosure, the inner enclosure is almost rectangular with rounded angles. The ditch is eight yards wide and four feet deep. The outer enclosure is less well defined – approximately seven yards wide and two feet deep.

The resulting island is thought to have contained a manor house and domestic buildings. A causeway crossed the southern arm of the ditch and the outer enclosure formed a paddock occupied by stock.

Map of Holywell showing Castle Dyke - bottom right of map
H 103A With the permission of Lincolnshire Archives

Forgotten People

Thought to have been a modest fortified manor house built of timber, it was probably built on the site of an existing Saxon manorial centre for civil administration lorded by the Saxon, Halfdene. Constructed with forced, unskilled labour, most such buildings took one to two thousand man-days of work. Rough-hewn oak formed the palisade of the outer walls. With traditional wattle and daub and a thatched roof, the building was crude and cramped but local peasants living in traditional cob buildings of mud and straw would have been in awe of such an imposing sight. A meeting place for the knight and his tenants, it was a place for arranging agricultural affairs and trying minor crimes.

After the conquest Castle Dyke may have become the home of a minor French knight. Any such knight was forced to give at least twenty days military service in wartime, be equipped with armour and have at least one war horse; a gelding or stallion much smaller than our horses of today. Often he captured his weapons and armour in battle. Second hand, dented with use, they showed his low status to major noblemen.

Living frugally, he existed on a simple diet of coarse bread and pottage; a one-pot stew to whatever was around was added. Little difference to the lifestyle of a Saxon thane, eating from wooden bowls in an unlit house and only a campfire for heating. Feast days were reserved for meeting and entertaining other knights and lords and for providing the opportunity for marrying off sons and daughters.

It was usual for any of the knight's sons after the age of seven, to leave the home away from the influence of their English mother. The eldest would live with another knight and learn manly arts. The second son often became a monk or cleric and any other sons could become sergeants or household servants in major houses or castles. The eldest son, when grown, often survived as a local squire and a justice of the peace.

HOLYWELL… BRIDGE VILLA/HOME FARM

Andrew and Mary Hoyle have lived at Home Farm since 1980. Succeeding Jack Straw, Andrew was employed as estate manager to William Lockwood of Holywell Hall.

When Mr and Mrs Lockwood sold Holywell in 1988 Andrew and Mary bought their house with an adjoining plot of land. Earlier described as Bridge Villa, the house was rebuilt in 1877 by Holywell's Charles Birch-Reynardson for farm bailiff Robert Baron.

An original Victorian post-box complete with flap is built into the house wall on the roadside. In 1849 the Post Office encouraged people to provide their own similar letterboxes.

When post-boxes were first installed they were painted green. Between 1874 and 1878 they were repainted red.

In the 1930s James Kerfoot, previous tenant of both Warren and Marshall's Farm in Careby arrived at Bridge Villa. Tenant to Mrs Fane, he farmed the land known as Home Farm.

Tenant: James Kerfoot

Part	29	Burnt Hills, inclusive of the small plantation and all fruit trees
	38	Lound Field
	67	Parkers Close
	72	Barons Home Close
Part	74	Mill Homestead Farm Buildings
	75	Long Piece
	76	Horse Close
	78	Coles Hill
Part	84	Long Docksight
	85	Mill Field
	87	Stackyard Field
	88	Garden
	90	19 acres or Cocked Hat
Part	91	Aunby Close
	96	New Field
	102 & 165	Pattinson's Holt
	106	Coach Pillars
	71	House and Garden
Aunby Parish		
	28 & 31	Walpole Close
	37a	Heath Towers
Holywell Parish		
	107	Twenty Acres

◀ *From farm records*

James Kerfoot married Matilda Chapman who lived at Pettywood Farm with her parents and three sisters. They met after Matilda and one of her sisters alerted James when spotting his favourite riding horse apparently in difficulty in the lake. He positioned a forty-foot ladder and reached out to rescue his horse but on seeing so many rescuers, the horse swam away and scrambled out.

Sisters Margery, Matilda with James, Bertha and Winnie
With the permission of Karen Cunningham

One afternoon after milking his cows in the cow shed behind Bridge Villa, James happened to glance across the lake. Agatha Fane and guests who were staying at the Hall were stooping to pick fallen walnuts.

He spun on his heel, ran across the bridge and through the gate. It was his field. He rented it. They were his walnuts.

James picked up the basket brimming with nuts. 'Sorry Ma'am. These are my walnuts. I can't let you...'

Mrs Fane straightened and fixed him with a piercing look. 'They're my walnuts.' She advanced and wrenched the basket from his hand.

James stepped back. His brow furrowed. She couldn't do this. 'See you in court then!' Seething with anger, he returned to his cows and released them on to the paddock.

The disagreement did go to court and Agatha Fane lost the case, the judge ruling that as tenant farmer James Kerfoot owned the crop, but as landlord, Mrs Fane owned the tree.

Mrs Fane had the tree cut down. James' tenancy was not renewed.

In 1935 the next tenant of Bridge Villa was Mr Kent who had previously farmed Pickworth Plain.

By this time Mr and Mrs Fane were leasing Holywell Hall to Major Hoare who ran the Kesteven Battalion Home Guard during the war.

Frank Kent remembers the lake being cleared out once a year. Men in two boats rowing parallel trawled up and down with scythes held between them, cutting the weed until the bottom of the lake was clearly seen. The weed was dragged on to the banks with rakes, then once dry spread on to fields as fertiliser.

Forgotten People

Five boathouses stood at various intervals alongside the lakes. One stood opposite Mill Farm, another was opposite the garden of Bridge Villa. The remainder were built close to the Hall. Only one remains now.

Once the lakes had been cleared of weed they were restocked with four hundred trout.

> Every weekend Frank would collect his rod from the shed and creep under the road bridge. Securing a firm footing on the concrete base he'd secretly fish.
>
> One day he heard brisk footsteps approaching. Frank kept very still. He knew who it was.
>
> Above him the Major's footsteps faltered to a halt. A long pause, then... 'Are they biting today, my boy?'

Water for Bridge Villa was piped from hillside spring water collected in a metal tank. A two-inch pipe lay across the bed of the lake, arriving on the bank in the garden with a bend in it so water could be collected in a bucket. All that remains of the tank is a circle of concrete in the field beside the lake. The centre has been filled with rubble to prevent sheep and lambs falling in.

Every Monday morning Frank crossed the road to open the gate by the road bridge to allow the major through. Major Hoare worked in London and caught the train from Little Bytham Station, returning on Fridays.

So always on a Monday Frank arrived at Careby School in one of the Major's two chauffeur-driven Rolls Royces. And if the chauffeur happened to pass him any other day, he'd give him a lift to school that day too.

After the war Frank's family moved to Lodge Farm, where they stayed until 1955.

Frank found employment at the sawmill next to the Mill Houses.

Diana Craghill lived in the main Mill House next door to the Brewsters, (who later moved to one of the newly built council houses in Careby.) Her father was groom for Colonel Sale's hunters. Colonel Sale had leased the empty stables adjoining the Mill House in the war.

Frank married Diana on the seventeenth of February 1951 and their reception, like so many others, was at Careby Village Hall.

The bridge at Holywell

HOLYWELL   MILL FARM

Mill Farm on the left as it is now, and below being restored in the early eighties.

Purchased from William and Catherine Lockwood in 1988, Mill Farm is home to Dick and Eileen Tinsley. In the early eighties the derelict Mill Houses had been reconstructed from Holywell Hall's dismantled piggeries and the archway to Holywell Hall's courtyard.

Above Mill Farm's front porch is the Latin inscription PERSPICVA VIRTVTIS VIA (Way of truth and virtue). This decoration was likely to have been removed from a building at the Hall; amongst plans dated

In the drained lake… Eileen Tinsley, 1990 and Richard Tinsley, 2010

1789 one item lists *'Decoration of 4 doorways – text not legible.'*

Another inscription set into the back wall of Mill Farm reads *'Samuel Pontin 1719'*. Research shows Pontin was a builder from Grantham.

Dick and Eileen and their family have spent much time and energy preserving and improving their beautiful lakes, woodland and pasture.

The first mention of a water mill at Holywell was in 1723 when Holywell's owner William Goodhall was on the verge of bankruptcy. Amongst the several mortgages raised he secured $400 from Reverend M. Birdmore on a messuage and lands with a watermill at Holywell.

Refilling the lake, June 2010

Goodhall's struggle with bankruptcy to save Holywell in 1728 was defeated. The entire estate was offered for sale and every property and piece of land detailed.

For the mill…
Edward Cole tenanted Mill Field. Dork Sike pasture (Docksight) was in tenure to John Oldham who'd also tenanted some Careby lands. [35]

One hundred and twenty years ago James Meredith was in charge of the water mill. Between the wars the mill was still operational. Three large stone buildings stood in the stackyard; one for drying timber, another for sawing and the third as a flour mill. Five sawmills and the flour mill were all driven by one water wheel and water was funnelled from the lake and under the road by a pipe.

The Mill Houses and old road to Careby – detail from Map H103B With the permission of Lincolnshire Archives

In 1947 only the sawmill was still operating driven by a tractor. The water wheel had become jammed and couldn't be freed.

After the sawmill closed, Colonel Sale ran his company Minneapolis Mowline Agricultural Machines from the stackyard: locals still remember his bright yellow tractors with red wheels.

35… *H110/2 With the permission of Lincolnshire Archives*

HOLLOW COTTAGE

Hollow Cottage is home to Sue and Dave Bryant. Like Mill Farm it was derelict when they bought it.

The map shows the site of the Hall's Hunt Kennels and two Dog Kennel Cottages. In 1861 a huntsman and dog feeder are recorded on the Holywell census.

It is believed that during WWII a couple living in one cottage owned a dog, their neighbours next door had chickens. Every so often a chicken would disappear. Despite denials from the dog's owner, the neighbour blamed their dog and relationships became strained.

One day the owner of the dog looked out of his window and saw his dog in the garden next door with the chickens.

Immediately he sought out his gun and shot his dog dead at exactly the moment his wife cried out their dog was chasing a fox out of their neighbour's garden.

For months afterwards the man's wife told her friend, the atmosphere in their house was like ice.

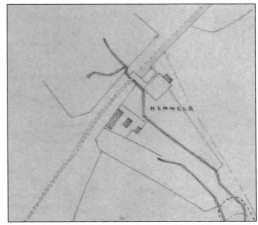

Hollow Cottage and the Kennels – detail from Map H103B with the permission of Lincolnshire Archives

HOLYWELL HALL

This enchanting country estate became home to Robert and Sally Gillespie in 2003.

Approached by a rural lane, the elegant Georgian manor is revealed after the drive wends through spectacular parkland until reaching a bridge crossing lakes brimming with wildlife.

With the tiny church tucked away to the left, the Hall stands splendidly above manicured lawns. Built of Clipsham stone, steps flanked by Tuscan columns approach the eastern front doorway. The doors open on to a spacious reception hall with a sparkling chandelier and magnificent staircase hall. Remodelled in the early 19th century, the impressive oak staircase splits left and right on to a galleried landing. Wall plaques with military trophies and swags relating to the Reynardson family adorn the walls.

The west wing was built in the 17th century. It has a separate entrance and when the main hall was built later, was used by live-in staff.

In 1994 the Hall underwent extensive restoration when Prince Yuri Galitzine, a member of the Russian Royal family, and his wife Dr Jean Shanks bought it for just under £4m.

Dr Jean Shanks, who was among the most distinguished pathologists in the country, founded Britain's only quoted independent pathology-laboratory company. A quiet and reserved person, she had great charm and among friends could be the life and soul of a party. By 1987 she employed two hundred and seventy-four staff handling up to two thousand patients a day. As resident of Braunston near Oakham, she'd always dreamed of owning Holywell Hall.

Under guidance from garden designer Bunny Guinness and interior designer Lulu Carter, the Prince and Princess lovingly restored the Hall. Once completed they lavishly entertained politicians and diplomats with shooting parties.

The Princess died in 1999 and following the Prince's death in 2002 Holywell Estate was put on the market.

The property included two farms, two cottages and eight hundred and ten acres of lakes, woodland and parkland. The grounds included an Orangery, Fishing Temple, boathouse, stables and an ancient tithe barn with a fine sculpted archway and lofty oak beams. Most stables had already been converted into offices but three remained, built in the traditional style with sleeping accommodation overhead for stable lads.

The Orangery faces south to overlook a glorious view extending beyond the lake. Behind the Orangery is a replanted flower garden, new orchard and a vegetable garden with greenhouses. Close by is a dovecote that used to supply dove eggs and young squabs collected for the table. Said to be the oldest building on the estate it is utilised as an apple store.

Vast walls capped with pantiles line the flower garden. When re-pointing, a row of

The view from The Orangery at Holywell Hall – beautiful even in winter!

bricks linked to a fireplace was discovered at the base of the south-facing wall. Vines were warmed by heat permeating along the brickwork.

A tributary of the River Glen feeds the parkland, and lakes separated by weirs are fed from springs. Before mains water was connected spring water was pumped manually via pump houses from Bridge Villa to another pump house by the lake and up to the Hall.

250AD: The Romans at Holywell

In March 2001, assistant gardener Alexander Mortimer and head gardener Brian Oldman made an exciting discovery. Digging out a water feature close to a spring on a slope overlooking the western end of the lake, an iron tap slagheap near to the epicentre of a Roman iron-smelting furnace was discovered.

Amateur volunteers of a local archaeological group were invited to walk the adjoining land. They found a quantity of Romano-British pottery and Roman coins and other small metal finds. Worked flints including a flint sickle 4000BC - 2351BC, indicated Neolithic Bronze Age activity. Close by was a flake, a primitive sharp tool struck from a core of flint using a deer antler.

The furnace area, thought to be sixty metres in diameter, produced slag and burnt stones too plentiful to collect.

Eleven Roman coins with a date-range from the 3rd to 4th centuries were discovered, together with iron nails, an iron horse/animal shoe, fragments of a Roman brooch and a metal cauldron, a large iron ring and a glass bottle fragment. Most were discovered with the use of a metal detector on an adjoining field. Some coins are in poor condition and not identifiable.

Roman Sestertius found at Holywell

The oldest coin found was a 2nd century Sestertius. This large heavy brass coin has a bearded bust on one side and an unidentifiable standing figure on the other. A fragment has been cut off; the usual practice when giving change. The meaning of sestertius was the coin's value; two and a half asses. Double sided, it was probably first issued by Posthumus, an emperor who died in AD258. Posthumus ruled a breakaway empire of Britain, Gaul and parts of Germany, and was keen to associate his regime with a reformed coinage system. He often took old Sesterius coins and over struck them with his own portrait.

After his reign the coinage system degenerated further until there were only antoninianii; very debased old coins.

Probus AD 276-282, a great soldier in Europe and Egypt but finally assassinated in 282, is depicted on another Holywell find. This coin is silver or silvered with a radiate bust with Probus on horseback raising his right hand, spear in his left, with a captive on the ground in front of horse. Like the majority of coins in Britain up to the mid 3rd century this coin came from Rome.

Roman Probus coin
Coins with kind permission
of Sally Gillespie

A Roman radiate coin of the late 3rd century was also identified. This was a common coin easily identified by the crown of sunrays.

A bronze coin of Constantine I reign (AD307-337) was found in Holywell Hall gardens. The value is unknown. An unidentifiable figure is on the reverse side with **IMP]CONSTANTINVS [P F AVG]** on the obverse. By this date coins were minted with idealistic portraits and not the true image of the emperor. The coin was minted at an important mint, Treviri in Germany from where copper alloy coins were imported to Britain.

A helmeted and cuirassed bust with **BEATA TRANQVILLITAS** around an altar is inscribed **VOTIS XX**. This coin also came from Treviri. The inclusion of a Christogram – an abbreviation of letters as a symbol of Christ marked a distinct change in the religion of the state.

The Magnentius coin found was minted at Amiens in France, a mint only operating during his brief reign of AD350-353. The coin is inexpertly made with mis-spelling of Magnentius, a Roman usurper and Commander who attracted Britain's loyalty because he tolerated both Christians and pagans. After his army's second defeat by Constantius, the son of Constantine the Great, Magnentius committed suicide by falling on his sword.

Roman
Constantine coin

The discovery of these coins and pottery provide strong evidence of Roman occupation at Holywell between the second and fourth centuries.

This evidence is corroborated a few hundred yards away. Bordering Pickworth Great Wood on land called Black Piece are the remains of a substantial courtyard Roman Villa.

In 1897 local resident Thomas Halliday first discovered signs of the villa on Sir David Davenport Handley's Clipsham land about three hundred yards distant from Careby and Holywell's parish boundary. It was again investigated after a trial boring by Clipsham Quarry Company and more excavation in the 1920s.

Archaeologist Mr Tabor and his team explored further until about 1950. Excavations revealed stone walls over one hundred and fifty feet long and two feet thick. A small room adjoining disclosed a human foetus.

From the National Monuments Record:

> *'Whilst quarrying for freestone at the Black Piece in September 1926, a large mound containing a two foot layer of ironstone and charcoal was discovered. Inside the mound were found oyster shells, tile fragments, Romano British pottery, Castor (ware from Castor to replace declining Samian pottery) and other potsherds, a stylus - a pointed metal pen for writing on a wax tablet and a very fine steelyard and lead weights. (A balance working on the lever principle.)*
>
> *'Soil marks over a considerable area indicate an ancient disturbance; the activity was probably that of iron-age workings and was in operation at least in the 2nd and 3rd centuries. A rough wall built of slag was discovered three years later and Samian[36] pottery.'*
>
> *'The site is about eighty metres across and a mass of spoil heaps under bushes. Several areas of current investigation are apparent, and at present exposed is a*

36... *Samian pottery produced the finest tableware of Roman Britain imported from France. Instantly recognisable by its smooth surface, rich red brown colour, sometimes finely detailed. These pots were generally press moulded.*

section of walling with foundations of a small square building at one end. Mr Tabor said his excavations have so far taken some forty years and are still proceeding. Excavations still in progress have revealed the undoubted remains of a probable courtyard villa with several phases of construction, destroyed by fire in the late 3rd century. After the destruction of the villa it appears to have been extensively robbed by an iron-working community whose habitation site has not yet been found but whose industrial debris covers the whole of the remains of the villa and surrounding area. The debris is mainly heavy iron slag and vast quantities of pottery and other artefacts dating occupation to AD 340-400 including another steelyard and a bronze buckle with two outward facing horse's heads dated the late 4th century. Fifty five coins were also found at the site ranging from Hadrian to Theidosius.' [37]*

Most of the floor of the villa was burnt to a deep brick red, and embedded deep in the cracks in the Collyweston slate floor were numerous roof and flue tiles. The roofing tiles included slabs of limestone and Collyweston slate. Some of the slates were circular, about eighteen inches in diameter and pierced by nails. Others were triangular and covered by a six-inch deposit of charcoal. Small pieces of wall plaster in deep maroon, also some with green and yellow decoration on a white base were also discovered.

Rutland County Museum keeps evidence of the habitation at the villa. Apart from the artefacts mentioned, hairpins, rings, tweezers, a bone knife handle, silver spoon, bracelets, a spearhead and a door latch are in the collection.

37... *By courtesy of Stamford Museum*

60 - 250AD: The Celts at Holywell

Springtime between AD 60 and AD 250. The place is a beautiful tree-lined valley with a wealth of natural springs. The Celts living there belonged to the Coritani tribe.

In the fading light, the few circular thatched houses stood in silhouette on the banks of the stream. Smoke lazily rose from the campfire. The ritual fire had been started with oak branches, rubbed and rotated against one another and then nine sacred woods had been added. These nine woods were the willow of the streams, hazel of the rocks, alder of the marshes, birch of the waterfalls, rowan of the shade, yew of resilience, elm of the brae and oak of the sun.

Brigid, a tawny-haired maiden, gathered sprigs of holly.

In the fire's glow, a hare crouched in a wooden cage. Conan had caught it earlier that day on the hill in preparation for their celebrations. He'd free it later.

The hare was their favourite animal, revered as a symbol of love, fertility and growth. Aldred, Conan's brother, said Queen Boudicca had taken a hare into battle to bring her luck against the invaders. Aldred was the news gatherer of the tribe and always knew what was going on.

Brigid loved Aldred. But she loved Conan more. He was a tall powerfully built man with reddish shoulder-length hair and grey-blue eyes. He'd put on his best thigh-length tunic and she'd made his cloak herself, even going to the length of collecting woad and dying the wool. It was striped blue and white and she'd secured it with a pin on his right shoulder. They were celebrating the full moon as well as the emergence of spring. At that very moment the moon lay low on the horizon.

Conan worked hard. He'd been put in charge of the iron-working furnace. Others turned wrought iron into tools. Brigid looked forward to seeing the jewellery and metal drinking horns when Conan finished working the latest batch of iron. He'd made the brooch she was wearing for tonight.

'Come on Brigid, play for us.' Conor looked at her expectantly, then picked up her lyre and handed it to her.

She'd made an effort, painted her nails, reddened her cheeks and darkened her blonde eyebrows with berry juice. Niamh braided her long hair and pinned it at the nape of her neck. She felt good in her new long tunic cinched at the waist with a belt, the brooch Conan had made, decorated with the outline of a hare, pinned at her shoulder.

She began to play a familiar tune and everyone joined in with the singing, even the little ones.

'Ssshh! Someone's coming!' Aldred held up his hand then pointed.

Brigid lay down her lyre and stood up. She couldn't see anything. Nervously two elderly members retreated into their roundhouse to hide behind the mud-daubed walls. They'd all heard about the Roman barbarians tramping north.

Blood-curdling screams. Her father clutched his chest, clawing at a spear driven deep inside him.

Men identically clad suddenly emerged from the trees, hordes of them bearing shields, yelling and pounding towards them, daggers or swords brandished above their helmets.

Brigid turned and ran and burrowed her way into a thicket. None of them stood a chance.

When the wailing ceased, the soldiers took the hare with them.

Two scouts from the Ninth Legion had spotted the smoke. Five thousand of us were camped at Stretton. There wasn't room at Caista, [Great Casterton] so we'd marched on. We were running low on weapons and from what the scouts reported there was an iron smelter only two miles away. Luck comes in different forms. Marching twenty-five miles a day humping sixty pounds of kit is no sport but at least we've got the mule, it carries our tent and the quern and other bits and pieces. Frankly, it's easier fighting than camping; digging trenches every night and inserting all those stakes is hard work for the pittance they pay us.

Those Celts didn't stand a chance. Maybe one or two ran away but we accounted for the rest. Eight of us enjoyed eating the hare; meat is a rarity for us, a change from pottage anyway.

Petrus was put in charge of building the villa. He chose a spot high up overlooking the valley where the Celts used to live. He made us dig out the earthworks; there was plenty of stone for the foundations and Viator was in charge of the under floor heating. We built underground chambers so hot air could circulate beneath the floor.

I quite like it here. Once we have the roof built, there'll be time to get down to the real business. I'm told there's a shortage of javelins and daggers. And they need more tools for digging trenches too. Sentius is supposed to be my assistant, but he hasn't a clue how to produce iron. I bet we'll be expected to make the daggers too.

'Well, those Celts knew a thing or two about finding ironstone.'

'What do you mean?'

'Really Sentius. I wish you'd pay attention. Didn't I tell you that the easiest place to find ironstone is on the banks of a stream? And look how many streams there are!'

'Natural springs, aren't they?'

'Never mind them. Look here at this furnace. See the chimney. Now we've got it to its proper height you can see it needs to be at least a gradus* tall, and there's an arch at the bottom to allow the slag to run off so we're ready to start work.'

'What do you want me to do Aquila?'

'You've prepared the charcoal, have you?'

Sentius nodded outside to the charred wood piled on the hillside. 'Will there be enough?'

'Well, you'll see, won't you? You need to bring it in.' Aquila picked up lumps of ironstone and began to lay them at the bottom of the furnace.

'Where do you want it?' Sentius's tunic was covered in ash as he struggled with an armload of charcoal.

'Cover up these stones, then go and get some more while I add in another layer.'

They filled the furnace and Aquila ignited the straw at the bottom. Once lit, he instructed Sentius to pump the bellows.

'We need to raise the temperature; it's got to be hot enough to form a bloom.'

'Bloom?'

'Yes. A Mixture of molten metal and waste. When it's hot enough we take it out and hammer and reheat until all the rubbish is driven off. Then it's my turn to start shaping the metal. Come on. Keep pumping.'

* Roman measurement 'gradus' = 0.74 metres

BLIND EYE QUARRY

Another iron foundry was discovered at Newell Wood's Blind Eye Quarry in 1961.

'A friend of mine who travelled for the Woolgrowers firm called one day at the home of the foreman of the quarries digging and loading pebbles to be used in glass making. The foreman was interested in an area of Little Newell Wood, about one mile from Holywell. The area was almost devoid of trees and was light compacted oolitic limestone. The fireman had discovered some nodules of iron and hoping to find treasure had started to dig. He dug but had no finds. My friends asked me to have a look and I decided it was worth a trial. So we pegged it out in squares and started to excavate. We were lucky to have the use of the tools from the factory. We were only able to work Sunday mornings so it was a slow job. We were lucky and exposed a rim of clay and working around it we were able to unearth a kiln. As we worked to the base of the kiln we uncovered the tyre hole and a piece of smelted iron that had been left at the bottom. We cleared the hard sand black area. We contacted the archaeological people at Leicester and they came and took samples for dating. They came up with the answer it was a Roman 4th century smelting kiln. A gentleman from Durham University also came and told us that this kiln was only the second found in this country. Pictures and report are in the Roman Journal.

We continued to work and a matter of twenty yards from the kiln we discovered four post holes with a large flat stone at the bottom of each and concluded that this was shelter and store for the workmen. This of course we connected with the Roman settlement at Gt. Casterton. I learnt afterwards that the presence of pebbles and oolitic limestone was due to a glacier breaking away from the Pennine chain and carving a valley right through to the North Sea. The rock in its path was crushed by the weight of the ice. Large rocks became pebbles, soft rocks became oolite from the limestone and the edge of the glacier left only a thin cover over the ironstone. This the Romans were able to find and work. The pebbles were used in the making of glass.'

This excavation was carried out by R. Grimwood, I. Smith and W. Stephenson.
By courtesy of Stamford Museum.

POTTERY SHERDS

Two thirds of the six hundred pottery sherds collected at Holywell were Roman grey wares dating from the 3rd to 4th centuries. Most of it was collected close to the iron-smelting site.

The scattering of medieval and early post medieval pottery is presumed to be rubbish from the centuries of population at Holywell. Until recent times it was traditional to scatter waste from the kitchens to manure surrounding fields and kitchen gardens.

Stanion and Lyveden pottery in Northamptonshire (c.1100-1399) were found as fragments of red brown to orange pots, evidence of movement and trade.

Stamford potters were the first users of glaze and they threw cooking pots, storage jars, bowls and jugs. Stamford Pottery, circa 900-13th century, (when there was a rapid redevelopment of pottery production coinciding with the formation of medieval villages), made wheel-thrown white ware, often with a yellow or pale green glaze. Theses pots are likely to have been waste from Holywell manor house tenanted by a knight.

Bourne produced Shelly Pottery from 1300: hard, smooth brick-red clay with a grey core giving a speckled appearance because of the use of fossil shells in the clay. Jugs, large bowls and cisterns for brewing beer were produced until the pottery burned down in 1637.

Midland Purple Ware used for cooking was made at Ticknall in South Derbyshire in late medieval times. Cistercian Ware produced pots for the table, including tygs. Drinking vessels with six handles, tygs were sometimes decorated with white clay motifs and were thin and hard and produced in coal-fired kilns able to reach much higher temperatures than traditional wood-fired burners. After firing, the pots were covered with a dark brown or purple-black glaze.

Sherds of Midland Yellow ware of the late 16th-18th century were also discovered. Midland Yellow specialised in chamber pots, candlesticks and pancheons. Using white slip and a clear lead glaze they resulted in a yellow finish.

So many diverse fragments show strong evidence of trade or exchange as well as social and economic status of those who lived at Holywell.

Thirty flint pieces were also found. They are thought likely to be of the Neolithic and Bronze Age because of the 'flake' technique used. With the exception of one large flint knife approximately five centimetres long, most were small. A 'thumb nail' scraper and a 'disc' scraper accompanied the first knife found. It is possible that these tools point towards a Bronze Age burial site near a boundary of Holywell and respecting a sacred place.

500AD: The Anglo Saxons at Holywell

Evidence of Anglo Saxons living locally was found at Holywell in the shape of an iron Cruciform brooch with the lower part missing. The brooch has been identified from 500 AD and made in England by Anglian and Jutish settlers who were confined to East Anglia, the East Midlands and Kent.

Cruciform brooches were worn singly on the breast to fasten an outer cloak. They have a square or rectangular head plate with one or three knobs. The lower part is always in the shape of an animal head with prominent eyes. Ninety-five per cent of brooches found date from the 5th or early 6th century.

A minority of brooches seem likely to be derived from plough-damaged burials but most have been assigned to casual loss. The Holywell brooch probably represents everyday wear to the early Anglo-Saxon inhabitants. The animal head is missing.

Selwyn's manor overlooked the valley. An obvious vantage point, it had been built many years earlier from hillside timber: an enormous rectangular hut, rough, crowded and uncomfortable with a line of planks hewn for the floor.

Rowena, Bliss and Edith had embroidered new large tapestries for the walls and smaller ones to cover the shutters at night for there was no glass to keep out the cold or prevent the possibility of wolves returning.

'Selwyn will be back soon.' Edith smoothed her long woollen tunic and hitched the belt at her waist. Fingering her knife she added, 'we'll soon need more wood for the fire. I'm cooking swan tonight.' She pointed at the iron cauldron suspended over the flames, the spiral of smoke almost non-existent now as it drifted up to the hole in the roof.

'I'll go.' Bliss gathered her cloak around her and fastened it on her shoulder with her favourite brooch. It had been handed down through generations; old and worn, the lower part of the cruciform was missing.

'Is everything ready?' Edith had tidied everything as best she could and was now pouring mead into flagons ready for tonight's feast. Simple wooden chests ran down the middle of the room and already Rowena had laden them with food. Selwyn always insisted on a feast when he returned from hunting. He said his men worked hard with the falcons and they deserved it.

'As ready as it can be.' Edith stood in the doorway to look across the valley. 'Wulf promised me he'd entertain us all with a couple of new songs. His father will play the harp.'

The hillside was bubbling with springs and water ran into the river below them. Through the trees she could see Selwyn astride his horse. Sunlight glinted on his gold plated sword. Two of his men held the falcons aloft and a third man led a horse carrying hordes of dead rabbits.

By the time the men arrived the women were ready. Aiden had found some eggs before he left; there were dishes of eels and rabbit over the fire cooked to perfection.

Bliss returned with an armful of wood. Tears spilled down her cheeks. 'If you go down to the river either of you: will you have a look and see if you can find my brooch. I've lost it.'

'I hope that doesn't mean we're in for a spell of bad luck,' said Edith. 'You know what they say.'

'Watch out! Selwyn's not in a good mood,' Rowena whispered to her as her thane stormed past.

Selwyn whipped round, his face fierce beneath his helmet. 'No. I'm not in a good mood. How would you feel if you'd just discovered the Danes setting up camp not far away? You'd better just hope they don't come to Bredestorp.'

Saxon brooch –
with kind permission
of Richard Tinsley

243

500 - 1575: Medieval Holywell

Germanic people invaded the Anglo Saxons as early as the 5th century. It is thought this is where the words 'dorp' or 'torp' come from. Brede means braid. Bredestorp; Holywell was the home of fine needlewomen.

Anglo Saxon needlework was recognised as the finest embroidery in Europe, and one reason why William the Conqueror's wife Matilde commissioned the Bayeux Tapestry.

Domesday

Holywell Hundred[38], Earl Morcar had 7 caruncles of land to the geld. There is land for 7 ploughs. It is SOKELAND of Castle Bytham. The men, Ingelrann and Earnwulf, have 1 plough there, and 6 sokemen and 1 villan and 5 bordars with 2 ploughs. There is 1 mill rendering 4s and 200 acres of scrubland. TRE worth £4; now 40s. tallage 12s.

The name Holywell is derived from Helewell – healing well. All over the country, springs and wells were venerated from early Saxon times, believed to be the source of a religious or magical experience. Holywell is thought to be on the site of a nunnery that existed by the sacred well.

Nuns were believed to have curative powers for many illnesses, particularly of the eyes. Sufferers were told that a pilgrimage to a holy shrine would cure them of illnesses if they acquired holy water from the place.

The ailing person visited or was taken to the well at the break of dawn, usually on Saints' days, Easter or Whitsun. A bent pin was often thrown into the water as an offering to the spirit of the well when the wish was made. This followed the ritual of approaching from the east and circling the well in silence a specified number of times to affect a cure. Sometimes the patient dipped a rag into the holy water to wipe the afflicted part then drape it on a nearby branch where it would rot while the sufferer regained health.

38... *Holywell Hundred was the term used for the administrative subdivision of the Shire with fiscal, judicial and military functions. The men of the Hundred were members of the Hundred Court. The term 'Hundred' is thought to mean roughly one hundred homesteads.*

At the time of the Conquest Holywell's occupant was Morcar who was descended from an English queen. William I gave Holywell to Drogo. After he fled the country it became part of the manor of Bytham held by Fortibus, the Earl of Albemarle. Holywell descended to his daughter Aveline who married Edward Plantagenet. Three years later King Edward I "having a mind to all her castles and land, came to an agreement with Aveline for them." With exception of four Lordships, the King took all Aveline's holdings including Holywell, paying her twenty thousand marks. Then in 1323 Roger Belers, knight, baron of the Exchequer, was granted Holywell along with Stretton. Both manors were regranted to him a year later, tail male, (property which would descend to a male heir) by service of a pair of gilt spurs.

In 1368 his son Roger succeeded him but died in 1380. With only a daughter to inherit, Holywell reverted to the Crown.

Whilst still a royal desmesne, Holywell's quarries together with Careby supplied stone for royal building projects at Windsor.

In 1381 Holywell was granted to the King's esquire William de Harpele for life.

In 1393 the churchwarden of Holywell Church, John Pountfrayt, appealed at court. Five layman and a chaplain who he accused on the night of 29 October, broke into the church of the Holy Cross and stole a missal valued at £10, two gold chalices valued at four marks, a procession book valued at half a mark, a psalter at three shillings and fourpence, a quire from a missal worth one shilling, two suplices, a bed cover worth 1s. 8d., two blankets 1s. 4d. two altar towels - half a mark, six quires from a cartulary - half a mark, a linen alter clothe and an ancient altar towel - 1s. 8d., a towel for the high altar with the name of the donor in blue beading - six shillings, a pair of sheets, 1s. 8d. and other belongings of the church worth £100. The same six were also accused of domestic robberies. The six were found guilty but five proved to be clergy. The other was hanged. None had any chattels so were they driven by need to misappropriate such sacred objects. Though what their religious observance might have been...[39]

1406	John Wakerley held the manor of Holywell and Stretton with all woods, rents and advowsons granted by the King's son Humphrey Duke of Gloucester.
1439	The Duke of Gloucester was still in possession.
1446	Holywell was granted to John Hemingburgh, the King's chief cook, for life.
1461	Hemingburgh received a similar grant from Henry VII. William, Lord Hastings was appointed steward.

In 1494 Sir John Hussey, Comptroller of the Royal Household, was granted the manor but in 1537 was executed for treason. His son William forfeited all lands except Holywell and Stretton.

After his father's death it was expected that all lands would be transferred back to the Crown.

William Hussey's daughter Margaret (Nele) married Richard Disney and in 1555 they were living at Holywell manor house. Their daughter Anne married Francis Columbell.

In 1568, in the reign of Elizabeth I, Anne Columbell now widowed, bought part of Holywell and its appurtenances from Hugh Selborne. Seven years later, Robert Goodlake, alias Goodhall, bought one chief messuage and seventeen

39... *Bibliography 1323 - A History of the County of Rutland Volume 2 by William Page 1935*

appurtenances at Holywell from Siriacus Disney. During the transaction some flaw was discovered in Disney's title to the estate.

It took two years for Goodhall to procure the Queen's pardon for obtaining the manor of Holywell without the Queen's licence. Goodhall learned that when Sir John Hussey found himself under fire he'd transferred the property in some irregular way to Richard Disney.

However, Goodhall was found to have bought Holywell legitimately and the sale of the manor went through.

Several generations of the Goodhall family lived at Holywell before Robert Goodhall married Mary Bolsworth in 1696. She bore him three children. Only William survived.

Born in 1698 William grew up during the struggle to keep the estate going, mortgaging and leasing lands and woods to relatives and acquaintances in Stamford and beyond. In the end young William became bankrupt and first leased then sold the estate to Lady Mary Barnadiston on 28th January 1728.

The Goodhalls were a huge family with numerous descendents, many christened, married and buried at Holywell Church during their one hundred and fifty-three years of residence.

Perhaps this is what gave the family a strong incentive to relocate the ailing church.

1698: Holywell Church

The first church of Holywell measuring forty by twenty feet was originally dedicated to St Mary. For many centuries it continued to be a chapelry belonging to the Parish Church of Castle Bytham. The first recording of it was in the appointment of a Master Richard Ringstede in the 13th century. He succeeded the deceased former rector Master Roger Hendernas.

In 1698 an application to the Chancellor of the Diocese of Lincoln was made to remove both the building and the burial ground because of flooding.

'To the Right Worshipful Doctor William Oldys, Chancellor of the Diocese of Lincoln: The Humble Petition of Robert Goodhall. Esq. And others, inhabitants within the village of Holywell… is situate in a peece of ground containing half an acre, which for many years last past hath happened to be so full of quick springs that the graves for burying the dead there either within or without the said chappell are commonly full of water before the corps of such as are to be buried there can be interred, and likewise the floor of the said chappell is frequently so overflown that neither the minister or inhabitants aforesaid can into the said chappell for prayers and other divine duties without wadeing to their seats. And whereas the aforesaid Robert Goodhall Esq. Owner of several lands and grounds within the said village, out of his

This return of the Commissioners was dated 24 January 1699. The matter was brought before the Consistorial Court, witnesses were examined and finally a decree was issued on the 4th April 1701 authorising the removal of the chapel from its former site and rebuilding it on the proposed new one, within the space of one year following the Feast of St John the Baptist next ensuing. The old church stated in the above quoted document was said to have been within two furlongs of the Water Mill.

pious inclination and for remedying the grievances aforesaid, is willing to give a very convenient peece of ground, and larger in quantity than that on which the said chappell now stands and (having the peece of ground on which the said chappell now stands in lieu and change) to settle the same for ever for the said chappell yard. And moreover, att his owne proper costs and charges, to remove the said chappell, with all the material thereof, and rebuild the same in all things as amply and fitly as the same was before, and otherwise to doo as to your discretion shall seem most fitt. Therefore we humbly pray your worship in order thereto that a commission of view may be granted, that the proceedings to this good work may have its desired end, and your petitioners shall ever pray,

ROBERT GOODHALL SEN, THOMAS BALY, ROBERT PARKINSON' [40]

Francis Pretious, vicar of Castle Bytham and Holywell, Robert Ffish, clerk of Little Bytham and William Cawthorne, rector of Careby were sent to visit the chapel. They found *'the walls thereof very much decayed by reason of ffresh springs arising therein'*.

'They likewise viewed the place sett out for the building of a new chappell upon and judge it very convenient for its purpose.'

In 1701 the rebuilt church erected close to Holywell Hall was dedicated to St Wilfred. The graves and head stones were also removed from what were described as quicksands. Many graves including those of the Goodhall family were transported to the present site close to Holywell Hall.

Two Norman pillars support the church's William and Mary bell turret. Perpendicular and Decorated styles reflect the re-used materials gathered from

40... *(Rector of Castle Bytham) John Wild's 'History of Castle Bytham 1871.'*

the original Holywell Church and the derelict Aunby chapel. The stained glass has been dated from the 14th to 16th centuries and includes two Netherlandish panels from Careby Church.

Holywell Church became a listed building in 1968, preserving the public right of way along the drive for Careby and Aunby residents to visit the church. In 1985 the church was taken out of the Diocese of Lincoln but banns can still be published and marriages solemnised providing the service of a rector is sought.

The worked stone and remains of the picket fence discovered when Holywell Lake was drained in 2010

Investigating the possible site of the original church, Richard Tinsley, sister Jenny and their father Dick discovered three ancient yew trees overgrown amongst a clump of trees on the north shore of the lake.

Yew was one of the nine sacred woods used in the ritual fires of the Celts. Historically it was used as a cardiac stimulant, an abortifacient, the making of bows and spears, for assassination and suicide and to poison fish and mammals on the tip of arrows. Renowned for longevity yew trees were traditionally planted beside graveyards as protection from evil spirits on their journey to the next world. Wands of yew banished malevolent spirits and spiritually purified the area.

In the summer of 2010 Richard Tinsley supervised the draining and extensive dredging of the lake opposite Mill Farm. The foundations of two stone pillars some forty feet apart were discovered in close proximity to the newly discovered yews. A section of worked stone was retrieved from the muddy depths of the drained lake and along the shore more building stone was discovered together with a line of picket fence.

1728 - 1797: Sam Reynardson

Soon after the church was rebuilt land became the most worthwhile and respectable investment. In 1728, shrewd Lady Barnadiston, a wealthy dame from Suffolk seized the opportunity and bought ailing Holywell estate for her favourite nephew, twenty-five year old Samuel Reynardson. She paid $11,200 for it. Another estate in Tottenham owned by the Reynardsons was also called Holywell so perhaps the coincidence had a hand in her decision. Perhaps too, she suspected even more land would soon come available in neighbouring Careby because of the Hatchers' financial straits.

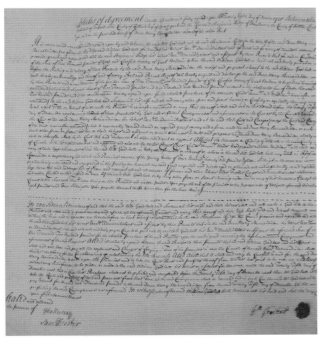

William Goodhall's particulars about Holywell Hall
Ref. H110/2 With the permission of Lincolnshire Archives

Sam was the only son and eldest surviving child of Jacob. Lady Barnadiston was sister to Jacob, a wealthy collector of customs in Bristol. Sam's grandfather was Abraham Reynardson, former Mayor of London. Abraham never disguised his royalist sympathies and was briefly imprisoned in the Tower during the civil wars of the sixteen forties.

William Goodhall's particulars showed Holywell Manor was a capital messuage with outhouses, stables, a newly built coach-house, a large garden well walled and planted with various fruit trees, an orchard, dovecote and fish ponds with a pleasant rivulet running through together with eight thousand acres. The land stretched all round the house between Clipsham, Castle Bytham, Aunby and Pickworth.

In addition to the manor house, three farmhouses and a messuage with a water corn mill were included in the sale along with tenanted lands and eighteen cottages, woods of young saplings, quarries, all to realise annual rents of £1,283.

Four years after purchasing Holywell, Sam Reynardson married Sarah Knipe. Sarah was the only surviving daughter of Sir Randolph Knipe and lived in Bedford Row, Holborn. She brought Sam a huge marriage settlement.

To Profit and Loss - see my wive's fortune.....£10,000.... /.....

As was the custom Sam kept careful account of all ingoings and outgoings, lists of window tax and hearth tax payments, revealing careful administration. Even wedding costs were accounted for.

By Jewells paid Seamer in full . A pair of Earrings 3 drops, ...£400.
A Stay buckle 24 Diamonds ....£96 10s.
Four Stay-buckles 28 stones each ....£140.
Making a pair of shoe buckles. 28 stones in each ....£5 10s.
3 rings and making plain gold ring £4 11s 6d

In the same year;

Victual bill £479
Sundries including chocolates: ....£21 5s. 6d.
Tea ....8s. 6d.
Five lottery tickets ....£36 16s. 3d.

£8,000 of Sarah's marriage settlement was to be spent on improving Holywell, building a new coach house, stables and a new bridge. Sam's mother Frances donated a similar amount, also stipulating it must be spent on the estate.

In 1746 Sam increased his acreage and added to his properties. He paid £1,900 for a portion of Careby Manor lands and houses. Soon shareholders in Careby Manor; Sir John Cust, who'd married a granddaughter of one of the Hatcher co-heiresses; and Henry Vernon and his wife sold out to Samuel Reynardson.

Then in 1754 when the remainder of Careby Manor was sold the majority of Careby lands came into Sam's possession.

But wealth doesn't always equal happiness. Sam's first-born, Samuel, died the day he was born in 1735 and Sarah Frances died aged three in 1748. They were buried in the new Holywell churchyard. Altogether, five of Sam's children died, although no others were buried at Holywell. Frances Elizabeth, Katherine, Samuel Charles and Jacob survived.

During this period part of the old manor house at Holywell was pulled down until only the west wing remained. Architect W. D. Legg was commissioned and plans drawn up and the rebuilding of the present Georgian Hall began.

Thomas Wright from Durham, astronomer, mathematician, instrument maker, architect and garden designer was commissioned to landscape the gardens.[41] The London-Palladian style Fishing Temple by the lake dated 1764 is identical to the 'menagerie' designed by James Gibbs at Hackwood Park in Hampshire. Gibbs had described the menagerie in his book of architecture in 1728. He also designed the Orangery, a similarly built five-bayed arcade.

The eastern spring-fed lake, the site of the original church, was designed in the mid-18th century as a fishpond. A boathouse stood almost opposite the messuage later to be rebuilt as Bridge Villa.

41... *Details of Wright's Holywell Horticultural Records can be found online at Holywell Hall Horticultural Records, Manuscript MS 77.2, John D. Rockefeller, Jr, Library, Colonial Williamsburg Foundation.*

Fishponds were an essential addition for houses of high status. After widening and damming a stream, the bed of a fishpond was lined with clay with a sluice at one end. Stocked with pike, bream, perch, roach and carp, all ponds were drained and cleaned annually.

Thomas Wright's eye for design created a winding drive through the park of fine trees. Yew, cedar, Scots pine, lime, beech, oak, sycamore and ash together with a vast plane tree near to the holy well create a stunning vista. The valley with sloping lawns, attractive islands, well-positioned bridges include the three-arch lower bridge covering a cascading dam. It is typical of a natural landscape favoured by 18th century garden designers.

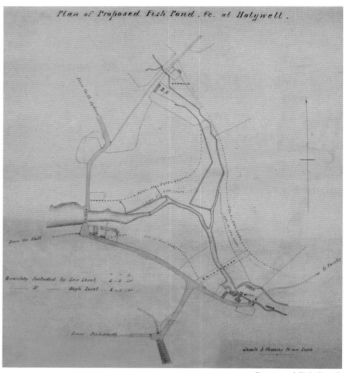

Proposed Fish Ponds at Holywell
Ref. H103B –
with the permission of Lincolnshire Archives

Sam Reynardson became a Fellow of the Royal Society of London formed to improve Natural Knowledge, a society generating research and discussion.

He also played an active part in local affairs becoming Justice of the Peace and Treasurer of the Southern Sessions Division of Kesteven. Reflecting his father's upbringing, the careful docketing and business-like notes indicating his legal mind, he was one of the Six Clerks in Chancery.

The Six Clerks Office in London was a public legal office serving the set of legal principles of the English Court of Chancery. The Court followed a set of loose rules to avoid the slow pace of change and possible harshness of common law. The Office had jurisdiction over all legal principles.

Sam's eye for detail included his investigation into up to date methods for running his estates. He bought and signed a first edition copy of 'The Modern Improvements in Agriculture' by Francis Forbes.[42] Carefully reading and annotating the text, he added notes of his own in the margins that related to his own farming practices at Holywell.

The book explains 'the principles of tillage and vegetation and the present practice of the most skilful husbandman in the culture of corn and pulse, and of the grasses, plants and roots for feeding cattle. It includes a comparative view of their uses and advantages from authentic experiments and the most improved methods of watering land, draining and other valuable improvements'.

In 1781, Sam's younger daughter Katherine married barrister Henry Partridge of the Middle Temple (one of the four Inns of Court).

As soon as Katherine woke up on Wednesday morning she felt a small flutter of panic deep within her chest. She stretched; today she was marrying Henry Partridge. Would living in London and Norfolk be anything like here? This secluded part of Lincolnshire? She very much doubted it.

Henry had been unfailingly polite, always seeking her comfort and happiness. He had proposed in a properly worded and prettily composed letter; she prayed her feelings would grow stronger and that Henry wouldn't just regard her as a possession.

42... *In December 2010 the signed copy of 'Modern Improvements in Agriculture' was for sale on the Internet for $600.*

She suspected her father had a hand in the arrangement though her sister had denied it.

'Oh no,' Frances exclaimed. 'Father doesn't need to concern himself with marrying you into high social circles. We have all we need.'

She and Henry had followed the correct procedure, applying to Father and Henry's parents for their approval. Mrs Partridge was Henry's father's second wife and they'd both warmly received her into their extended family.

Katherine propped herself on one elbow. Her silk wedding dress hung on the back of the door. She slumped against the pillows. Of the palest blue, the dress was of a simple style. Made with a shorter waist to the dresses she was used to; the bosom and hips were padded with muslin. A false rump and small hoops filled out the skirt. The hem wasn't completely sewn.

Yesterday, her maid Lizzie insisted, 'It's bad luck; no one sews the last stitch until it is time to wear a wedding dress.'

Katherine slipped out of bed and pulled back the drapes. Mist rose from the lake and sunlight sparkled on the tops of the trees. Father's dogs were scampering across the lawn to flush ducks settling on the bank.

A sigh escaped her lips. Yes, excitement for what lay ahead. But how sad she was to leave such a beautiful place. She bit her lip as she caught her reflection in the mirror. Lizzie had wanted to cover it over.

'Why?' Katherine laughed shakily. 'Everyone else will see me, don't you think I shall wish to see what I look like in such a splendid dress?'

Lizzie looked down at her feet. Mumbling she said, 'if I may say what others say, seeing your reflection on your wedding day will make you susceptible to evil spirits.'

Katherine shook her head after the maid left the room. Lizzie wasn't coming with her to Norfolk. She would not miss her gloominess. She picked up her hairbrush and brushed her long dark curls. The lace streamers carefully laid over the back of a chair would be fastened into her hair before the ceremony. Frances had offered to do it. Her sister had been so solicitous since their mother passed away. Oh, it seemed so long ago now that Katherine barely remembered her.

'Don't forget you must sew Mr Partridge's shirt, Katherine,' Frances had reminded her when they were preparing to cut the silk for her dress.

Made of the same material, it hung ready for her maid to wrap carefully and transport to her betrothed to wear this afternoon.

Katherine gathered her wedding dress between her fingers, sweeping the hem off the floor. Outside the sun had long disappeared and a shower of rain dampened the grass.

It was time. Her bridesmaids gathered round her in the vast hall. She could hear the fiddler outside, waiting, striking up a merry tune.

Father tucked her hand round his arm and squeezed her fingers. She nodded. She was ready.

'Don't let go.' They walked down the steps to cross the pile of broken dishes that had been hurled there the night before. Katherine suspected Lizzie had a hand in that. Father wasn't strong on superstition; she caught the shake of his head as they negotiated the shards of pottery. All she needed now was a chimney sweep and a lucky black cat and her marriage would be full of good fortune.

'Dear Father,' she whispered. 'Hold on to me tight. I'm not used to these shoes. I'm afraid I might slip stepping across the wet grass.'

It took barely a moment to reach the Church of St Wilfred. The fiddler stilled his violin and the warm stone gleamed a welcome. A soft breeze blew off the lake and a swan stretched and ruffled its feathers on the bank.

Katherine took a deep breath. As they paused between the massive pillars at the entrance to the tiny church, broad-brimmed hats swivelled towards them.

Father beamed with pride.

Then came the short walk towards the altar. Henry stood waiting, resplendent in a fine blue silk suit, tightly fitting and cut away to form curving tails. Instead of a cravat he wore a stiff stock and a closely curled powdered wig, dressed high and tied at the back. Under the coat Katherine could just make out the blue silk shirt she had sewn and a hint of embroidered waistcoat.

After the ceremony Henry allowed a small smile as arm in arm they walked solemnly back to the Hall to greet their guests. Katherine offered her cheek to Alice, old Mrs Partridge – she was sure they'd get on.

It was while dancing the 'wreath dance', that Katherine remembered her promises in the eyes of God. She'd tried to take in the lengthy scriptures from the Bible that emphasised their love of Christ. The wreath symbolised her maidenhood; she'd lose that tonight.

She twisted her wedding ring; it felt strange on her finger.

Katherine's sister Frances Elizabeth married Edward Reeve of Hanover Square in 1784.

Her brother Samuel Charles had already died unmarried in Lisbon at the age of thirty-six. Sam's wife Sarah died in 1763 and only surviving son Jacob eventually took over Holywell.

Jacob, Katherine and Frances and their families often visited, their names recorded as witnesses in Holywell's parish register.

Aged ninety-three Sam died on November 18th 1797. Robert Makepeace, goldsmith and jeweller of Lincoln's Inn Fields made nineteen gold mourning rings for the mourners.

1742 - 1811: Jacob Reynardson

Sam's son Jacob was born in 1742. He married Anne Cust on October 2nd 1777, strengthening the connection between the Hatchers' former Careby lands and Holywell. Anne, daughter of deceased Speaker Sir John Cust, had lived close by at Belton near Grantham.

By way of marriage settlement Sam awarded Jacob £10,000 and the manors of Holywell, Swineshead and Thorpe and lands in Hogsthorpe and elsewhere in Lincolnshire. Anne brought £2,000 to the marriage.

One of Jemima Reynardson's flower paintings – H56/1 With the permission of Lincolnshire Archives

Jacob and Anne married at Erddig near Wrexham where Anne was staying at the time, visiting Anne's younger sister Elizabeth. She'd married Philip Yorke of Erddig six years previously. The Yorke family became closely connected with Holywell and Careby Church.

The newly married Mr and Mrs Reynardson do not appear to have lived at Holywell, but in Great Ormond Street, London. The previous year at the age of thirty-two, Jacob had become one of the Four Clerks of the Privy Seal. The crown appointed the position with tenure for life. As a high officer of state Jacob was jointly responsible for all pardons and charters passed. The documents were traditionally stamped with the Privy Seal first recognised in the reign of King John.

Jacob and Anne produced five daughters; Ethelred Anne the eldest was born in 1778. Lucy Charlotte died and was buried at Holywell aged four. Katherine Sarah married rich landowner Wyrley Birch of Wretham Hall in Norfolk and Elizabeth died unmarried in 1837. Jemina had artistic leanings and learned painting. A portfolio marked 'Jemima's flowers, pray do not touch the drawings' survives.

Following the death of his father Jacob took a real interest in Holywell. In 1779 he commissioned a series of maps drawn by Edward Gibbons and Edward Arden.

He became very friendly with Dr Willis who lived at Greatford Hall. Letters were exchanged regarding Jacob's invention of a measuring wheel and Francis discussed his inventions.

While Jacob was staying with the Cust family at Belton the following letter was redirected from Holywell. Outlining medical treatments of the time, it mentions the afflictions befalling Jacob's brother-in-law. Ninepence was paid for the letter's arrival by mail coach.

'I hope however that Mr Partridge is in way of recovery though his progress is slower than his friends could wish. Dr Alderson of Hull published about three or four years ago an essay on 'The Rhus Toxicodendron pubescent poison oak or sumach' with cases showing its efficiency in the cure of paralysis and the diseases of extreme debility, printed at Hull and sold by Johnson of St Paul's Ch yard, London. Dr A relates reversal cases in which the leaves of this plant were given with success and in one instance, where the patient was a man of 47, was reduced to a state of that of a child of six months both as to mental as well as bodily powers.

'Our friend is undoubtedly in the way of good advice at Bath, however, the information respecting the success of new medicine in extraordinary cases can do no harm, tho it may not be thought proper to recourse to it.

'I have myself for upwards of two years been trying various remedies for a desperate complaint, the stone in the bladder, though hitherto with little success. On the autumn of 1798 I began taking a solvent, which I preserved (some short interruptions excepted) for ten months – at last it disagreed with me so much that I was obliged to leave it off: and upon the whole in rather a worse state than when I began it.

'My strength does not seem impaired and I have the perfect use of my limbs but am for obvious reasons so restrained in the exercise of my locomotive power that my walks are now limited to a few turns round my garden.

'As to great adventure – after the snow was gone I walked more than twice. The first time was on 2nd April when I met with two Highwaymen; the second time about a month later when I called on our neighbour but met with no adventure - good or bad.

'The summer preceding I spent at Clifton drinking the Hot Well Water.

'I am not surprised that you heard report of my death! Having been buried there these eighteen months would naturally create the presumption of my being dead – Mrs C is well and writes with me in kind wishes to Mrs R and yourself and family. We hope in more prosperous times – if such should ever arrive, that we may effect a visit.

I am very truly and faithfully Mr R C
Shirley March 11th 1800

Letter to Jacob Reynardson
H110/7 With the permission of Lincolnshire Archives

261

Enclosure

Already owner of most of Careby Parish, Jacob became responsible for the enclosure of land at Aunby. Much ancient arable ridge and furrow had disappeared although aerial evidence of ridge and furrow ploughing strips on land near Robert's Field still remain.

Sections of the parish had already been enclosed. Villagers toiled on the remainder of the land, sometimes a family looking after several strips, not necessarily all in one place. Separated by grass paths the strips were a furlong in length and twenty-two yards wide, equivalent to an acre. Crops grown were decided at village meetings and if the strips were not kept weed free there'd be disputes.

Also attached to the houses were 'closes'; small areas of enclosed land, orchards, paddocks or gardens that had existed for many centuries. Three Calves Closes to the south of Careby village street were amalgamated by the Reynardsons into the larger Calves Close Meadow now enclosed on two sides by the railway and the river.

The smallholders or labourers who worked these closes or strips believed they'd lose their independence once the Enclosure Act of 1801 became law. Former smallholders losing land because of enclosure were now employed to man machinery, plough, sow, hoe, and harvest crops. Becoming extra stockmen, dairymen and shepherds, enclosure meant more labour and more wages, not less. Fences, ditches, even roads had to be constructed, providing work for the landless labourers.

The process of obtaining an act of enclosure had previously been time consuming. Any owner of between three-quarters and four-fifths of land in a village had to produce a petition giving notice of his intention to enclose.

Ever since 1774 the law stated the petition must be affixed to the church door for three consecutive Sundays in late August or early September. Once the Bill was drafted it was read twice in the House of Commons. Objections were considered. After a third reading it was passed to the House of Lords then the Bill was given Royal Assent before becoming an Act of Parliament.

In 1802 Jacob Reynardson applied to enclose all the manor lands at Aunby. This would concentrate the farm in one place, rather than be interspersed by land tenanted and owned by Lord Willoughby of Ancaster.

Before any land could be officially enclosed, between three and twelve commissioners were appointed, depending on the amount to be inspected. The commissioners employed surveyors and clerks who drew up plans to show all fields and strips. Owners or tenants were recorded on each map and once a group of lands to be enclosed were inspected the commissioners reported back to Parliament.

At a series of meetings each claim was considered and a decision made. Then after the land had been allocated for enclosure a new map was drawn up, displaying the new boundaries and location of new paths and roads. All enclosures were passed under one Act of Parliament.

The map overleaf shows the Castle Bytham to Holywell road running past the Hall and through the park; the road to Little Bytham from Holywell is also shown.

When Jacob Reynardson died in 1811, son-in-law Lieutenant-General Thomas Birch-Reynardson became the new owner of Holywell. He'd married Jacob's eldest daughter Ethelred Anne in 1806. Before Sam Reynardson died he'd been anxious that the family name should continue.

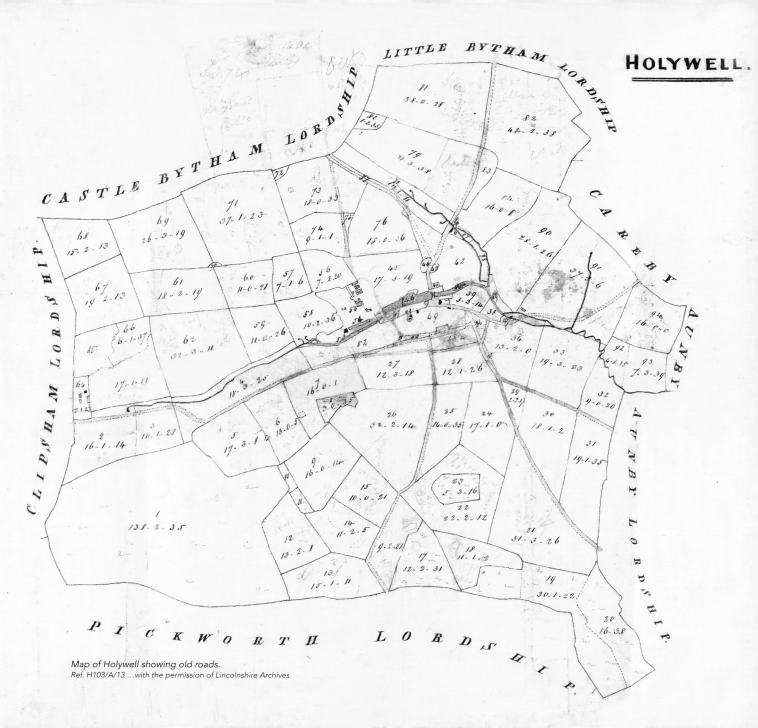

Map of Holywell showing old roads.
Ref. H103/A/13 …with the permission of Lincolnshire Archives

1806‑1847: THE GENERAL

Ethelred Anne married high-ranking officer, Major-General Thomas Birch in 1806. The second son of a respectable Warwickshire family, he'd inherited property in Birmingham.

To begin with, as an army wife, Ethelred Anne shared her husband's lodgings.

Thomas was quartered at Colchester with the 16th Queen's Light Dragoons, a regiment mounted on light cavalry horses for reconnaissance, scouting and flank-guard duties. The 16th and 17th Regiments were extensively engaged with France. The 16th Light Dragoons formed part of Wellington's army, winning major battle honours.

In 1815 they fought in the final defeat of Napoleon in Belgium and their timely intervention prevented total destruction of the 'Heavy Brigade'.

Cornet Beckwith of the 16th said, *'No-one was ever in such a fight before. I think Bonaparte is ruined. We charged four times.'* The regiment returned in December 1815 and two months later embarked for Ireland. In 1822 the 16th Queen's Light Dragoons were posted to India.

During this time Ethelred Anne bore Thomas nine children. The first was Ethelred Frances, born in 1809. Charles was born a year later at Lexdon near Colchester.

When Jacob died, Ethelred Anne and Thomas made Holywell their home subject to the demands of the newly promoted General's military career. The children were brought up at Holywell, although the boys were sent to Charterhouse and Eton.

Later, according to Charles in his book 'Down the Road,' General Birch-Reynardson was *'a first rate man on a horse, a first rate judge of a horse, first rate seat on a horse and the best hand on a horse I have ever known.'* [43]

43... *'Sports and Anecdotes of Bygone Days.' Charles Birch-Reynardson.*

FORGOTTEN PEOPLE

A steward at Lord Exeter's Stamford Racecourse, the General was responsible for those taking part to adhere to the rules of racing. The racegoers included Daniel Lambert – famed for his weight (which was 52 stone when he died). People flocked to Stamford, staying at the numerous inns in the town. Stamford's Assembly Rooms was venue for race night dances. Next to the George Hotel, cock fighting took place in the pit constructed at Lord Exeter's direction. Boxing matches were held alongside the racecourse straight mile of Wittering Heath.

'There were but few paid jockeys, the generality being either the gentleman who owned the horses, or some gentleman friend, or occasionally some groom or coachman belonging to some of the gentlemen, and sometimes a young gentlemen farmer would try his hand.

For instance, Lord Wilton would ride, and every one knows that as a jockey, or across country, he was not to be beaten. Then there would be Osbaldiston, the Squire, as he was called, Colonel Lowther, Black White, old Platel, a solicitor from Peterborough, and others whose names I forget, and who are long since dead and gone. The principle amusements on the course used to be pea and thimble, pricking the garter, and a good deal of boxing, fighting with a legitimate ring and ropes and a very fine amusement it used to be, to see two fellows strip and go at it and punch each other's heads into twice the size they ought to be.' [44]

General Birch-Reynardson loved hunting, keeping a stable of fine horses at Holywell. He also spent time with his friend Dr John Willis, eldest son of the highly regarded Dr Francis Willis, doctor to 'mad' King George.

The King often stayed as a patient at Shillingthorpe Hall, built as a lunatic asylum next to Willis's home at Greatford Hall.

[44]... *'Sports and Anecdotes of Bygone Days.' Charles Birch-Reynardson.*

With Aunby far behind, skylarks warbled and soared above them. The General's horse moved rhythmically beneath him. He allowed the reins to slacken. 'You are comfortably off now then, old friend?' He risked a glance at his companion.

John Willis slowed his horse to a walk and swept off his wide-brimmed, tall conical hat. The pressure from the rim had created a groove across his forehead and his long sideburns and curls at the side of his head were damp.

'You could say that. Though Greatford Hall is an expense to keep going. But we've a fine pack of harriers and good horses. In thanks for all Father did for King George and also in thanks to me over the years since Father died, I've been awarded £650 a year for the rest of my life. Mustn't grumble.'

The poor mad old King had been a frequent visitor to Dr Willis's private madhouses. His death was a merciful release. General Birch-Reynardson pursed his lips. 'The King was most generous.'

'We did what we could for him,' Willis murmured, his voice heavy with regret.

The General thought Willis a good and kind man, a most agreeable companion. Full of fun and anecdote, courteous and gentle in manner, he dressed well; snug leather breeches with ties and buttons at the knees with a fashionable cropped riding coat over a double-breasted waistcoat. Who could fault him? Everyone liked him.

They rode on in silence to join the lane leading to the road into Holywell Park. Mature woodland and rolling acres of ripening corn filled the landscape with the vibrancy of summer.

As the two men turned off the byway both horses jinked sideways.

'Hallo! What the deuce have we got here?'

Harnessed tandem-fashion, two donkeys were zigzagging across the lane. The lead donkey kept stopping and turning round to peer at a boy seated on cushions piled high on a curious two-wheeled gig. The gig seemed to be constructed from a green garden chair and a wheelbarrow and the child was waving a whip in an attempt to keep the donkeys straight.

'Charles!' The General thundered at his son. 'What are you up to?'

'Go easy on him,' the doctor murmured. 'Most enterprising of the boy. He's got this far on his own.'

The donkeys moved along nicely towards them.

Charles laid down his whip. It looked as if it had been put together from odds and ends found in the General's drawer. The boy bit his lip and didn't speak.

His father rode alongside. 'Surely you don't want to learn to be a coachman? And driving a tandem too! Of all things in the world a tandem is the most dangerous and most slang. I never saw a tandem in my life that I did not expect to see the leader turn into a madhouse!' The General had difficulty keeping his mirth to himself.

'Sorry Father. I wanted to practise…'

'Humph. You'd better fall in behind us.' The General winked at the doctor while Charles struggled to turn the donkeys round.

'You are a foolish fellow.' The General smothered a laugh. 'Coach driving indeed!'

On another occasion whilst visiting Stamford….

'Leaving Mr. Gilchrist, Clare went next door, to Mr. Drury [45] *, and, entering the shop, fell back with astonishment on hearing a tall aristocratic-looking elderly gentleman inquire for 'John Clare's Poems.' It sounded like sweet music to his ear, the cracked voice of the old gentleman.*

Mr. Drury, not noticing the entrance of Clare, took a small octavo volume from the top of a parcel of similar books lying on his counter, and handed it to the

45… *Boots the chemist stands on the site of Drury's old bookshop.*

gentleman, informing his customer at the same time that the poems were 'universally applauded both by the critics of London and the public.' John kept firm in his corner near the door; he thought his friend Drury the most eloquent speaker he had ever heard.

'And, pray, who is this John Clare?' asked the tall aristocratic-looking gentleman.

'He is ...' began Mr. Drury, but suddenly stopped short, seeing a whole row of his books tumble to the ground.

John Clare, in his terrible excitement, had pressed too close towards an overhanging shelf of heavily bound folios and quartos, which came down with a tremendous crash. It seemed as if an earthquake was overturning the 'New Public Library;' and the astonishment of the owner did not subside when he saw his poetical friend creeping out from under the ruins of five-score dictionaries, gazetteers, and account-books.

Having somewhat recovered his composure, Mr. Drury, with a grave mien, turned towards the tall gentleman, exclaiming, 'I beg to introduce to you Mr. Clare, the poet.'

The gentleman burst out laughing at the intensely ludicrous scene before him; yet checked himself instantly, seeing the colour mount into Clare's face. 'I beg you a thousand pardons, Mr. Clare,' he exclaimed; 'I hope you have not been hurt.'

And as if to compensate for his rude hilarity, the tall gentleman entered into a conversation with Clare, ending by an invitation to visit him at his residence on the following day: 'Mr. Drury will give you my address; good morning.'

John Clare made no reply, and only bowed; he did not feel much liking for his new acquaintance. However, when Mr. Drury told him that the stranger was General Birch-Reynardson, a gentleman of large property, residing near Stamford, on an estate called Holywell Park, and that his acquaintance might be of the greatest benefit for the success of his book, if not for himself, Clare consented to pay the desired visit. The allusion to his published poems by Mr. Drury was pleasant to his ears, and Clare eagerly sat down to examine his book.

He stayed some hours at the shop, and it was arranged that early on the next morning he should call again to get ready for the important visit to General Reynardson.

Early on the day following, John Clare made his appearance at Mr. Drury's shop. The busy tradesman had already provided an outfit for his friend, whom he meant to patronize more than ever, now that his poems promised to be successful. In the course of half an hour, John found himself clothed in garments such as he had never before worn. He had a black coat, waistcoat, and trousers, a silk necktie, and a noble, though very uncomfortable, high hat; while his heavy shoes seemed changed by a covering of brilliant polish. Surveying his figure, thus altered, in a looking-glass, John was greatly satisfied with himself, and with a proud step marched off towards Holywell Park.

General Birch Reynardson received him with great affability; at once took him by the hand, and led him into the library.

It was the finest collection of books Clare had ever seen, and he warmly expressed his admiration of it. After a while, the General took a small quarto, bound in red morocco, from the shelves, and showing it to his guest, asked him what he thought of the contents. They were poems written by the General's father; and Clare, seeing the fact stated on the title-page, was polite enough to declare them to be very beautiful. Another red-morocco volume thereupon came down from the shelves, full of manuscript poetry of the General's own composition. John Clare began to see that genius was hereditary in the family, and expressing as much to his host, earned a grateful smile, and a warm pressure of the hand. He was asked next to promenade in the gardens till dinner was ready.

The gardens of Holywell Park were laid out with great taste, and John Clare *soon lost himself in admiration of the many beautiful views opened before him. While wandering along the banks of an artificial lake, fed by a cascade at the upper end, he was joined by a young lady of extraordinary beauty. He believed it was the wife of the General; yet, though showing the deepest respect to the lady who addressed him while walking at his side, he could not help looking up into her face now and then, in mute admiration of her exquisite loveliness.*

The General, after a while, joined the promenaders, when John, somewhat to his surprise, learnt that his fair companion was not the hostess of the establishment, but the governess. Notwithstanding the presence of the master of the house, the young lady continued speaking to Clare in the freest and most unrestrained manner, bewitching him alike by the tones of her voice and the soft words of flattering praise she poured into his ear. She told him that she had read twice through the volume of poetry which the General had brought home the preceding evening, having sat up for this purpose the greater part of the night.

Clare's face got scarlet when he heard these bewitching words; never before had praise sounded so sweet to his ear; never before had it come to him from such honeyed lips. He was beside himself for joy, when, as a proof of her good memory, she began reciting one of his poems: 'My love, thou art a nosegay sweet.' And when she came to the last line, 'And everlasting love thee,' Clare's eyes and those of the beautiful girl met, and he felt her glances burning into his very soul.

The General did not seem to take much notice of his companions, being busy picking up stones in the footpath, and examining the state of the grass on the borders of his flower beds. On returning towards the house, he informed Clare that the servants were about sitting down to their dinner, and told him to join them in the hall. The young governess appeared intensely surprised at the words; she looked up, first at the General and then at Clare. Probably it seemed to her a gross insult that a poet should be sent to take his meal with the footmen and scullery-maids. But Clare's face looked bright and serene; to him, as much as to the master of the house, it appeared perfectly natural to be returned to his proper social sphere, after a momentary dream-like rise into higher social regions.

He walked into the hall, and humbly sat down at the lower end of the servants' table. The big lackeys whispered among themselves, looking with a haughty air upon the base intruder. John Clare heeded it not; his soul was far away in a world of bliss. Before him, in his imagination still hovered that sweet beautiful face which he had seen in the gardens; in his ear still sounded the soft tones of her voice: 'And everlasting love thee.' Thus he sat at the table, among the footmen and kitchen wenches, tasting neither food nor drink - an object of utter contempt to his neighbours.

Before long, however, there came a message from the housekeeper's room, inviting Clare to proceed to the select apartments of this potent lady. He followed the servant mechanically, careless where he was going; but was joyfully surprised on entering the room to see his dream changed into reality. There, opposite the table, sat his beautiful garden-companion, smiling more sweetly, and looking more exquisitely enchanting than ever.

She stretched out her little white hand, and Clare sat down near her, utterly unmindful of the presence of the mistress of the apartment, the lady housekeeper. The latter felt somewhat offended in her dignity, yet overlooked it for the moment, being desirous to proffer a request. Having succeeded in rousing Clare's attention, she informed her visitor, with becoming condescension, that she was very fond of poetry; also that she had a son who was very fond of poetry. But it so happened that, though very fond of reading verses, neither she nor her son was able to produce any. Now hearing, from her friend the governess, that there was a poet in the house, she had taken the liberty to send for him, to do some trifling work. What she wanted was an address of filial love, as touching and *affectionate as possible; this she would send to her son, and her dear son would return it to her, signed by his own name. She hoped it could be done at once, while she was getting the tea ready.*

Could it be done at once? Clare started on hearing himself addressed a second time by the high-toned lady - he did not remember a word of all that had been said to him. But he bowed in silence, and the dignified elderly person left the room to make the tea, firmly persuaded that her poetry would be got ready in the meantime. When she was gone, Clare looked up, and found a pair of burning eyes fixed upon him. He tried to speak, but could not; the words, rising from his heart seemed to perish on his tongue. After a long pause, the young governess, flushed with emotion, found courage to address her neighbour: 'I hope to see you again, Mr. Clare; I hope you will write to me sometimes.' He had no time to reply before the bell rang and a servant entered the room, reporting that General Birch-Reynardson wished to see John Clare before leaving.

The intimation was understood. John went up to the library, bowed before his stately host, muttered a few words of thanks, he knew not exactly for what, and left the house. When the gate closed after him, he felt as if expelled from the Garden of Eden. Slowly he walked up the road, when suddenly a white figure started up on his path.

The young governess again stood before Clare. 'I could not hear of your going,' cried the beautiful girl, her bright face suffused with blushes, and her long auburn hair fluttering in the wind; 'I could not hear of your going, without saying good-bye.'

Clare again tried to speak, and again the words died upon his lips. But she continued addressing him. 'Oh, do not forget to write to me,' she said earnestly, with a tinge of melancholy in her soft voice. It thrilled through his soul, and opened his lips at last.

'I will write,' he answered, 'and I will send you some new poems.' Thus saying, he bent forward and took both her hands, and their eyes met, full of unspeakable passion. But a sudden noise from the distance startled Clare and his fair companion. There was a man on horseback coming up with full speed, riding in the direction of Holywell Park. The young governess softly loosened her hands, turned a last fond look upon the poet, and fled away like a frightened hind into a neighbouring wood.'

'Life of John Clare' by Frederick Martin 1830-1883

Commenting on religious customs at Holywell, Charles wrote:

'only 98 inhabitants lived in Holywell and the church ceremonies were very limited. A solitary wedding in the course of twelve months and the same may be said of funerals. Events of this kind here excite considerable interest. The Reverend John Reynardson is the present incumbent of this church and the Domestic Chaplain to the family; prayers being offered up every morning in the Hall of the Mansion when the whole household assemble. Such are the laudable proceedings at Holywell. On Sunday evenings they are assembled in the dining room when either General Reynardson himself or the Rev. John Reynardson reads a sermon previously to the offering up of the evening orisons.'

General Birch-Reynardson became High Sheriff of Rutland before he died in 1847. Ethelred Anne outlived him by seven years.

Through the tales of the General's eldest son Charles Thomas Samuel Birch-Reynardson, the story continues.

1810 - 1889: CHARLIE THE COACHMAN

'I was born so long ago in camp near Colchester, where my Father was then quartered with the 16th Light Dragoons, now 16th Lancers. On the 10th November 1810 I first drew my breath, and was born with both eyes open, and having kept them pretty wide open ever since that memorable time, and having been pretty wide awake for more than seventy five years, and as, up to the present time, I have never been obliged to wear spectacles, or even clearers, either to read or write' [46]

Thirteen-year-old Charles loathed Charterhouse, his first school in London.

'In those days it was a regular prison, and in the dirtiest part of London, and close to Smithfield. The unfortunate boys never wore hats, went bareheaded and generally looked as if their fathers must have been chimney sweeps. In winter the playground was some inches deep in black sludge. Wet through and cold as we were a change of raiment was unknown.' [47]

'Did you really think you would die?' George hacked at the ice with his heel in perfect time with each word.

'No.' Charles caught a vague aroma of frying bacon. What he wouldn't give for a second breakfast.

Edward nodded. 'Mama thought so. She was most worried when you were ill.' He stamped his feet on the pavement outside Stamford's George Hotel.

Lamps flickered, casting pools of light in the darkness. Shovelled snow lay piled at both sides of the road. The crisp air froze in Charles's nostrils. He sniffed. 'I can't feel my fingers. Why did Isaac drop us off so early?'

'To make sure we didn't miss the coach of course.' George huddled deeper into his greatcoat, his nose glowing with the cold.

46... *'Sports and Anecdotes of Bygone Days.' Charles Birch-Reynardson.*
47... *Down the Road.*

Still wearing her robe Mama had hugged them close and Father stood in the porch and waved them off. Father encouraged independence. Mama cried. Driving with their coachman to Stamford the sky was as dark as pitch except for stars floating like jewels in a black sea.

The day stretched ahead; no chance of reaching the George and Blue Boar in Holborn before nine or ten o'clock tonight. Charles bit his lip and prayed Eton would be an improvement on Charterhouse. The thought of returning to that place sent a shiver scorching down his spine. He imagined prison could be no worse. But did prisoners have their bare bottoms roasted over a fire? He thought not.

Bullies had knocked him about but the worst of it was when he'd been tossed in a blanket up to the ceiling and fallen through the huge tear that appeared. He'd struck his head on the floor. Desperately ill he'd been sent home. Everyone imagined he would die.

He glanced at his younger brothers. Bored, they were shoving against each other under the disapproving gaze of a waiting bespectacled gentleman. As twins they stuck together. Bullies hadn't succeeded in intimidating them.

The gentleman moved towards the edge of the pavement as soon as the regular tattoo of horses' hooves drummed over the town bridge. The cream and black Regent coach with its relentless rumble of iron-shod wheels was drawn by four sweating horses spiralling clouds of hot breath into the lamplight.

The guard lifted his horn to his lips and the long drawn out note warned of the coach's arrival. Enviously Charles watched old Mr Barker manipulate the reins to steer his team towards the rear of the hotel.

'Five minutes. That's all it will take for Whincup [48] to change the horses.' Edward hopped up and down in the gutter, carefully avoiding lumps of frozen horse dung.

The door of the Hotel opened and passengers began to filter out on to the pavement.

48… *Whincup - Father and son, landlords at the George for eighty years*

Charles stood impatient, the anticipation of the chance to take the reins almost too much to bear. When the horses pulled up under the gallows, the guard held open the door of the coach and then with a cheery grin, let down the step before helping the gentleman and three ladies clamber inside. Luggage was piled on top of the coach until it resembled a stage-wagon.

'I'm not going inside.' Mama had insisted they travel inside the coach. 'I'm going to ride up on the box.' Charles elbowed past his brothers and scrambled up. He sat down beside the coachman with George and Edward squeezing together beside him.

A deep bed of straw cushioned their feet and warmed their toes. Vast John Barker winked down at Charles. Last term he'd encouraged him to take hold of the reins as they drew into the George Hotel yard.

At Huntingdon they'd change horses, perhaps Mr Barker would give him the chance to take the reins again. Charles was desperate to learn about handling a team of horses under the coachman's watchful eye.

He'd have to swear his brothers to secrecy. Father had a horror of coachmen, believing them drinkers of brandy and water who swore like moss-troopers [49] and had one tooth knocked out so they could spit.

Colonel Edward Birch Reynardson 1855

Charles's younger brother John also boarded at Charterhouse where he was a Gownboy. A schoolhouse for boys of scholarly status; Gownboy allowed boys to be free to be themselves and develop as best they could.

Both John and George eventually took Holy Orders: George becoming a rector in Kent: John at Holywell and Careby.

Brother Edward followed his father into the army. He rose to the rank of Colonel with command of the Grenadier Guards at the Battle of Inkermann in the Crimean War. Fought in the Ukraine on November 5th 1854 the war

---

49... *moss troopers – bandits resisting the Cromwellian occupation, particularly on the Scottish border.*

combined French and English forces against the Russians. Despite fog and their forces outnumbered they took the Russian guns and won the battle.

Henry became a barrister and had rooms in the Temple in 1846. Like Katherine Reynardson he married a member of the Partridge family and lived at Adwell Manor, near Oxford, becoming High Sheriff of Oxfordshire.

William, born in 1819, did not survive childhood. A personal account of Holywell and its occupants written by a family member in 1844 records, '*This darling child died October 1825 of a fractured skull, occasioned by a kick from a horse, after lying seven weeks in patient suffering – he was a child of greatest promise*'.

Charles had three sisters. Unmarried sister Emma Lucy stayed at Careby Rectory with John, possibly after their mother died in 1854. After John's marriage to Sophie in 1862, Emma Lucy went to live at Adwell Manor where she later died.

Ethelred Frances was the third member of the family to marry into Norfolk's Partridge family. She had two children with husband Henry Champion, both christened at Holywell but she died and was buried at Holywell in 1846 at age of thirty-seven.

In 1853 Matilda Caroline married Robert Stopford, son of the Hon. and Reverend Richard Bruce Stopford. Their daughter Evelyn Perry erected a memorial to them in Careby Church and also commemorated their son Lt. Colonel Horace Robert Stopford of the Coldstream Guards, killed at the Battle of Modder River in South Africa in 1899.

At Charterhouse Charles and his brothers often over-looked the street to see a Charlie [50] standing with his horn lantern in his watchbox and a rattle stuck in his belt.

50... *early watchman to prevent crime*

The boys let down their nightcaps attached to a length of string. With the sixpence placed inside, Old Charlie on the corner of Wilderness Row bought them tarts, plums, apples and other contraband eatables, filling the nightcaps to be hauled back up again.

At the end of term a hackney coach was chartered overnight for an early start in the morning. '…*with its pair of worn out dog horses smelling of King Froust and sometimes, I fear, of subjects taken by the body snatchers from some graveyard to the hospital for dissection.*'[51]

The hackney coach proceeded from Harley or Wimpole Street from where the Regent Coach[52] left at six o'clock. Gas was still in its infancy:

'…*there is thick fog; and, after groping along in nearly outer darkness, we at length turn into the yard and find the horses put to. Piles of luggage are being placed on the top and into the fore and hind boot of the coach. Where the luggage for four in and twelve out used to go I will leave you to make out, for I never could.*

'*We got out of the yard. Down Holborn Hill to the left up Cow Lane, through Smithfield, and make the best of our way to the Peacock at Islington, meeting droves of bullocks, sheep, and all sorts of conveyances from Smithfield. The steam from the horses, the breath from the horses, the cattle, and the sheep, added to the dimness of the lamps and dense fog, and turned everything into worse than darkness.*

'*A noise assails your ears as coach after coach pulls up. Up came the old hostler with a horn lantern and called out their names as they arrived on the scene.*

'*York Highflyer, Leeds Union, York Express, Stamford Regent, Truth and Daylight, all with their lamps lit, and all smoking and steaming so you could hardly see the horses. The coaches clattering over the stones, the horses feet clattering along to the sound of the merry-keyed bugles upon which the guards played remarkably well.*

51… *Down the Road*
52… *In the Regent's heyday, the journey from London to Stamford took nine hours twenty minutes including changes.*

'On we go in the fog, the steam rising from the horses as if one were sitting over one of Barclays and Perkins's largest brewing coppers till we get to Highgate Archway. If you are not too cold and wet to see, on looking round, you see London about four miles off in such a yellow smoke and fog no artist has attempted to paint.

'Off we go again, the Regent being due in Stamford at eight the same evening.' [53]

After unmerciful bullying and victim of the accident with the blanket Charles was taken away from Charterhouse and sent to Eton. The coach journeys continued. The boys experienced alarming floods and deep snow.

At one stop old coachman John Barker [54] could not get his team to start. No amount of persuasion did any good. At last he said to Bill the guard, 'Get us a couple of wisps of straw and a lantern.'

Bill set the straw on fire under the refractory horses and the effect was electrical. Away they went at once as if the devil had kicked them sideways.

In summer, driving the coach up Alconbury Hill by Monks Wood with the fat old coachman by Charles's side murmuring encouragement, 'Good, old friend. Keep them going,' they saw the usual incredible number of fork-tailed kites. They soared in almost every direction and some even squatted in the road. Charles dreamed of an outdoor life as a coachman but knew it was unlikely his father would ever allow it.

'...Father naturally did not wish to see his son become a blackguard; and, as I was his eldest son, he thought the propensity I was showing of becoming a disciple of Jehu might bring disgrace upon his house, which was a house much given to hunting and equitation of all kinds.' [53]

53... *Down the Road*
54... *John Barker was buried in St Michael's churchyard, Stamford*

Close together in age, Charles, George, Henry and John shot, fished, swam and rode together.

'I remember when almost a boy and with my brothers out shooting, one of them thinking he might run short of powder, after having shaken his flask and not being quite satisfied as to its contents, unscrewed the top when a spark from a cigar fell into it and there was of course a real blow up. The flask was blown to pieces over the hedge, his hair and face considerably singed and scarified, but no one was killed or seriously injured. The same good Providence has watched over him ever since for he was second in command of the Grenadier Guards at the Alma.' [55]

The boys tasted almost everything. Mice weren't bad, rats about the same. They didn't mind squirrels and hedgehogs were rather good. The only thing that beat them was fox. When they were out with the hounds they got Lambert, first whip, to cut out the fox's tongue and next day had it boiled for luncheon. But they couldn't eat it because of the smell.

Their father kept a stud of lightweight horses and encouraged the boys to ride and hunt. It wasn't long before Charles was allowed to ride one of his hunters, togged out with white cord breeches, top boots and a swallow-tailed red coat.

'We have arrived at the meet and have mounted our horses, an old stamp of an animal and what would seem in these days an antiquated kind of 'gee' but he is full of beans and fit to go; he has short legs and his square cut short tail displays his rounded quarters to advantage; he has more timber about him than is generally seen theses days in a thoroughbred; weedy animals who owe their good coats to hot water and Turkish Baths than to the use of strap-oil and elbow grease.'

55... *'Sports and Anecdotes of Bygone Days.' Charles Birch-Reynardson.*

'...*they would ride up to the meet in their white cord breeches, with either what were called mud boots or spatterdashes to keep their boots free from mud, swallow-tailed coats (no one wore cutaways in those days) and tall chimney-pot hats which had as much nap on them as there is on many a Southdown sheep's back, and which were much in the shape of a garden pot – regular chimney pots. The said hats were wonderful to behold, not only from their height and shape, but also for their marvellous discomfort for when they got wet through they became soft as tripe and as heavy as a sheet of lead and a mixture of something like gum or glue would trickle down one's face and neck. They took a deal of drying and ironing with a hot iron to get them into any kind of shape again.*

'*No man in those days would have a servant behind him with half a hundred-weight of sandwiches and half a butt of sherry. A small packet of sandwiches or a few gingerbread nuts in the pocket of his swallow-tailed coat was all he required.*

'*The Melton men, many of whom are great dandies are almost refulgent in their white cords, white buckskin gloves and well-brushed hats, for their grooms have given them a tickle up for the occasion; their well-polished boots have also had a lick-over.*'

Describing the hunting parson…

'*Bent on mischief, a certain dapper little man in black. His hat, shining like satin, his white cord breeches particularly well cut and fitting without a wrinkle below the knees, where they are tied in a most artistic manner by a white leather bow. But all this is nearly eclipsed by the white choker that encompasses his neck, which is as white as driven snow, about four inches deep, starched to the consistency of pasteboard and folded across in front with a simple small round jet pin, like a bead on a gold stem. This is surmounted by a pair of well-starched milky white fine stan' up collars. The choker seems as if it will choke him and the stan' up collars seem to bid fair to cut his ears off.*

‘He has performed a marriage and a christening before he set off and has a funeral at three o'clock, ridden seven miles to the meet, or rather the covert he thought they would draw.' [56]

On occasion Cottesmore Hunt met at Holywell Hall. Charles kept up with the action, sticking close to Jack Lambert, the hunt's whipper-in who was responsible for the behaviour and control of the hounds. With eyes like a hawk watching if any hound stepped out of line, Lambert punished it with a peculiar left-handed cut. The Master, the good old Earl, Sir Richard Sutton, couldn't bear to hear a hound punished; nor could he abide swearing.

With Pickworth behind them horses clattered down the lane towards the point of Castle Dyke Wood where it met the Holywell road. Hounds bayed in full cry running with their heads down, brown, black and white bodies flashing through the trees.

Charles sat tall in the saddle, struggling to keep up with Lambert who was shouting and cursing more than usual. They overtook the former Master, Lord Lonsdale.

'Oh Lambert, Lambert, can't you do all that without swearing?' he said.

The whipper-in touched his hat. 'No my lord, damned if I can, they do roile me so.'

Ahead on the corner where the two lanes met, several bystanders stood halloaing and shouting and waving their arms.

Charles glimpsed the fox slink away across the lane. Bland, a son of one his father's tenants at Aunby, was standing in the middle of the lane, screeching like a wounded animal.

56... *'Sports and Anecdotes of Bygone Days.' Charles Birch-Reynardson.*

Charles shook his head at him. What a poor attempt at a view halloa.

Lambert snatched up his reins and charged at young Bland. 'Oh dear! Oh dear! Shut your mouth; shut your mouth or by God I'll ride down your throat!'

Sometimes Lambert showed a softer side…

With hounds in full cry the horses blew hard as the fox streaked across the stubble from Holywell to Aunby.

In the soft light of dusk scores of red-coated riders sped south past Vale Farm and up the hill towards Pickworth Drift. To the sounds of the Master blowing his horn, shouts and curses and the pound of galloping hooves, the wind tore Lambert's cries from his mouth.

'Damned varmint's heading for Turnpole Wood. After him!'

Lambert's horse rose over the hedge bordering the Drift. Young Charles dug in his spurs and his horse put in an enormous leap before almost crumpling on landing. Sweat from the horse's neck stung the boy's face as he struggled to maintain his balance.

Determined not to miss any of the action and heedless of low branches flaying his cheeks, Charles rode hard on the heels of the whipper-in. They both crashed through the trees in time to see the brush of the fox disappearing into a hole in the ground.

Before curses had left Lambert's lips six hounds had tumbled after the fox.

With a roar he stopped any more following.

Tongues lolling, the rest of the pack milled round the hole. The Master pulled up breathless and red-faced, the remaining Hunt followers halting discreetly behind him, their crumpled chimney-pot hats rammed hard on their heads.

Lambert leapt off his horse and threw the reins at Charles. Hounds yelped and scattered as he made space to lie face down and peer into the blackness.

His arms vanished, groping into the hole.

After a full minute he clambered to his feet and shook his head. 'Jack! Where's Jack Abbey?'

A whiskery old man urged his horse forward.

Lambert caught the horse's reins and spoke urgently. 'You must go to Pickworth Jack and ask Mr Thraves to lend you a ladder and some ropes and a lantern. And don't forget to bring a tinderbox and matches in case the lantern should go out.'

Charles wondered if they'd have enough light to locate the fox.

Hoof beats faded as Abbey galloped hard down the Drift.

'Goodnight.'

'Goodnight.' In the gloom most followers nudged their horses homewards and plodded away.

Charles dismounted and leaned against his horse for warmth, the comforting smell of horses' sweat filling his nostrils. Lambert tied his horse to a tree. Men that remained unwrapped gingerbread and brought out flasks. Hounds jostled for tossed scraps. Laughter echoed through the trees.

A horse whinnied and Charles made out a rider coming steadily towards them. Jack Abbey carried a ladder over his shoulder, ropes and a horn lantern and a bundle of tallow-dipped candles were strapped on the front of his saddle.

'About time!' Lambert lurched forward in the gathering darkness and snatched up the ladder. He spun round and slithered it down into the hole before straightening up to look round.

'Sir!' Lambert glanced at Charles to indicate Abbey who'd dismounted and was lighting the lantern. 'If you don't mind holding that lantern for me sir I might be able to see what I'm doing.'

Charles tied up his horse then followed Lambert down the ladder, the flickering light illuminating a cavern as large as any stable.

Excited hounds rampaged round his feet, their long bony tails striking against his legs. All hounds seemed unhurt except for one hanging back against slimy green limestone dripping with wet.

Charles glanced up. A circular grey gleam of sky. The light of the lantern casting an eerie glow on stalactites. From somewhere under his feet the sound of rushing water.

'Throw down that rope!' Lambert shouted.

The rope snaked down and the whipper-in grasped two muddy hounds and coupled them together. When he'd bound their legs tight he cupped his hands round his mouth and yelled hoarsely, 'Haul them upwards if you please.'

Soon all six hounds were out.

More riders bid goodnight.

'Now then sir.' Lambert grimaced at the mud streaking Charles's coat. 'Where's that damned fox gone? Sir, if you please, if you'll let me have the lantern for a moment.'

Lambert cast the light to illuminate the fissured limestone walls of the cavern, swinging the lantern high and low. 'Hah! Got 'im! There he is, sir! See him?'

Charles moved forward to join him and spotted a quivering bundle of fur deep in the crevice of a rock.

Lambert shouted, 'Someone up there lower my whip.'

Then setting the lantern down he doubled the long plaited thong to fashion a loop.

Charles held his breath while he shone the lantern and stood motionless as Lambert poked the whip into the crevice. After several attempts the whipper-in managed to fasten the loop round the fox's neck.

What they would do when they got it out? As the thought crossed Charles's mind, Lambert reached in to grab the fox's brush. Endeavouring to escape the fox twisted violently but somehow Lambert held on.

A surge of revulsion flooded through Charles as the last few inches of the fox's brush came off in Lambert's hand.

'Damn you! Damn you. You'll not get away from me.'

The fox skittered out of sight.

'We must have been here for an hour already. Shall you not give up?' Charles felt the dankness seeping through his coat tails. His fine leather boots weren't enough to prevent the numb feeling of cold either.

'Give up? How else will it get out? No sir. I'd sooner spend the night here than not get my fox out.'

Lambert squelched to the bottom of the ladder. 'Jack! Will you come on down?'

'Master's taken the hounds home,' Jack wheezed, his feet hesitant on the rungs. He descended to the floor and wrung his hands. 'He said for you to catch him up.'

'I will when we've finished here.'

The three of them spread out across the floor. Lambert flicked his whip and the fox darted backwards and forwards in its efforts to evade capture. Once it dodged between old Jack's feet and he was too slow to catch it but after numerous wild grabs the fox was finally secured in Lambert's arms.

He grasped it by the back of its neck to avoid the row of teeth visible between drawn back lips. 'It's a vixen. She's a fighter, isn't she?' His face softened and he glanced at Charles. 'Be a shame to kill her now sir. I'm going to let her go. Let her live to fight another day.'

Then with the vixen still squirming in his arms, Lambert mounted the ladder and thrust her out into the darkness.

Wearily the three of them trudged to their horses. The flickering lantern cast a ghostly light on the ladder swinging over Jack Abbey's shoulder.

Before untying his horse Lambert paused.

'You know the tradition. You must have the brush sir.' He reached into his pocket then placed the tapering end of the vixen's tail into Charles's hand.
Father would be pleased.

Charles took the brush home and had it mounted. For years it sat on the shelf in the library of Holywell Hall.

Charles's travels to and from Eton continued to whet his appetite to become a coachman. When old John Barker retired and set up a staging post at Welwyn, John Hennessy drove the Regent and continued with Charles's illegal lessons.

The boys would leave the George and Blue Boar at Holborn, always riding outside with the coachman whatever the weather. In early summer they left London with smoke rising from chimneys in endless blue puffs. Every now and again the smell of pinewood from the little white bundles of kindling so well known to housemaids would drift across the air mixed with the smell of an early breakfast.

At Islington they'd stop for a few minutes to take up passengers and parcels. Then they'd be off again, the sun shining, no great tall ugly chimneys pouring black smoke; the early morning air exhilarating as they trotted along.

Charles could barely contain his impatience till they reached Barnet. He knew that after a glass of rum and milk at the inn John Hennessy would say, 'Now then sir, you shall work the stage. Catch hold of them and don't let the apron catch the old mare, or she'll kick the boot in.'

Charles would pick up the reins and John's shrill whistle would wake up the four horses and make them skip into their collars. Throwing his thong lightly under the near side bar Charles reminded the leader to do his share of work.

Horses, Horses

'I hope you won't be dirtying that new pink today.' Lambert touched his hat most politely as if to say, I should not wonder if you come a cropper with that smart new coat on.

Charles had no time to respond; hounds were away, streaming after a fox running towards Oakham. It turned towards Langham and the field charged up the lane to Burley on the Hill. Once past the blacksmith's shop the fox fled into Burley grounds before twisting back to the road and racing for the cottage on the corner. It leapt over the wall with hounds closing in.

'It's done for,' shouted Lambert.

But the fox sprang on to the backs of the hounds and scrambled over the wall and away towards Exton. With hounds in full cry the hunt galloped parallel to the Cottesmore road. The fox turned swiftly as if it meant to go towards Ashwell then doubled back and dodged down a pathway snaking behind the village of Cottesmore.

Charles stuck close to Lambert, determined to keep up but mindful of the wet and greasy footpath. Zigzag, so called because of the way she stood in her stable, felt tired beneath him.

Ahead was a stile with a footboard and a drop on the far side leading into the back lane to the village. Lambert dug in his spurs and charged at the obstacle and his horse rose. Too late Charles saw the young green ashpole nailed across the top.

Vaguely he heard voices call out. 'Don't go there! Don't go there!'

'Over,' murmured Charles to himself as he sensed the mare wanting to refuse. He kept her head straight and rammed in his spurs.

Zigzag hit the ash pole with her knees and somersaulted into the lane.

Cannons fired, thunder rolled, cymbals clashed in his head while church bells and mighty water rushed into his ears, submerging him. Lightning of all colours streaked through his head while men in red and black and green coats peered down.

Charles regained consciousness in a hot slipper bath in a room in Cottesmore. Lady Frederick Bentinck and Miss Thompson, a friend of Lord Lonsdale, bent over him.

One of them was pouring a black cordial mixture down his throat.

He struggled to sit up and coughed. Pain streaked down his side. He recognised the taste of the mixture: cardamom and aloes. Dr Willis used nothing else for drenching everybody who came under his notice.

Charles spluttered the mixture down thinking that at least it was better than blooding.

I've had a near squeak of it. Thank the Lord my parents are away. No doubt everyone thinks I'm killed because my horse has fallen on me.

When Charles could bear to move he was sent home in the Master's carriage. Staff put him to bed for a week. They reported; a good deal bruised the colour of plum but no bones were broken.

Charles's luck finally ran out.

He broke his leg – he doesn't say how – and was forced to hobble about on two sticks for several years. His hip 'ankylosed' and became too stiff for him to ever mount a horse again.

'The greater number of my contemporaries who were at Eton with me remember a youth upon a pair of young and active legs, my body and carriage straight as a fishing rod. Those who were not born in that remote period believe from seeing me, used a coaching term "with a wheel up", for I have been lame from an accident

for more than sixty years, and consider me to "have been dropped by a nurse when a baby".

Till the age of nineteen I was in possession of as good a pair of legs as other people. As soon as I was old enough I was put on a rocking horse, from that wooden affair I was put upon a donkey who used to make the point of kicking me off three or four times a day; I was promoted to a pony with merely a sheepskin and surcingle round it then to a saddle and stirrups and ultimately to one of my father's hunters with white cord breeches, top boots and a swallow-tailed red coat. I could generally hold my own across country with the best of 'em.'

At the early age of twenty I became a confirmed cripple, and from the fact of my hip bone having become fixed in the socket; I have never since been able to get up on a horse but feel thankful I have been able to enjoy other sports, I have been able to drive coaches, shoot and fish in a moderate way and enjoy many amusements which did not require that I should actually be on top of a horse.' [57]

On leaving Eton, Charles told his headmaster that he planned to follow his father into the army instead of going to Cambridge University. He was headed for the Guards.

Finally, well enough, but unacceptable for an army career, he was forced to enter Trinity College. There he discovered most of his contemporaries were either leaving or left. He came across an old Etonian and complained about his loathing for Greek and Latin.

His old friend gave him advice. 'Never go to anything you are told,' he said, 'except to Hall. You must go to Hall to get marked in or you'll lose your term. But don't go to anything else till you're told or sent for. Some of the dons will soon send for you to ask why you haven't been to lectures or chapels and it will be all in good time for you to go then.'

57... *'Sports and Anecdotes of Bygone Days.' Charles Birch-Reynardson.*

Charles mentally agreed and determined never to go to chapel at seven in the morning. How could he? The Stamford and Leicester coach started at seven and he couldn't be in chapel and drive the coach from Cambridge. He'd make sure he always walked with two sticks in Hall although by now he could do very well with one.

Inevitably, the Dean finally sent for him. Charles convinced him that he couldn't possibly walk with even two sticks over the shiny marble floor of the chapel in case he fell.

The Dean was sympathetic and excused him all chapels.

Charles didn't feel at all guilty. He was learning a useful trade, wasn't he?

Often he drove Cambridge men to Fitzwilliam meets and one morning when he pulled up at the George Hotel, his father saw him. He didn't say much. Charles hoped that perhaps he'd believe coaching was part of the training he was receiving at university.

On September 1st 1835 Charles Birch-Reynardson married Anne Yorke of Erddig, continuing the connection between the families since his grandfather Jacob had married Anne Cust.

Charles and Anne lived in Shropshire close to the great Holyhead Road. An old friend allowed him to indulge his passion for driving coaches and gave him character references to drive the Holyhead Mail. A fast coach, it averaged eleven miles every hour between Holyhead and Shrewsbury.

Charles also drove the Welshpool to Liverpool stagecoaches. They seated four passengers inside and twelve out, excluding the coachman and guard. The fore boot and hind boot were packed with parcels, the roof piled high;

but not too high, allowing passage beneath the archways of inns. Boxes, carpetbags, gun cases, hampers and luggage hung over the sides, secured with a tarpaulin and held fast with a leather strap. Lamp irons sometimes hung, along with baskets of pheasant and hare dangling down. Underneath, a cradle swung for extras that would go nowhere else.

Whilst living at Erdigg Anne bore him three children.

In 1843 Charles felt the urge to travel abroad, full of visions of driving his own coach all over the world.

He bought a large yellow coach for one hundred and thirteen sovereigns, together with a four-horse harness, intending to buy horses on the other side of the water. Eventually his money ran low as he and his wife and a much-loved maid and nanny to the children travelled from Switzerland and on to Rome. After nearly four years he grew faint-hearted. They all returned to England with baby Charles who'd been born in Milan in 1845.

The family settled near Christchurch in Hampshire but when young Charles was five years old Anne died. The nursemaid became even more important to the children.

After the death of General Birch-Reynardson Charles and his young family and the nurse moved to Holywell. The much-loved coach Charles had valued at £80 was auctioned for six guineas. Despite entering it at several sales it seemed that the coming of the railway deterred anyone from buying it.

Several years later, on a sporting visit to Ireland, the widowed Charles met Victoria Dodwell and he remarried in 1867. Victoria only lived a further four years and was buried at Holywell on 30th August 1871.

Charles became crippled with arthritis but was content to watch his four children grow up and three of them marry. His son became a Colonel in the Grenadier Guards and served in India. As an old man Charles continued to enjoy the tranquil rural surroundings, often with the aid of a telescope.

'A litter of cubs were laid up in a gravel pit, on the side of a hill within sight of my front door, and when they had grown big enough to come out of their earth and play about I could see them quite distinctly. Their father and mother were particularly fond of some little white call ducks that I had, and from the fact of the earth being within two hundred yards of a piece of water on which my little ducks used to breed, out of twenty-four they took eighteen, and I have more than once seen the little robbers dragging and carrying my poor little ducks about, and running after each other and playing about with them in their mouths in the middle of the day.

I wrote to West, who then hunted the Cottesmore hounds and begged him to come over and have a look at them. This he did and after much watching and waiting about two of the little fellows put in an appearance.

'Now then.' I said, ' let us go and see what they've got in their larder.'

On arriving at the earth there were plenty of white feathers, legs and heads of hares and rabbits and horribile dictu, part of a lamb!

'Why, you don't mean to say that foxes will eat lamb?' said I appealing to West.

'Well, not as a rule sir,' said he, 'unless they could get mint sauce with it.' [58]

Charles asked one of his tenants whether he had any complaints about foxes.

"'Well sir,' he said, 'my mother is terribly put out about them. They've taken, she says, a hundred chickens this year and that's a good many in one year sir.'

'Well' I said, 'Did you say anything to the Master of the hounds?'

58... *'Sports and Anecdotes of Bygone Days.' Charles Birch-Reynardson.*

'Oh yes sir. I told him but he don't care about our chickens.'
'Why did you think that?'
'Oh sir, all he said was you should shut your chickens up.'
'We do sir, said I, but they take them in the daytime.'
'Then, damn you, he says, you shouldn't keep chickens at all.' [59]

For his own amusement Charles put together memories as a gentleman coachman in 'Down the Road'. Illustrating the book were paintings of the coaches he drove, immortalised by Henry Alken.

Charles Thomas Samuel Birch-Reynardson continued writing and two years before his death published 'Sports and Anecdotes of Bygone Days in England, Scotland, Ireland, Italy and the Sunny South.'

He was buried at Holywell on the 25th April 1889 to lie with his forefathers in the vault beneath the church.

The second half of the 19th century had brought change; the growth of steam power and the resulting spread of the factory system altering the land. Country life ceased to be the traditional life of the nation. In Careby Parish pockets of the old life linger.

Many Holywell cottages have disappeared but the sublime valley with its lakes and streams have been preserved.

The woods planted in 1732 now creak with age. A woodcock with its extraordinary frog-like croak wings away in the dawn, a fox inspects a rabbit hole and deer rustle through the trees.

59... *'Sports and Anecdotes of Bygone Days.' Charles Birch-Reynardson.*

FORGOTTEN PEOPLE

A single crow flaps past,
Black spectre skims the cobalt sky.
Marching from the valley
Tall pines stride on ridge up high.

A narrow path meanders
Past seasoned piles of birch.
Fungi sprout on ancient trees
Like scalloped autumn skirts.

In dimness badgers trundle
Through slender shafts of light
Glance on fox cubs slinking
Hunting late at night.

Sleek, well-fed bodies wear
Gleaming chestnut coats.
Muzzles twitch to test the air,
Detect pale bird on post.

Wings spread in silent flight,
Amber feathers flecked and soft,
Ghostly body of the Barn Owl
Swoops home to chicks in loft.

Stag flits amongst the trees
Alarmed with tail held high.
Speckled hide magnificent
'Neath moonlit midnight sky.

Russet dappled mothers
Half grown fawns at foot
Flee to brambles, twisted trunks;
Too soon for autumn rut.

Dawn heralds plaintive calls
Buzzards pee-yeou to their young
Circling high with lazy flaps
Above the rising sun.

Midges whirring gaining height
Incessant their ritual dance.
Spinning through shafts of sunlight
To coos of pigeons' chants.

Tall stag maintains his vigil,
Patient; liquid eyes awake
Man disturbs his watchfulness.
He flees towards the lake.

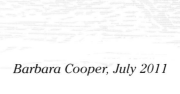

Barbara Cooper, July 2011

Bibliography

Lincolnshire Archives

The History of Castle Bytham: Its Ancient Fortress and Manor – John Wild

The History of Castle Bytham (update 2000) – Richard Foers MBE JP

The Rural Economy of England – Joan Thirsk

The Cottage Homes of England – Helen Allingham and Stewart Dick

The Common Stream: Two Thousand Years of the English Village

Lord Willoughby's Railway; The Edenham Branch – R.E. Pearson and J.G. Ruddock

Down the Road; Or, Reminiscences of a Gentleman Coachman and

Sports and Anecdotes of Bygone Days in England, Scotland, Ireland, Italy, and the

Sunny South – Charles Thomas Samuel Birch-Reynardson

Kelly's Directory 1896

Whites of Lincolnshire 1872

Census Returns 1841-1901

Acknowledgements

Mark Bennet – Lincoln Historic Environment Record

Jeremy Coote – Pitt Rivers Museum

Bob and Margaret Creasey

Rupert Elmore

Jonathan and Mrs Forman

Sally Gillespie

Brian Hall

Houses of Parliament – Parliamentary Archives

Elaine Jones – Rutland Local History and Record Society

Frank Kent

Janice Lea

Simon Lowis

Stamford Museum

Rutland Museum

Brian Oldman – Holywell Hall head gardener

Alan and Clare Price

Richard Tinsley

University of Leicester Library

Francesca Vinter – Tate Publishing

Helen Wells – Assistant planning archaeologist

Malcolm and Janet Wood

Tony Wright – Photographer

FORGOTTEN PEOPLE